Julian Mott ◀
Anne Leeming ◀
Edited by Helen Williams ◀

information communication & technology

for AQA AS Level

second edition

Hodder Murray
A MEMBER OF THE HODDER HEADLINE GROUP

The Publishers would like to thank the following for permission to reproduce copyright material:
Photo credits
p.1, 2, 258 and **260** Julian Mott; **p.23** *t* Photofusion Picture Library/Alamy, *b* © Npower Ltd 2006; **p.24** *t* Network Photographers/Alamy, *b* © Pallava Bagla/Corbis; **p.25** Peter Titmuss/Alamy; **p.32** James King-Holmes/Science Photo Library; **p.33** *t* Fiona Hanson/PA/Empics, *b* © Steve Chenn/Corbis; **p.42, 75** and **76** Anne Leeming; **p.57** Robert Harding Picture Library Ltd/Alamy; **p.74** © Royalty-Free/Corbis; **p.127** *t* Powered by Light/Alan Spencer/Alamy; **p.138** © Npower Ltd 2006; **p.207** educationphotos.co.uk/walmsley; **p.216** Jerry Bergman/Rex Features; **p.219** *c* and *b* Hewlett Packard; **p.221** *t* educationphotos.co.uk/walmsley; **p.222** Mark Douet/Stone /Getty Images.
Acknowledgements
p.86 and **87** Copyright © 2003-2005 McAfee, Inc., 535 Oakmead Parkway, Sunnyvale, California 94085. All rights reserved; **p.109** Copyright © Guardian Newspapers Limited 2006; **p.180** Copyright © 2005–2006 Mozilla Corporation. All rights reserved. The Firebird logo is a trademark of the Mozilla Foundation.
All AQA material is reproduced by permission of the Assessment and Qualifications Alliance.

Every effort has been made to trace all copyright holders, but if any have been inadvertently overlooked the Publishers will be pleased to make the necessary arrangements at the first opportunity.

Although every effort has been made to ensure that website addresses are correct at time of going to press, Hodder Murray cannot be held responsible for the content of any website mentioned in this book. It is sometimes possible to find a relocated web page by typing in the address of the home page for a website in the URL window of your browser.

In order to access teacher support materials for this book, please go to www.ict4aqa.co.uk and register your teacher details online. We will then contact your centre to verify the information provided is accurate and send you a password that will provide you with access to the site. It is important that you provide a valid e-mail address when submitting your details.

Examination support and mark schemes can be found on the AQA website www.aqa.org.uk/qual/gceasa/inf_assess.html

Orders: please contact Bookpoint Ltd, 130 Milton Park, Abingdon, Oxon OX14 4SB. Telephone: (44) 01235 827720. Fax: (44) 01235 400454. Lines are open 9.00 – 5.00, Monday to Saturday, with a 24-hour message answering service. Visit our website at www.hoddereducation.co.uk
© Julian Mott, Anne Leeming 2002, 2006
First published in 2002 by
Hodder Murray, an imprint of Hodder Education,
an Hachette livre UK company,
338 Euston Road
London NW1 3BH

This Second Edition first published 2006

Impression number   5 4 3
Year   2010 2009 2008 2007

Cover photo TEK Image/Science Photo Library
Typeset in 11/14pt Stone Informal by Pantek Arts Ltd, Maidstone, Kent
Printed and bound in Italy

A catalogue record for this title is available from the British Library

ISBN: 978 0340 907252

Contents

Knowledge, information and data

What is information and communication technology? ◄

▶ Information and Communication Technology (ICT) is normally associated with computers. In fact ICT means using any form of digital technology for the collection, storage, processing and sending of information.

This can be using computers or other devices such as MP3 players, mobile phones or satellite television.

What do we mean by data? ◄

▶ Data means recorded facts – usually a series of values produced as a result of an event or transaction.

For example, if I buy an item in a supermarket a lot of data is collected such as:

- my loyalty card number
- the bar code numbers for each item bought
- the number of the credit card used to pay for the goods.

All this data has been generated by an event – me buying some items in a supermarket.

If I pay a cheque into my bank account, this is a transaction that collects data such as:

- my bank account number and sort code
- the bank account number and sort code for the cheque paid in
- the amount of the cheque.
- Account numbers such as 0244 78200 04191 1 or 07379082 are data.
- Postcodes such as DE13 0LL and W1A 1AA are data.
- Barcodes such as 50 00231 036422 and 31 05634 412412 are data.
- Numbers, letters, names, dates are all examples of data.

The meaning of the data may not be obvious and on their own items of data may not be much use. However, data is very useful when it is processed to create *information*.

Figure 1.1 Examples of data

What is information? ◀

▶ Information is data that has been processed and given a *context*, which makes it understandable to the user.

For example:

When a barcode is scanned at a till, it is simply data being entered into a computer. The computer program looks up the name of the item and its price which are then displayed on the till. This is information because the data has been processed and a context added so that it is meaningful.

Both the examples shown in Figure 1.2 are meaningful to the user.

Figure 1.2 Examples of information

What is knowledge? ◀

▶ Knowledge is a set of rules allowing people to use information to make decisions.

A shop has 50 items in stock. The shop manager knows from experience that 60 of these items are sold every day so decides to order some more stock. This is *knowledge*.

Data	Information	Knowledge
25th October	My antivirus software expires on 25th October	I have decided to update my antivirus software because it runs out on 25th October
Mr John Hiley	I have sold some items to Mr John Hiley	I need to deliver the goods to Mr John Hiley and to send him an invoice

Activity 1

a) Give an example of a decision based on each of the examples of information shown in figure 1.2.

b) Give three examples of your own (not the ones above) of data, information and knowledge.

c) I purchase a music CD from an on-line store. State three items of data generated by the transaction.

Input, process and output

▶ All ICT systems work on the basis of three stages: input, process and output.

Input means entering data into the computer. For example, data could be bank account numbers, a barcode or a string of letters.

Processing means manipulating this data into information that is in a form that is understandable to the user. This might be by looking up the details of the product whose code has been entered or by performing a calculation on numbers that have been entered.

Output means presenting this information to the user or the outside world. It must be in a form the user can understand, so it must have a context. It is information. It could be printed, displayed on a screen or in another form.

For example:

■ In a school or college, attendance might be collected and typed into a computer at each class. (*Input*)
■ At the end of the week all the collected attendance data is processed. This might include: summarising, calculating, storing and sorting the data. (*Process*)
■ At the end of the week, tutor group (form) lists are printed showing each student's overall attendance during the week. (*Output*)

Activity 2

Copy the grid below and fill in possible entries for the missing cells.

Context	What data is input?	What is the processing?	What information is output?
1. Payroll	Employee name, hours worked	Calculate pay, work out tax, etc	Payslip
2. Household electricity supply			Bill
3. Examination board	Marks for exam papers		
4. Salesman's visits			Day's list of appointments
5. Booking a holiday online			
6. Going to a cash machine			

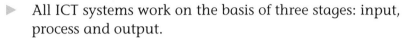

Feedback

▶ ICT also uses feedback which means using the output from a computer to influence the input.

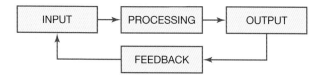

Figure 1.3
Feedback diagram

■ The barcode of an item sold is scanned at a supermarket checkout. *(Input)*
■ The store's computer system updates its stock levels by reducing the stock level of this product by 1. *(Process)*
■ A list of products and stock levels is printed out; the manager decides to order additional stock. *(Output)*
■ When the new stock is delivered, details are entered into the computer. *(Input)*

This is an example of the use of feedback. The output from the computer influences the input.

example

A computer-based learning program provides on-screen facts to users, who then have to answer a series of questions – **input**.

The computer system works out if the answers are correct and calculates the user's score. This is **processing** data into a form understood by the user – whether the answer is correct or not and the score.

For each answer an audible bleep is heard; a low tone for a wrong answer and high note for a correct answer. The updated score appears in the top right-hand corner of the screen. These are **outputs**. They provide **information** to the user.

After the user has answered all the questions, they will move on to another set of questions. There are different sets of questions depending on how well they did in the previous test. The output has affected the input – this is **feedback**.

Direct and indirect data capture ◀

Data capture means the collection of data to enter into a computer. Data can be captured directly or indirectly.

Direct data capture is the collection of data for a particular purpose.

An example of direct data capture is:

■ reading barcodes at a supermarket till so that the cashier knows how much to charge the customer.

Indirect data capture is the collection of data as a by-product from another purpose.

An example of indirect data capture is:

■ using data from reading barcodes at a supermarket till to work out stock levels.

Why things go wrong ◀

If data is entered incorrectly, whether accidentally or deliberately, the information output will be incorrect. Information is only as accurate as the data that was entered. If the data source is wrong, the information output will be wrong. This is sometimes referred to as **GIGO – Garbage In, Garbage Out**.

Stories abound of things going wrong with computers. A warehouse/production system at Rootes Group in the 1960s didn't know the difference between feet and inches – some components turned out 12 times bigger than they should have been.

NASA made a similar mistake when trying to send a rocket to Mars. Some measurements were in inches and some in centimetres. Let's just say that the rocket didn't land as expected.

Encoding information ◀

Encoding information means putting it into codes.

In a computer, all information is represented in some form of machine-readable code so that it can be processed. In a digital computer, these codes are made up of binary digits (bits), which can be written as either 0 or 1.

Most computers use ASCII (pronounced as-key) code to store letters and other characters. This is a binary code some of which is shown over the page.

Letter	Binary	Decimal
A	01000001	65
B	01000010	66
C	01000011	67
D	01000100	68
E	01000101	69
F	01000110	70
G	01000111	71
H	01001000	72
I	01001001	73

So the word HID is stored in the computer as 01001000 01001001 01000100.

ASCII stands for American Standard Code for Information Interchange. You can see more of the code at

http://www.asciitable.com/

The following are all examples of files stored in the computer in binary code:

- digital pictures such as bitmaps, jpg or gif files
- digital videos such as mpg or avi files
- sound files such as wav or mp3 files.

Activity 3

a) Create a very small digital image (you could just crop an existing image) and save it (for example in jpg format).

b) Load up text editing software such as Notepad.

c) Open the image file in Notepad.

d) You will see the machine-readable code for the image. It is not in binary but each character of the code represents a longer binary code.

We can't understand it! Can you?

You can try this with sound files, such as *wav*, as well.

Value judgements

A value judgement is when you give a value to something. It is entirely your opinion and may differ completely from someone else's opinion. Examples of value judgements are if you say something is nice, attractive or ugly.

If someone says, 'I get up at 7 o'clock each morning,' this is not a value judgement but a statement of fact. If they say, 'I get up *early* each morning,' this is a value judgement.

A milkman used to getting up at 3.30 wouldn't describe 7 o'clock as *early*. A student used to getting up at 11 o'clock might describe 7 o'clock as *very early*.

Coding value judgements

Businesses are interested in our opinions. Do we like the taste of a product? Is the packaging attractive? Is it too expensive? These are some of the questions a market researcher might ask members of the public before a new product is launched. Information from this research will later be used to determine the price, the image and even whether the product is produced at all. It is likely that there will be a limited choice of responses such as:

This new product will cost £1.65. Is it:

1. ☐ much too cheap
2. ☐ too cheap
3. ☐ about right
4. ☐ too expensive
5. ☐ much too expensive

What happens if the customer thinks it is a little bit too expensive? Do they choose 'about right' or 'too expensive?'

Coding value judgements like this leads to a limited number of answers, none of which may be appropriate. The results may not be meaningful because different people will have different opinions about what 'too expensive' and 'much too expensive' mean.

Worked exam question

1 Every ICT task involves the input of data, which is then processed and information is output.

Using an example of an ICT task with which you are familiar:

a) State what the task is (1)

b) Give one example of data that is input, stating how it is input (2)

c) Describe one process needed to fulfil the task (2)

d) Give one example of information output, stating how it is output. (2)

June 2004 ICT1

► **EXAMINER'S GUIDANCE**

a) This question is difficult because you have to think of an ICT task. There are dozens of tasks you could choose. Sometimes it is easier if you are told the task such as stock control in a supermarket, printing a bank statement or preparing a wage slip. Remember to answer in sentences.

► **SAMPLE ANSWER**

An example of an ICT task is to produce wage slips for a small bakery employing 25 people.

b) One example of data input is the number of hours worked by each employee in a week. As the bakery is small this data is typed in at a keyboard.

► **EXAMINER'S GUIDANCE**

c) Describing the processing means going further than just saying, 'The process is to work out the wages.'

► **SAMPLE ANSWER**

One process needed to fulfil the task would be to multiply the hours worked by the rate per hour for each employee. This will calculate their gross pay.

d) One example of information output is the pay for each employee. This will be printed on a payslip.

SUMMARY

- ▶ **Data means raw facts and figures.**
- ▶ **Information means data which has been processed to give it a context which gives it a meaning.**
- ▶ **Knowledge is a set of rules for using information to make decisions.**
- ▶ **Data can arise directly or indirectly.**
- ▶ **A poor data source will lead to poor information.**
- ▶ **Information is often encoded in machine-readable form when it is stored in a computer system.**
- ▶ **Coding information reduces the accuracy and may make it meaningless.**

Chapter 1 Questions

1. Explain the difference between the following terms as used in ICT. Use an ICT example to illustrate your answer for each term.
   a) data   (2)
   b) information   (2)
   c) knowledge   (2)

2. A checkout operator in a supermarket scans the barcodes of items being purchased by customers. The scanner is linked to an Electronic Point of Sale (EPOS) system. The software that is used contains functions to look up the prices and descriptions of the products that are scanned in order to produce an itemised receipt for the customer. The software also produces a daily sales summary report for the store manager.
   a) Give one item of data that is entered into the EPOS system.   (1)
   b) Give two items of information that are produced by the EPOS system.   (2)
   c) Describe one use of the daily sales summary report for the store manager.   (2)

   June 2003 ICT1

3. Data input to an ICT system can take many forms such as pictures, sounds, numbers and letters. In all cases the data has to be encoded.
   Using an example, explain why data needs to be encoded.

   (2)

   June 2002 ICT1

4. The expression 'Garbage in, garbage out', or 'GIGO', is often used in connection with information processing systems. Explain, using an example, what is meant by this expression.   (4)

   June 2001 ICT1

5. Three components of an Information Processing System are input, processing and output. State what is meant by:
   a) input
   b) processing
   c) output
   and give an example of each one.   (6)

   January 2001 ICT1

6. Encoding value judgements can lead to reduced accuracy. As a result information from a questionnaire is inaccurate. Explain, with the use of two appropriate examples, why this may happen.   (4)

2 The value, importance and control of information

Quality of information

▶ Information is said to be of good quality if it is **accurate**, **up to date** and **relevant** for a particular use.

Accuracy

How accurate it needs to be will depend upon the use being made of the information. For example, the information in a bank statement must be exactly right to the nearest penny otherwise the account holder could make inappropriate decisions over spending and would be fully justified in complaining to the bank. When reporting overall A-level pass rates at a school a figure to the nearest 1% would usually be sufficiently accurate.

Up to date

If information is out of date, then wrong decisions can be made. It is very important that all reports produced include a date; in certain circumstances, a time is also required. This enables the reader of the report to know exactly when it was produced. Information changes over time and without a date the reader might make a wrong decision, unaware that the information is out of date.

If a list of names and addresses, used for mail shots, is five years out of date many letters will be sent to a wrong address as the person named may have moved or even died during that time. It would be a waste of time and money for a company to send out letters to these addresses. The older the mailing list, the fewer the 'hits' there would be.

In order to determine the number of AS ICT classes to run in a college, the administrator would need to know the number of students wishing to follow the course this year. Last year's figures might be quite different; if they were used instead of this year's numbers then too few classes might be set up.

A sales manager for a large company selling office furniture throughout the UK will need to decide which salesmen have been doing badly and need extra support and which products to choose for extra production or promotion. Using information based on an earlier month's figures rather than the most recent would result in incorrect decisions that could lead to further reduced sales and profit.

When an employee of a cinema is taking a booking for the evening performance of a film, he needs to know which seats are still available at the time of booking, not the ones that were available at the start of the day.

Relevant for particular use

Information that is essential in one situation may have no use in another. For example, information intended for a branch manager of a supermarket, showing checkout till usage to allow him to allocate staff over a weekly period, would not be of use to the regional manager wanting to see the efficiency of all branches.

A figure showing the percentage pass rate in ICT A-level for all pupils in a school would be useful for teachers when planning and reviewing their work. However, a detailed list showing each student's mark in every module would be needed when advising individual students whether or not to resit modules.

Activity 1

For each of the following situations given below, state why the information might lead to an inappropriate decision being made. Describe the possible consequences of the decision.

1. The purchasing manager of a mail order company is looking at a list of stock levels for his products before placing orders prior to the Christmas rush. The list was produced in June.
2. Two trained nursery teachers are considering setting up a new nursery school in the local area to start in September 2007. They have information from the local council of the number of children under the age of eleven in the local area which was produced in June 2005.
3. A bakery wishes to determine ways of increasing profits. They want to know whether they could sell more loaves and which are the most popular. The manager is given the number of loaves, of each type, baked each day for the last 12 months.
4. The manager of a holiday company has to pre-book places in hotels for the 2008 season. He has the results of a market research survey of holiday preferences from members of the public that was carried out in 2002.

Information as a commodity

Information can have a financial value. In many ways it is a commodity such as oil, gold or wheat.

An organisation may build up a database consisting of names and addresses of customers or contacts that would be valuable to another organisation.

For example, a charity might have a list of names and addresses of donors that another organisation could use to target individuals by mailing letters to advertise an event likely to be of interest to the donors. Such a targeted mailing would be more effective than sending out letters to everyone living in the area as the letters sent in the targeted mailing would only go to people who are likely to be interested in the event. Money would be saved as fewer letters would need to be sent.

The organisation could collect the name and address information for itself, rather than purchase it from the charity, perhaps by undertaking a survey. However, this method of obtaining the information would be more expensive and time consuming than purchasing it from the charity. The information will only have a monetary value for a time, whilst it is sufficiently up to date to ensure that most names and addresses are still current. As time passes many people may have moved house or their circumstances or interests will change. More letters (and therefore more money) will be wasted and eventually the time and money spent on the mail shot will no longer be worthwhile.

Whether or not information has monetary value to an organisation will depend upon the potential use to which it can be put.

case study 1
▶ Supermarket loyalty cards

The use of loyalty cards is common in supermarkets and other large stores. Customers have to fill in an application form to obtain a card; this requires them to give their name, address and other information. The loyalty card is used whenever a customer purchases goods and points are allocated according to the amount spent. The points can then be used to make further purchases.

The use of loyalty cards means that special offer information and vouchers can be sent to customers. The types of goods bought can be linked to a customer. The loyalty card identifies the customer. Its identity number is input into the computerised till when details of purchases have been gathered from the bar codes on the products. Thus the special offers sent to a customer can be for products that are likely to be of interest.

This information relating to the purchasing patterns of a customer is of use to other organisations besides the supermarket itself. For example, a list of names and addresses of people who regularly purchase cat food would be valuable to a company selling pet insurance products.

1. List three other types of company that would be interested in purchasing the list of names and addresses of pet owners.
2. List five types of company that would be interested in purchasing a list of names and addresses of people who regularly buy baby food. Explain why it would be important that the list should not be more than three months old.
3. Explain why it is worthwhile for the organisations listed above to buy the list of names and addresses from the supermarket.

Obtaining information

▶ Whenever goods are purchased by telephone, mail order or online via the Internet, data about the customer is gathered; whenever a form requesting a 'special offer' for goods or information is cut out from a newspaper or magazine, whenever a person enters a competition the consumer's details are likely to be stored electronically.

Organisations have a legal requirement to ask customers if their data can be passed on to others. This is often done by using a tick box with a message such as:

'Information gathered in this way may be used to target specific customers through direct mail'.

case study 2
▶ Porsche Cars

Porsche Cars Great Britain (PCGB) imports all Porsches into Britain and owns five Porsche dealerships. Sales are small compared with volume manufacturers such as Ford or Vauxhall.

PCGB know that the people most likely to buy one of their cars are people who have bought one in the past. These people obviously have an interest in sports cars and presumably have the necessary income to purchase one.

This means that PCGB spend 80 per cent of their marketing budget on direct mail targeting previous customers. They have built up a large database of 22,000 current Porsche owners, over half of all Porsche owners in the country. These owners receive a copy of Marque, PCGB's magazine. This is an important part of their marketing strategy. Industry sources suggest that sixty per cent of customers will buy from you again simply because you keep in touch.

Keeping a database like this is quite legal but PCGB must comply with the Data Protection Act (see Chapter 9).

1. Give three reasons why PCGB use this method of promoting their cars rather than advertise on television as volume car manufacturers do.

2. Give three further products, other than cars, that might best be marketed in this way.

3. Describe the measures PCGB would need to take to ensure that their database of customers is kept accurate and up to date.

Activity 2

■ Write down in which of the following situations you, or a family member, have given personal data.

Buying insurance – for house, car, holiday or pet	Purchasing goods on-line via the Internet	Applying for college or University
Purchasing extended warranty for goods such as mobile phone or iPod	Booking ticket for a concert over the telephone	Registering with a doctor or dentist
Filling in an application for a 'free holiday' advertised in a magazine	Taking part in a telephone survey	Filling in a free meal voucher in a restaurant

■ For three of the above, list the data items that were collected. Explain what use would have been made of the information in each case.

■ Describe five further ways in which personal data could be collected.

Free information

◄

▶ Much information is freely available to the public. The electoral register is compiled by local councils and lists the names and addresses of people entitled to vote in elections. A section might look like this:

Paddock View, Pillsbury, P85 3RH

1 Paddock View	Albert Mitchell
1 Paddock View	Doris Mitchell
2 Paddock View	Sally Bryant
3 Paddock View	Graham Williams
3 Paddock View	Sally Williams
3 Paddock View	Daniel Williams
3 Paddock View	Adam Williams (10 August)
4 Paddock View	William Hunter
4 Paddock View	Shirley Hunter

There are a number of things that can be deduced from this information which businesses might find valuable. For example, all nine people live in Pillsbury. A local restaurant might see them as potential customers. A date appears after Adam Williams' name. This means that he will be old enough to vote on that day and so is approaching 18. He might be a potential customer for the local nightclub.

Information on recent births, engagements, marriages and deaths appear in local newspapers. Local government departments will also give information on building planning applications.

Information is valuable and there are costs involved in collecting it. Even when information is available free, for example the electoral register, there are labour costs in entering the data and converting it into a suitable electronic format. The electoral register on paper is not very convenient.

Companies like Millennium Data Ltd (http://www.marketinglists.com/eroll.htm) resell the electoral roll in electronic format. They say this electronic format is useful for:

- direct marketing campaigns
- political campaigns
- data analysis, capture and validation
- software development.

Telephone directories contain alphabetic lists of subscribers together with their telephone number. It is not practical to use such a directory to obtain the name and address of the holder of a particular number. However, when the data are stored electronically such searches can easily be performed. There are companies who will scan in telephone directories and sell customers the information in electronic format.

Data on all house purchases are stored by the land registry. A number of companies have websites that allow users, for a fee, to find the value of recent sales of houses near to them. Try the sites – http://www.myhouseprice.com and http://www.ourproperty.co.uk (see figure 2.1).

The more information that is required and the more detailed the information, the more it will cost to obtain. If the data are collected through a survey the cost will depend on the size of the sample and the number of questions asked.

Figure 2.1 Property website

Keeping information up to date ◀

Information has to be up to date to be useful. Keeping the information up to date will affect the costs of producing the information. The costs arise from the need to:

- Collect up-to-date data
- Enter the data into the system
- Delete out-of-date data.

Traditionally many computer systems operated in batch mode (see Chapter 16) in which data was collected over a period of time, a day, a week or even a month before processing took place. The information then produced was only as up to date as the most recent processing run. Transaction processing updates with new data as it arises, processing each change as it occurs. Information produced from a transaction processing system is always as up to date as possible, but such a system is more costly to run as faster processing, more sophisticated hardware and faster communications might be required.

An organisation will need to have systems in place to ensure that changes in data can be collected. This can prove to be very complicated and time consuming as changes can include altered marital status and perhaps a change in surname, a change in telephone number as well as an address change. Very often when a patient attends a doctor's or dentist's clinic the receptionist will quickly check basic data with them to ensure that it is up to date.

It is very important that a school or college has up-to-date information about its students. Up-to-date contact addresses and telephone numbers are essential. A system would be in place whereby students could fill in a form whenever any changes occur. However, such a method would not be foolproof. As a way of catching missed changes, every student might be given a printout of their personal details and qualifications every year or even every term for checking. Any changes would be added and the student would be expected to sign the form. The data held electronically would then be updated. Such a process would cost money. Each student's details would need to be printed out and distributed; missing students would need to be chased up; every sheet would need to be checked for changes and the changes entered. The data could be kept even more up to date if the printouts were issued and checked every week but the cost in both time and money would make this unproductive for the few changes that would be highlighted each week.

Many organisations try to gather address changes and other details from customers by including a form with every invoice that allows the customer to enter changes easily. It is then a simple matter for this changed data to be entered onto the database.

Name and address lists used for targeted mailing will soon get out of date. Systems need to be put in place that will enable entries to be deleted when no longer current and new names added. Organisations which keep a database of customers will probably record a date when the customer last made contact in some way – by making a purchase or an enquiry. In this way, those people who had made no contact for a set period of time could be deleted from the database.

The control of information ◀

Legal obligations

Whenever personal data is held on individuals by any kind of organisation, that organisation has legal obligations that are described in detail in Chapter 9. These legal obligations determine what can be done with data.

Importantly, the data cannot be passed or sold to other organisations without the permission of the data subject, the person to whom the data refers.

The data subject has the right to view the data and require any inaccuracies to be corrected. This means that the holder of the data must have systems in place that allow the subject to view the data held on them and for any necessary changes to be made.

Value of selling information that should not be disclosed

Information that is protected by law from disclosure can still have a commercial value, even though the selling of the information is illegal.

In June 2005 a number of workers in an offshore call centre were found to be selling private information from UK bank accounts. Apparently a computer expert was buying the PIN and credit card numbers, private addresses and passport details of British account holders from call centre employees, then selling them to would-be identity thieves who would access the accounts illegally. The cost of the details of one confidential account was stated to be £3.

In May 2003 the *Guardian* newspaper reported that a US company had been obtaining personal data on millions of citizens in Latin America and selling it to the US administration. Allegedly the company received at least £6m in return for the data. Apparently the data consisted of Mexico's entire list of voters, including dates of birth and passport numbers, as well as Colombia's citizen identification database. It is illegal under Colombian law for government agencies to disclose such information, except in response to a request for data on a named individual.

There is a market in buying and selling lists of mobile phone numbers which are then used for marketing purposes. It is likely that some sellers of mobile ring tones and games also sell on lists of valid mobile numbers as the threat of detection, and penalty if caught, is low.

Even though there are tough laws on data protection in the UK there are concerns that data, such as credit card details, held on computer files can be purchased by unscrupulous businesses.

Information can be so valuable that reputable companies may take illegal steps to get it. 'Industrial espionage' to obtain information from a competitor is not unusual. Accurate information would be very useful to a rival company.

Theft of computer data is a real possibility. Every major company in the UK has been the target of some attempt to steal data stored on its computers. If information is valuable, as with any commodity, it is important that it is kept securely, and access to it is controlled.

SUMMARY

> ▶ Good information should be accurate, up to date and relevant for its particular use.

> ▶ Information is a commodity that can have a monetary value. The value depends on its accuracy, potential use and its intended use.

> ▶ Information that is freely available may have a monetary value when it has been converted into a more useful electronic format.

> ▶ Ensuring that information is up to date can be time consuming and costly.

> ▶ Holders of personal data have legal obligations in respect of that data. Information cannot be sold without the permission of the data subject.

> ▶ Information that is protected by law from disclosure can still have a commercial value.

Chapter 2 Questions

1. A report has been produced by an information system for the sales manager of a company. He then complains that he does not know when the report was produced, or how up to date the contents of the report are.

   a) Explain why it is important to have the date it was produced shown on a report. (2)

   b) Explain, using an example for each one:

      i) why up-to-date information will be important to the sales manager

      ii) why the age of the data used to produce any graphs included in the report will be important. (2)

      June 2004 ICT1

2. State **three** factors that affect the value and importance of information. Give an example that shows clearly how each factor affects the information's value. (6)

3. A supermarket stock control computer system updates its stock levels every evening based on that day's sales. Describe **two** possible consequences of the supermarket using out-of-date data. (4)

4. The owners of a hotel are considering organising some special deals for 2006. They use data obtained from the customers who stayed in the hotel during the year 2002 to decide what to offer.

   a) Explain why the data from 2002 might not be suitable for use when deciding on the special deals to be offered for 2006.

   b) Explain what the effect on the hotel might be if it used the data from 2002. (4)

   January 2005 ICT1

Why are computers used so often?

▷ Computer systems are machines that process data and turn it into information. What is it about computer systems that has meant that they play such a large part in twenty-first century life? The main reasons are:

- they are fast
- they can search very quickly
- they have vast storage capacity
- they are very accurate
- they perform repetitive tasks well
- they are automatic
- they can combine data
- they can link to other computer systems.

- **They are fast**. Computer systems process data very quickly – certainly much, much faster than a human could do it. This means they can also process large volumes of data. Not only that but they keep getting faster with the processor speed doubling about every 18 months. As computer systems get faster there are more and more applications for which they can be used.

  Accurate, detailed weather forecasts could not be produced without very fast computer systems. They run simulation programs that manipulate data on many different weather factors. To be of any use, a weather forecasting program has to run faster than real time. It is no good getting a forecast for Monday morning's weather on Tuesday, or even on Monday afternoon!

- **They can search very quickly**. Computer systems can search through large volumes of data very quickly. For example, files can be located based on the name of the file, the date of creation or particular text stored within the file.

  Consider a computer system used by the police that stores details of the fingerprints of hundreds of thousands of people in digitally coded form. When a fingerprint is detected at the scene of a crime a search needs to be made to see if the print matches any that are held. Without a computer system this task could not be undertaken for all the thousands of stored prints within a realistic time.

■ **They have vast storage capacity**. There are a variety of ways of storing data in a computer system, all of which store large amounts of data in a very small space. Data can be stored in the computer's internal memory (RAM). This data is lost when the computer is turned off.

Data can be stored more permanently using backing store media such as the hard disk, CD-ROM or DVD.

For example, a film can easily be stored on one DVD. Today, even a modestly priced home microcomputer has sufficient storage capacity to enable a user to run a program such as an action game that has very realistic animated graphics. Such graphical images require large amounts of storage space.

■ **They are very accurate**. Although there is the possibility of hardware failure or software errors, computer systems are much more accurate in processing data than humans because they can perform repetitive tasks without becoming bored or tired. If a piece of software such as a spreadsheet is set up to perform a task such as adding up a list of numbers, it will come up with the same result every time the same figures are entered. A human, on the other hand, is quite likely to get the result wrong sometimes, particularly if they have been working for a long time and are tired.

■ **They perform repetitive tasks well**. Many computer applications involve repetitive tasks such as printing bank statements or calculating wages for employees. Unlike humans who tend to find doing repetitive tasks boring, computer systems are very good at repeating calculation after calculation. Paying wages for 5,000 people is no harder than paying wages for five people when using a computer system.

■ **They are automatic**. Computer systems work automatically and need little human supervision. They can work 24 hours a day, 7 days a week and can be programmed to perform certain tasks without an operator being present. For example, many organisations will arrange for file backup to be carried out automatically at night.

■ **They can combine data.** Data from different sources can be combined to provide high quality information in a variety of output formats. In a school or college a student attendance system collects data on the presence of each student in each of their classes. The data from all classes can be combined and sorted to produce a weekly summary for each student of their attendance in all classes.

■ **They can link to other computer systems**. Computer systems can link to other computer systems and other electronic devices, almost anywhere in the world. This has also increased the number of applications for which computer systems can be used.

Wireless connections are becoming more commonly used. They are more flexible but can only be used over short distances and performance does not match hard-wired systems.

The Internet allows users to communicate with other users worldwide via e-mail as well as to access and transfer huge amount of data through the *World Wide Web.* A holiday company will store details of all available holidays together with bookings that have been made on a central computer system. This will be available to travel agents in many different locations who can link their computer system to the central data store. This enables a travel agent both to have access to up-to-date information on holiday availability, and to make immediate bookings while their client is with them.

All these characteristics mean that computer systems can be used in many situations today and they provide information of a high quality. Many tasks currently carried out were impossible before the development of computer systems. Accurate weather forecasting, managing international chains of supermarkets and processing financial transactions are all tasks that could not have been performed without computer systems.

Activity 1

4. In recent years we have seen an increase in the amount of direct mail we receive. Sometimes this is called junk mail. Explain why **five** of the capabilities at the start of this chapter have helped expansion of junk mail. An example is shown below. (10)

Capability	Explanation
Computer systems can search very quickly	A supermarket, sending out direct mail about a new pet food they are selling, can **search** through customer records to find those customers who have bought pet food before. Only these customers will receive the direct mail.

Each of the following five case studies describes a particular computer application. Read each carefully, then answer the questions.

case study 1
▶ Public lending library

A lending library in Wintown has a very large stock of books, DVDs, CDs, audio tapes and videos that are loaned to members for a fixed time period. The computer system used to manage the flow of data in the library is linked via a wide area network to the central county computer.

The computer system records details of all loaned and returned items. Whenever a loan is made the system checks that it will not exceed the member's allowable loan limit; also the member will be reminded if they have any overdue items.

An electronic catalogue of all items held by the library is maintained for the use of both staff and members. The central county computer can be accessed to extend the search for a book countywide.

Once a week a mail merge program is run that produces letters to be sent to all those members who have items that are over a month overdue.

Every six months a summary is produced for the senior librarian that provides statistics on borrowing patterns. A list is also produced that contains the details of all items that have not been borrowed during the last period.

1. What is a mail merge?
2. Refer to the list of capabilities given at the start of the chapter. **Explain** which apply to the Wintown library system.

case study 2
▶ Gas billing system

A gas company delivers gas to over half a million customers. Details of all customers are held on the computer system and every three months bills are printed out and sent to the appropriate householders. Each bill is worked out from a reading taken from an individual property.

Details of any payment made are used to update a customer's record. If payment is not made within a defined period the customer is sent a further bill as a reminder.

Each meter reader has a hand held device that she uses to record the number read from the meter. The device already contains details of the customer and house. At the end of the day the meter reader attaches their device to a connecter that is installed at their home. This is then connected via a telephone line to the company's wide area network. Details of the readings she has made are transferred to the central computer system and details of the households that she is to visit the next day are downloaded to the device.

1. What information, apart from the recent meter reading, will be needed to produce a customer's bill?
2. Refer to the list of capabilities given at the start of the chapter. **Explain** which apply to the gas billing system.

case study 3
▶ Hospital patient records

A new computer system costing £6.2 billion is being installed in the NHS. The system will store records for 50 million patients. By 2010 medical staff will be able to access and update information on their patients from every doctor's surgery and every hospital in England. Wireless access will allow doctors to access the system as they visit different hospital wards.

A number of different medical personnel will use the system:

- A clerk records details of appointments and visits to outpatients clinics.
- The ward clerk enters details of a patient's stay in a ward.
- The radiographer stores details of X-rays.
- Laboratory staff enter results of blood and other pathology tests carried out.
- Ward nurses and doctors enter details of medications issued and treatments undertaken.
- GPs can refer to all the information relating to a patient under their care.

1. State two advantages of using the computer based system described over a manual one.
2. Why will each patient need to be allocated a unique patient number?
3. Refer to the list of capabilities given at the start of the chapter. **Explain** which apply to the NHS patient record system.

case study 4
▶ Aid agency

An aid agency provides help to people in need around the world after a disaster such as a flood, earthquake or famine has taken place.

Local field stations are set up and whenever possible these are equipped with a computer system or hand-held palmtop computers. These allow for fast communication links so that e-mails can be sent giving details of the latest situation and what aid is needed.

The agency maintains a database of skilled volunteers such as doctors, engineers or builders who would be prepared to travel to help out if an emergency were to arise.

A further database containing details of potential donors is maintained and when an emergency does occur a mail merge is used to circulate them asking for donations.

- Refer to the list of capabilities given at the start of the chapter. **Explain** which apply to the aid agency systems.

case study 5
▶ Airline bookings

Every airline maintains a centralised booking system for its flights; travel agents all around the world can access the system to find out about seat availability as well as make a booking. Travellers can cut out the travel agent by searching for flights over the Internet and booking directly using the airline's web site.

Bookings can be made several months in advance. For many large airlines there will be thousands of flights available for booking at any one time.

Whenever a booking is made a number of details relating to the passengers is recorded, including dietary requirements. Seat numbers can be allocated, the total cost including airport fees and other charges is calculated and payment made by credit card.

Many systems allow the travel agent to print the ticket for the customer at the time of booking. Travellers who book over the Internet do not get a ticket but receive a reference to give when they check in. Some airlines allow passengers to print their own boarding cards and check-in documents using a touch-screen computer system.

When the passenger arrives at the airport he checks in, his luggage is booked in and has a label attached that holds details of airport destination along with an identification code. All the details are recorded on the computer system.

A number of lists need to be produced which include:
■ a full passenger list for check-in clerks
■ a list showing special dietary requirements for the caterers
■ a list of passengers needing special service together with their seat numbers.

1. What is the baggage code used for?
2. Refer to the list of capabilities given at the start of the chapter. **Explain** which apply to the airline booking system.
3. What problems could arise from having a booking system that is dependent upon computer systems?

Response speed ◀

▷ The speed of response is very important in many modern computer systems. A police officer might want to know quickly if a particular car is stolen. When withdrawing money from a cash machine a customer does not want to wait a long time for the computer system to process the data and check whether enough money is available in their account.

Fast response times are important in computer systems that involve feedback; for example, in a stock exchange system which allows shares to be bought and sold electronically. Share prices go up and down all the time depending on how many have been bought or sold. Share prices are adjusted automatically.

This is feedback – the output (details of shares bought and sold) affects the input (share prices). Fast response times are essential for this to work successfully.

Electronic funds transfer ◀

▶ Payment for goods can be made in a number of ways:

- by cash
- by cheque
- by credit or debit card.

The use of computer systems has allowed for the development in the payment of goods by means other than cash. Many payments are made electronically in shops and supermarkets, ticket offices, restaurants and via the Internet.

Banks throughout the world have large mainframe computers that process customer accounts. Software that enables electronic funds transfer (EFT) to take place has been written especially for these computer systems. The international nature of banking, with banks in every time zone, means that EFT systems run 24 hours a day.

When a person wishes to make a payment using EFT, their card is first 'swiped' through a reader that reads the details from the magnetic strip. (Internet purchasers will type in their card number.) The purchaser then has to enter their PIN number. The reader is linked via a wide area network to a central bank computer system that checks the details of the proposed transaction against the state of the individual's bank account.

If there are sufficient funds in the account to cover the payment an authorisation code is sent back. The response needs to be returned within a few seconds otherwise the customer will become impatient and a long queue may build up at the point of sale.

If the response authorises the payment, the sale is then completed. This process is an example of feedback; the salesperson is able to carry out the sale in the knowledge that the payment is authorised by the bank. If the card is rejected for some reason, this is also feedback that influences the next step. The sale could be abandoned or further ID requested.

The software written for EFT is capable of handling large numbers of transactions per second.

Limitations of information and communication technology

Although modern-day computer systems have phenomenal capabilities, there are limitations in the use of ICT systems. Stories abound of computer systems not being able to carry out what they are designed to do.

The main limitations are:

- hardware limitations
- software limitations
- communications limitations
- inappropriate design
- poor data control mechanisms.

Hardware limitations

The speed at which a computer system performs depends on its components. The speed of a computer's processor and the size of its internal memory are important. A slow processor speed would delay processes like searching for a particular item or sorting into order. A small memory would limit the possibility of multi-tasking – running several programs at once. Laptop batteries need recharging, without which they will not work.

However, technological developments continue; processor speeds are continually getting faster, memory is getting bigger and batteries contain more charge.

Some printers are slow with a smaller buffer memory. They are not suitable for large images. Some screens may be too small. Laptop screens may not be visible from certain angles.

Even when hardware is suitable, failure is not uncommon. The result of such failure can be severe, for example, disk failure can lead to the loss of data if backup copies have not been kept.

Software limitations

Data may not be transferable from one software application to another. This may mean that data has to be entered twice.

Software errors can make a system fail or behave in an unpredictable manner. This can happen because the software has been rushed onto the market without being fully tested. This is often done for commercial reasons, perhaps to beat a competitor.

Communications limitations

There have been huge developments in communications technology over the last few years. However communications can still cause a bottleneck in a system. Connection speeds, for example, to the Internet or a computer network will affect performance, particularly if large files are being downloaded. Wireless network connections are not as fast as hard-wired connections.

Inappropriate design

Poorly designed systems will not achieve what they set out to do. A system can be poorly designed as a result of inadequate investigation. Perhaps some possible data inputs have not been considered or the results have been calculated in the wrong way. Remember the computer is only a dumb tool and will only do what it is programmed to do. If the programming is wrong, the output will be wrong.

Poor data control mechanisms

However, the biggest limitation of computer systems is that they are used by humans. Computers will only process the data that is entered into the system. If the wrong data is entered into the computer system, the wrong information will come out.

It is vital to have appropriate data control mechanisms that detect human errors, if a computer system is to produce reliable and accurate information. Validation (see chapter 12) can be used to detect any data that has been entered that is not sensible. However, it is difficult to prevent or pick up all errors.

Backup copies of data must be kept in case of data loss. Backups must be checked to make sure that the backup systems are working.

Hardware limitations of the Internet ◀

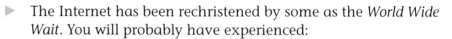

▶ The Internet has been rechristened by some as the *World Wide Wait*. You will probably have experienced:

- waiting for web pages to load particularly if using a dial-up connection
- some pages and/or images not loading at all
- the connection being lost while you are using the 'net'
- having to wait even longer in the afternoon or evening because America is 'online'
- not being able to connect to your Internet Service Provider because the lines are 'busy'.

Even broadband services are not perfect. You may still have to wait some time while graphics, particularly videos, load.

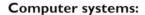

Activity 2

Visit a newspaper or magazine site on the Internet such as http://www.computerweekly.co.uk/ or http://www.computing.co.uk and search for 'computer error'. Find three examples.

For each example determine the cause of the error.

SUMMARY

Computer systems:

▷ **are fast**

▷ **can store and process vast amounts of data**

▷ **can search very quickly**

▷ **are very accurate**

▷ **perform repetitive tasks well**

▷ **are automatic**

▷ **can work 24 hours a day, 7 days a week**

▷ **can be programmed to perform certain tasks at night without an operator being present**

▷ **handle large volumes of data.**

However, there are limitations to the use of ICT. Factors include:

▷ **hardware**

▷ **software**

▷ **communications**

▷ **inappropriate design**

▷ **poor data control mechanisms.**

Chapter 3 Questions

1. Your aunt has only recently purchased her first computer and is looking forward to using it. She has written to you asking if she is likely to have any problems using it. Write a response describing to her:

a) one possible hardware limitation (2)

b) one possible software limitation (2)

c) one possible communications limitation. (2)

2. When Mrs Brown received her gas bill she found that it was for £10,000, which she knew was not correct. When she telephoned the gas company to complain, the explanation she received was that 'the computer had got it wrong'. Describe a more likely explanation. (2)

June 2005 ICT1

3. Describe one hardware limitation of using:

a) the Internet (2)

b) a floppy disk (2)

c) a network printer (2)

d) a laptop computer. (2)

4. Most employers now use computer systems to calculate their employees' wages and pay them straight into the employee's bank account. Describe **four** capabilities of ICT which makes electronic payment advantageous to the employer. (8)

5. Over half the world's e-mails are believed to be **spam**. This is unrequested advertising sent to collections of e-mail addresses offering to sell you anything from medication to a university degree. Describe three capabilities of ICT which have made spam so prevalent. (6)

6. 'Computer systems are only as good as the people who use them.'

a) State one procedure that can be used to prevent data loss. (1)

b) State one control mechanism that can be used to prevent unauthorised access. (1)

7. A hospital is planning to provide all its doctors with hand-held portable computers. These computers will be able to be used anywhere in the hospital to access patient information and order medicines.

a) List **two** benefits to the hospital of introducing this system. (2)

b) Explain **one** disadvantage to the doctor of introducing this system. (2)

▶ ICT has already had a great effect on society, for example, in the fields of employment, leisure and communications. This trend is likely to increase as processors get faster, computer memory gets bigger and their price becomes comparatively cheaper. In this chapter we look at some of the ways ICT has affected the way we live and work.

The growth of the use of ICT has brought many general benefits that apply to many aspects of life and work. It has improved communication through the use of networks. Vast quantities of data can be stored and information made available more quickly and in more than one place. It is easier to present information in a professional form and a variety of ways which can enhance an organisation's image as well as improve the quality of decision making.

On the other hand, an over-reliance on ICT can cause some problems; when for some reason the technology is not available, perhaps through breakdown, normal business cannot continue. The storage of large amounts of data can result in information being accessed inappropriately.

ICT and manufacturing ◀

▶ The benefits of ICT can be seen in the manufacturing industry as computers are able to work 24 hours every day and perform repetitive tasks quickly to a high degree of accuracy.

Many industries now use **Computer-Aided Design/Computer-Aided Manufacturing (CAD/CAM)** where the output from a CAD process is input to control a manufacturing process. Benetton, the fashion company, uses a CAD system to produce a template for items such as a pair of jeans in a range of sizes. The CAD system automatically calculates the best way to lay the templates on the fabric so as to minimise the wastage of materials used and cuts the time taken to produce these templates from 24 to 2 hours. Benetton links its CAD system to its CAM system. This enables designs created on the CAD system to be transferred directly to computer-controlled knitting machines, so increasing the flexibility of the systems still further.

Benetton finds that the quality of the computer-manufactured products is higher and more consistent leading to increased productivity as fewer garments are wasted. The use of CAM should optimise the use of raw materials, so cutting down on wastage.

Figure 4.1 CAD/CAM system

ICT and commerce

▷ Business today is unrecognisable compared with business in the days before computers. The electronic office is an obvious example of the effect of ICT on business. A modern office is likely to have a computer on every desk. The work carried out in offices is generally the receipt, processing, storage and dispatch of information. The computer can do all these things more efficiently than traditional methods. The use of **word processing** and **desktop publishing packages** has meant that even very small businesses can produce material in a very professional manner and so enhance their image with both existing and potential customers. A document can be stored for later use and does not need to be retyped if it were needed again, perhaps with minor changes.

Computer systems are used to produce an invoice that shows the amount owed by customers. If the software is not properly specified, or inadequately tested, bizarre invoices can be produced. There have been reports of a customer being sent a request for payment of a very small amount, say £0.05 or even £0.00, and then further reminders sent until a payment for that amount is received. Having to write a cheque for £0.00 can understandably exasperate a customer!

In most large shops an **Electronic Point of Sale (EPOS)** system is used. This has a scanner that is used to read the bar code that identifies the product. The software uses functions to look up the price and description of the product and produces an itemised receipt for the customer. This lists the description of every item purchased, together with its price and the overall total that the customer has spent. The software also maintains sales and stock level information for use by the store manager. By linking to an **Electronic Funds Transfer (EFT)** system

Figure 4.2 Supermarket 'Chip and PIN' card reader

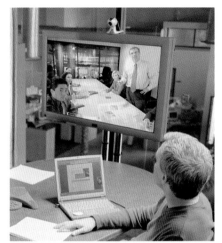

Figure 4.3 A videoconferencing session in action

an EFTPOS till allows customers to purchase goods using credit or debit cards as their credit worthiness can be checked on-line. The new '**Chip and PIN**' cards provide security for the customer who has to enter a secret 4-digit code (see figure 4.2).

The arrival of fax, e-mail and satellite links has completely changed how businesses and some individuals communicate. Businesses now advertise their fax numbers and e-mail addresses prominently, which makes it easier for customers to keep in touch. It would seem logical that this would affect the level of traditional communications, particularly letters sent by post.

The growth of the Internet has provided organisations with many opportunities. The use of videoconferencing allows meetings to take place without the time or cost of travel. **Videoconferencing** makes use of a webcam, a video camera that captures images which can be transmitted across the Internet, and a screen. The use of **e-mail** provides a cheaper way of keeping in touch with customers than using normal mail. It can be used to confirm transactions, inform of dispatch of goods as well as to alert customers of new products and special offers. However, the growth in such use of e-mail is now growing so much that it can be annoying for customers who find their mail boxes fill up with unwanted messages from companies.

Products can be ordered on-line using the Internet. This can make the potential market for a product very large – even worldwide. **Electronic Data Interchange (EDI)** is a system of sending orders, paying invoices and sending information electronically. In this way data can be transferred nearly instantaneously. Money can be transferred electronically to pay for goods and services. These are all examples of e-commerce (electronic commerce) or e-shopping (see page 53), which is revolutionising how businesses order and sell products.

Shopping via the Internet is taking an increasing share of the market. It is not just hi-tech and multinational companies such as Amazon that use e-commerce to sell goods. Businesses can set up their own website to market their products. The site can be used to make customers aware of special offers. A family-owned butchers from Yorkshire, Jack Scaife, started to use an Internet site (http://www.jackscaife.co.uk) to sell its bacon, sending deliveries all over the world. Soon e-commerce was bringing in £200,000 worth of sales from a site that cost only £250 a year to maintain.

Computer systems can be very expensive to develop and install. A corner shop that installed a very sophisticated bar coded POS system found that the benefits that followed did not make up for the very large installation cost as there was no scope for reducing staffing.

Computerised stock control has enabled supermarkets to reduce costs by reducing stock levels and selling a greater range of products than before. Computers in the shops and warehouses are linked through a wide area network. When a store's stock for an item falls below a preset level the store computer automatically sends an electronic message to the warehouse to initiate the transfer of new stocks to the specific supermarket. The warehouse computer will produce a 'picking list', a document used by warehouse staff to select items to be dispatched. In many warehouses the 'picking' is done by a computer-controlled robot.

However, dependence on ICT can cause problems if a failure in a system occurs. Many large stores, such as supermarkets, now use only EPOS tills that are linked to a central computer that holds a database of stock levels and prices. There have been many cases when a store has had to ask all its customers to leave the store because a computer failure has made all the tills inoperable.

Banking ◀

▶ The number of transactions carried out by banks has grown so rapidly that they could not now operate without computers. Banks transfer money electronically. Most workers are paid directly into their bank account by computer. Many regular payments such as mortgages, utilities and insurance premiums are transferred electronically from an individual's bank account to the company's bank account as a direct debit or a standing order. This means that an individual does not have to worry about remembering to pay bills, risking extra charges if they forget to pay.

Cash is not as important as it used to be (see Case Study 1). Most individuals do not need to carry as much cash as before thanks to credit and debit cards. The bank keeps detailed records of purchases made by a customer using their card. A customer is sent a list of all transactions every month which helps them in their financial planning. These records can be used by customers to show proof of purchase of a product if they have not kept the receipt and wish to return the product.

If a person does run out of cash, they can visit an **Automated Teller Machine (ATM)** at any time. Before banks introduced ATMs, they had to employ more people to act as tellers who worked at a desk and dispensed money to customers. The customers would have to queue up until a teller was free, fill in a withdrawal form and show identification before they were given cash by the teller.

The development of ATMs has brought benefits to both customers and banks. Customers now have access to cash at any time of the day or night, which is much more convenient. It saves time for the customer who no longer needs to queue at the bank counter behind someone who is depositing 20 bags of small coins! The bank reduces its need for staff or can use its tellers for other tasks. It can close some branches and just provide an ATM device which reduces costs. Many banks have used the space and staffing freed up by the installation of ATMs to develop new services which are useful to customers and increase profits.

There are also drawbacks to the use of ATMs. There has been a growth in fraud and card theft as well as attacks on customers who have just withdrawn money. Many customers preferred the more personal approach when human tellers were used. There have also been occasions when computer failure has occurred putting many ATMs out of action.

Home or **online banking** means that users with access to the Internet can check their bank account balances, transfer money between accounts and pay bills from home. This can be much more convenient than having to visit a bank in person and transactions can be carried out more quickly than by using the normal postal service. **Online** banking has the added convenience of its services being available at any time from anywhere in the world. However, many people are unwilling to use **online** banking as they are afraid of fraud and other security issues.

ICT has also affected our shopping habits in other ways. The widespread use of credit cards means it is possible to shop and pay for goods without leaving home. Cable and digital TV shopping channels and the Internet have provided new ways of finding out what to buy instead of the traditional catalogues.

Activity 1

Draw up a table showing the benefits and drawbacks of using ICT in the manufacturing industry. For each point, give an example to back this up from the text. Try to think of a further example of your own.

Help! This can appear quite a difficult task at first. The best thing to do is to read through the text, paragraph by paragraph, looking for specific benefits and drawbacks from examples and then write them down in more general terms. Some ideas are included for you.

Benefit	Example from text	Other example
Reduces staffing requirements	Document can be reproduced, with some changes without need for retyping	
Increases speed of data transfer	Use of EDI can transfer electronic data almost instantaneously.	
Increased convenience to customers		

Drawbacks	Example from text	Other example
High set-up costs		
Inadequately tested systems can cause loss of confidence in company		
Loss of business due to computer failure		

case study 1
▶ The cashless society

There have been many developments in ICT that are leading to a society without cash. These include:

- credit cards where computers store financial details
- cheques which are processed by computers using MICR (Magnetic Ink Character Recognition)
- direct debits used to pay regular bills are generated by computer
- wages and salaries are paid by electronic transfer and not in cash
- phonecards can be used for telephone calls
- smart cards containing a microchip can be used for automatic debit and credit (see below)
- electronic funds transfer connects the shop with the banks' computers.

A company called Mondex launched an experiment in Swindon hailed as the start of the cashless society. Local people were issued with a Mondex card, described as an 'electronic purse' that could be charged with cash and then used to pay for goods and services, for a monthly fee of £1.50. After three months, just 4 per cent of householders had the card and a total of only £250,000 had been spent using Mondex.

A rival company, Visa International, one of the world's largest credit card providers, started a similar experiment in Leeds. Visa Cash, a chip-based plastic card, allowed users to make everyday purchases of small items such as a newspaper or a pint of milk, without having to scrape around for the right change. Holders of the Visa Cash card can 'load' the card's electronic chip from their bank account, up to a limit of £100, at any of 3,000 specially designed automated telling machines.

1. Why do you think the residents of Swindon were unwilling to use the Mondex cash card?
2. Many people welcome the fact that they do not have to carry around large amounts of currency. Why do you think this is so?
3. Other members of society feel 'left out' of the move towards a cashless society as they cannot have, or do not want to have, credit and debit cards. Identify the categories of the population who might feel this way and give reasons why they might do so.
4. Make a list of all the transactions that you think will continue to require cash in the future; for example, giving pocket money to young children.
5. Describe the benefits and drawbacks of a cashless society. When preparing your answer consider different categories of people – the young, those on a low income, the elderly.

ICT and medicine ◀ ▼

> Computers are used in the administration of hospitals and doctors' surgeries, storing patients' records. Pharmacists keep records of customers and their prescriptions. When a patient's records are needed by a health professional they will always be available, unlike paper-based records that can only be viewed in one place at a time. The use of electronic records can lead to concerns about the consequences of storing inaccurate data and the increased threats to the security of the data.

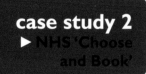

case study 2
▶ **NHS 'Choose and Book'**

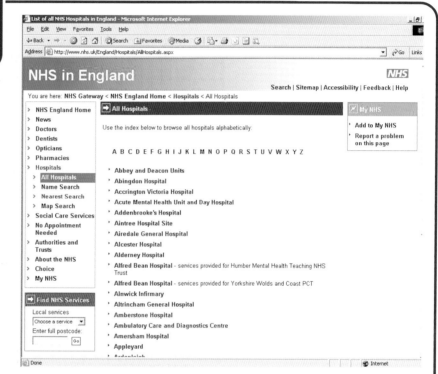

Figure 4.4 The NHS website

An Internet booking system for NHS services called 'Choose and Book' is a new national service that aims to provide an electronic booking system with a choice of time, date and place for a patient's first appointment as an outpatient. This new system is designed to give patients a much greater involvement in the making of decisions about their treatment

Patients can choose from one of four or five hospitals and information on these hospitals should be available to General Practice doctors and other staff, as well as patients on http://www.nhs.uk. Patients have the choice of booking their hospital appointment electronically when they are at the doctor's surgery with the help of the GP, or they can book later by themselves using the Internet.

1. Find out more about the new system on http://www.chooseandbook.nhs.uk
2. Explain the main benefits of the 'Choose and Book' system.
3. Imagine that you were in charge of the team who were implementing this new system. What would be your main actions to ensure that the system worked as intended?

Some hospitals are now experimenting with storing medical records on smart cards kept by the patient and taken with them every time they visit a doctor, dentist, pharmacist or hospital. The smart card can store a complete medical history and can be updated at the end of each visit.

Benefits of using computerised medical records	Drawbacks of using computerised medical records
Information is always available, cannot be lost, or left sitting on a desk.	If the computer network goes down, information is unavailable. This could be inconvenient or even prove life threatening.
Information is available to users in different locations, such as doctor in clinic, nurse in ward or radiologist in x-ray department.	All staff will need training in the use of the software.
Information can be displayed in a variety of ways to meet different users' needs.	Part time or agency staff may not be trained and cannot access vital information.
Information can be easily read (unlike some doctors' handwriting!).	Some staff may be resistant or fearful of using ICT.
Results from tests in hospital departments can be added to a patient's record as soon as the test is complete and thus be available immediately to the doctor.	It is very expensive to set up.
Levels of access can limit amount of data that users can view. A clinic receptionist would not be given access to details of a patient's medical condition.	

ICT also helps in the diagnosis and monitoring of patients' illnesses. Expert systems can be set up to help in diagnosis by asking questions about symptoms and using the answers to draw conclusions. Computer controlled ultra sound scanners enable doctors to screen patients very accurately. X-ray film is being replaced by on-screen digital pictures. Computers can be used for continuous monitoring of patients' bodily functions such as blood pressure, pulse and respiration rates. Such systems provide instant feedback of information and can free up nurses to carry out other duties.

ICT in the home

Computers have changed many people's leisure activities; a high percentage of households now have a home computer and/or games console. These offer a new form of entertainment. For example, many home users use software to trace and record their family tree, to plan a journey by accessing route planning and mapping software or access information from an encyclopaedia held on a CD-ROM. Digital photography, with photographs taken using digital cameras, stored and printed in the home is increasing in popularity.

Home use of the Internet is also growing. The use of e-mail to keep in touch with family and friends around the world is becoming increasingly popular. Home users can also book holidays, carry out their personal banking and order goods from a supermarket that will be delivered to their door. Such e-commerce facilities save time and people can carry out these tasks at a time that is suitable to them.

Activity 2

Carry out a survey of ten home computer users who have access to the Internet. Find out how many hours a week they link up to the Internet. List the different features and services they use. Enter your results into a spreadsheet and display graphically.

Many people now routinely make many purchases on-line, a process known as e-shopping. There is very little that cannot be ordered and paid for in this way. A company such as Amazon have been successfully selling books and other products for a number of years. A prospective shopper can browse through available products or search for specific items. On making a choice, an item can be placed in a 'shopping basket' – a list of desired items. When the shopper wishes to make a firm order, he selects an icon that transfers him to a web page called a 'checkout'. At this point choices in the trolley can be kept or discarded. The shopper then moves on to a further page where details of delivery address and payment details are entered.

E-shopping allows the shopper to make purchases without having to leave home. It allows access to products that might be hard to find in their local area. Those who have difficulty getting to shops, due to poor health, family commitments or time constraints are enabled by e-shopping to make the purchases they desire. For the sellers they are no longer limited to a local pool of potential purchasers and do not have to maintain the overhead of mailing expensive catalogues needed for mail order.

Some people are put off e-shopping because of worries over security issues relating to the use of credit and debit cards over the Internet. Others do not like to choose items without seeing them physically.

Access to the Internet also provides leisure opportunities. Development of chat rooms, applications such as friends re-united and online games provide many opportunities to the home user. Of course, there are dangers as well as benefits from such a wealth of facilities. Many parents worry that their children spend so much time sitting at a computer or games console that their health may be damaged; there are many sites, such as those displaying pornography that are unsuitable for children. Chat rooms, while providing a useful opportunity for exchanging ideas, can be misused by unscrupulous people.

Activity 3

Explore four different e-shopping sites on the web. Try a variety of sites – include a small specialist site as well as a large food retailer.

1. Describe the common features that you find.
2. A member of your family is trying to decide whether or not to become an e-shopper. To make sure that they make a reasoned decision, list three benefits of e-shopping and three drawbacks.

ICT and education ◄

▶ Computers are commonly used by pupils and students in schools, colleges and universities to research topics and produce word processed reports. The World Wide Web has become a major research tool. Most students at university are provided with free Internet access. This means that students access material, both provided by their tutors and from a wider base, at any time. This makes them more independent and less reliant on their tutors. There is also less pressure on the library for books when all the students on a course are preparing for the same assignment as the students can access material stored on the World Wide Web. If they have to miss lectures they can access the notes on-line. The tutors can contact students using e-mail which is quicker, more reliable and cheaper than sending out printed notes. Students can submit word processed work attached to an e-mail; this is less likely to get lost and the time of submission is recorded.

ICT has improved education in other ways. Intelligent tutoring systems enable the computer to give the student information, ask questions, record scores and work at the individual's pace.

Computer communications provide new opportunities for distance learning. Students can send their work to their tutors by e-mail and receive back annotations and comments. Videoconferencing may be used for lectures, enabling two-way communication and discussion. This is particularly useful in remote and underpopulated areas. Students in schools or colleges can undertake courses which are not viable to run in their own institution as there are not enough students wishing to study the subject. From a college viewpoint, the use of distance learning increases the potential market for their courses.

Computer Based Training (CBT) is a sophisticated way of learning with help from ICT. A simulated aircraft cockpit used for pilot training is an example of CBT, which is cost-effective and less dangerous than the real thing. The number of computer based learning packages that are available is growing very fast as modern computers have the processing power and storage capacity to support fast moving and realistic graphics.

Many schools are using electronic means for registering their students in class. Such methods can provide up-to-date attendance information brought together from a number of classes. This provides a valuable overview of an individual student's attendance as well as providing the opportunity of studying trends in class attendance.

Schools and colleges enter students for public examinations electronically using EDI. Files are sent to the exam boards with details of students and the modules that they are entering. Later on the results are sent back to the institution, in encrypted form, via the Internet where they are imported into a local database. The results are then printed out for the students.

Students applying to university through UCAS are likely to do so electronically using the **EAS (Electronic Application System).** Using this the student fills in an online form, entering personal details, course choice details, lists of qualifications gained and examinations to be taken, and a personal statement. Once this has been completed the student's reference is added by a teacher. The application is then sent electronically to UCAS who forward it to the chosen institutions.

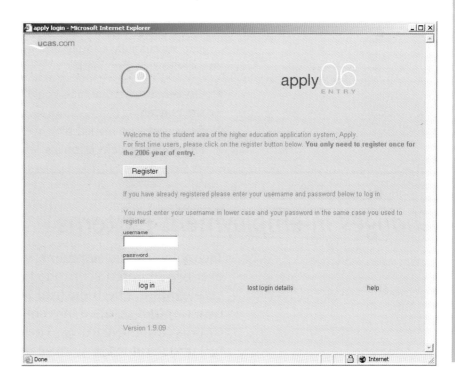

Figure 4.5 Applying for a place at university through UCAS

case study 3
▶ Studying online

Jane works in Africa as the pharmacist in an Aids research project team. For her work she needed to extend her knowledge of certain drugs. There were no suitable courses available to her locally. She could have flown to the US or Europe to attend a course. This would have meant that she would have had to take several weeks away from work and would have cost the charity for which she worked a considerable amount of money.

Instead Jane enrolled on an online course run by a university in the United States. The course was designed to take 60 hours of study. The university had run the course delivered in the traditional way before expanding to include online delivery. The online delivery had expanded the potential market for their course, as any English speaker with access to the Internet could apply, and had provided an increase in income for the university. Once the course was set up and all the materials produced, the course cost less to run online than by using traditional methods.

Jane was able to study in the evening at home after work; she linked to the Internet and accessed her learning materials online. The course was divided into sections and at the end of each section there were questions to check her understanding and progress.

Jane was assigned a tutor; she communicated with him through e-mail attaching her word processed assignments when they were completed. Of course, she was not able to have face to face support from her tutor.

Online study can cause a student to feel isolated as they do not meet and work with fellow students. To help get around this problem, several online discussion groups were set up so that students could share ideas and obtain help and support from each other. As the students on the course were spread around the world, Jane had to choose a group whose members would be awake when she was!

Jane successfully completed the course and acquired the extra knowledge that she needed to carry out her role in the research team.

1. List other ways that Jane could have acquired the knowledge that she needed.
2. Explain why online learning was the best option for her.
3. Identify drawbacks of online learning.

Changes in employment patterns ◀

▶ Technological developments since the Industrial Revolution over two hundred years ago have led to changing patterns of employment. The Industrial Revolution led to the building of factories that resulted in a shift in the population from the countryside to the towns. The development of the computer has also changed patterns of work and it has affected nearly every part of industry and commerce.

Some skills have disappeared completely. For example, in the printing industry, typesetting used to be a skilled operation using hot metal. It was performed by print workers who had undergone a seven-year apprenticeship. Now it can be done in the office using a desktop publishing program and a standard PC. This has resulted in greater job flexibility and the breakdown of the traditional demarcation lines between printers and journalists. Football pools checkers are no longer needed as the job can be done automatically.

Some jobs may have changed little, such as gardeners or delivery drivers, but they still may be affected by such inventions as computer-controlled greenhouses or automated stock control. Other jobs such as supermarket checkout operator, bank clerk or secretary have changed considerably. This has usually meant that existing staff have had to retrain to use ICT.

Teleworking ◄

Teleworking means using ICT to work from home. It has been made possible by advances in technology and networking such as fibre optics, faster modems, fax, palm-top computers, satellite systems, internal e-mail and teleconferencing. Working from home has been common for a long time in some industries, such as sales representatives, telephone sales and the self-employed. Now teleworking has extended home working to other industries.

It is now possible for authors, journalists, computer programmers, accountants and word-processor operators to do their work by teleworking.

BT estimates that there are around 1.3 million teleworkers in Britain, made up of 650,000 self-employed persons, 150,000 company employees and 500,000 mobile workers such as sales staff.

The Britannia Building Society has implemented a new policy for its text creation department – what used to be called the typing pool. Dictation of letters is now done over the phone, stored and then transmitted to the teleworker's home. The completed documents are typed at home and submitted by e-mail. Britannia say that the system works really well and it is easy to monitor the work rate and error rate of the teleworkers.

It is common for teleworkers to spend part of their working time at the office and part at home. Typically such a person would work at home for three days and be at the office for two. Many companies use a method of '**hot-desking**', where instead of having a workstation for every employee, teleworkers share the use of a number of computers. For the employer, teleworking saves the cost of office provision such as desks, chairs, floor space, heating and car parking space.

The pool of available labour for a job is hugely increased if teleworkers are employed. British Airways flight booking takes place in Bombay, proving you don't even need to be in the same continent. Much computer programming and testing for British companies is done in Asia.

There are obvious advantages in teleworking for the employee such as flexible working hours, avoiding time-wasting rush hour travel as well as the associated costs. Some childcare problems can be eased. Teleworkers are no longer tied to living in crowded cities where housing costs are very high but can live in the location of their choice.

However, the lack of the social side of work can be a disadvantage for many employees as many people make friends through their work. Not everyone is good at getting down to work by themselves and some find it hard to be part of a team at such a long distance. Much informal training takes place in a workplace without the participants really knowing about it. There is a real danger for many people that the distinction between work and private life gets blurred and work takes up more and more of their time, affecting the quality of life and producing stress. Teleworking demands new skills and training is essential if it is to be successful.

In the long term, if teleworking were to become the way the majority of people worked there would be implications for society. Reduced travel would be environmentally friendly, and could cut pollution and perhaps lead to the end of cities and offices as we know them.

case study 4
► Teleworking in Action

Rosemary works as an events organiser for a London museum based in the east side of London; she lives in the west side of the city. Travelling to work involves Rosemary taking three trains and walking for a total of 20 minutes. On a good day she can complete the journey in under an hour and fifteen minutes but she often meets delays that can add up to an hour to her journey time. She finds the travelling tiring and stressful and resents wasting so much time in unproductive activity. When she made the journey on a daily basis, if she awoke feeling slightly unwell she would have to stay at home and miss a day's work as she did not feel that she could cope with the travel.

Rosemary negotiated with the museum to become a teleworker for two days a week. Now she stays at home on a Tuesday and a Wednesday. She is able to plan, produce reports and contact external providers without interruption from her colleagues. She has a home computer with Internet access that she uses to keep in touch with her colleagues via e-mail.

Rosemary makes good use of the travel hours saved on a Tuesday and Wednesday. She usually gets up at her normal time and either goes for a morning run when she would otherwise be sitting on a train or else starts work early and then meets up with a friend for a long lunch break.

The balance of working three days at the museum and two days at home suits Rosemary. She would not like to work at home every day as she would miss interacting with her colleagues.

1. Summarise the benefits of teleworking to Rosemary.
2. List any benefits to the museum.
3. List five jobs where teleworking would be appropriate, explaining why.
4. List five jobs where teleworking would *not* be appropriate, explaining why.

	Benefits of teleworking	Drawbacks to teleworking
To the employee	No need to travel – less stress, saves time and money Flexible hours – work around family commitments Can live where you like	Lose social contact with work associates Boundaries between work and home can get blurred leading to stress Distractions may make it hard to work at home
To the employer	Reduced office costs (NB 'hot-desking') Less absenteeism Wider pool for recruitment as location no longer important	Can be harder to keep track of employees' work Potential lack of company spirit
To society	Less travel leads to reduced pollution Family commitments covered in the home Reduced concentration of population near employment	Reduced human interaction at work

SUMMARY

The term 'electronic office' is used to describe how ICT dominates a modern office

ICT developments affecting commerce include:

▶ EDI, where commercial data is transferred electronically between companies

▶ e-commerce where trade is carried out over the Internet

▶ computerised stock control and reordering.

In banks, computers are replacing human workers while most people are paid directly into their bank account by computer. An increasing number of other transactions take place electronically.

Some people predict a cashless society.

ICT is widely used in medicine:

- ► Much administrative work is performed by computer.
- ► Expert systems are used as an aid to diagnosis.
- ► Computers are used to monitor the bodily functions of patients.

ICT is playing a growing role in leisure in the home, where the Internet is used by many people who explore the World Wide Web and send e-mails to friends and family.

In education, ICT supports online learning, CBT is used extensively in training, the Internet and encyclopaedia CD-ROMs are used for research purposes.

ICT plays a major role in educational administration.

Teleworking is the name given to the use of ICT to work from home.

ICT brings many advantages but there are also drawbacks that must be acknowledged and understood.

Chapter 4 Questions

1. For each of the following areas, state **one** advantage and **one** disadvantage of the use of ICT. Your advantages and disadvantages must be different for each area:
   a) education (2)
   b) leisure in the home (2)
   c) industry (2)
   d) medicine (2)
   e) teleworking. (2)
   June 2004 ICT1

2. A checkout operator in a supermarket scans the bar codes of items being purchased by customers. The scanner is linked to an electronic point of sale (EPOS) system. The software that is used contains functions to look up the prices and descriptions of the products that are scanned in order to produce an itemised receipt for the customer. The software also produces a daily sales summary report for the store manager.
   a) Give **one** item of data that is entered into the EPOS system. (1)
   b) Give **two** items of information that are produced by the EPOS system. (2)
   c) Describe one use of the daily sales summary report for the store manager. (2)
   June 2003 ICT1

3. Describe **three** ways in which the Police use ICT in the detection of crime. For each way give an advantage to the Police of using ICT. (9)

4. Describe **three** different ways in which a company might make use of the Internet to benefit its business. (6)
   Jan 2005 ICT1

5. a) The use of automated teller machines (ATMs), provided by banks and building societies, has become a common way for people to obtain cash. State:
      i) One advantage to the bank or building society of installing ATMs (1)
      ii) Two advantages to the customer of using ATMs (2)
   b) The use of ICT has allowed banks and building societies to keep detailed records of purchases that people make using credit or debit cards. Explain one reason why this is a benefit. (2)
   June 2002 ICT1

6. Mr Patel has bought a DVD on fishing from a company on the Internet. He has now started to receive e-mails about fishing holidays and is receiving fishing catalogues through the post.
   a) Explain why Mr Patel has started to receive the e-mails and the catalogues. (2)
   b) State what most people are likely to be worried about when ordering goods using credit cards. (1)
   c) Describe two measures that a company can take to help give customers confidence in using online facilities. (4)
   d) Describe **two** advantages to a company of selling its goods online. (4)
   June 2005 ICT1

7. Describe **two** different ways in which the Internet has helped the authors in writing this book. (6)

5 The role of communication systems

Global communications

◄ All organisations and individuals need to communicate, to send information to and receive information from other organisations or individuals.

Information technology has transformed the way we communicate. New methods of communication have been developed, each with its own features and advantages such as:

- e-mail
- fax
- Internet
- Internet conferencing
- messenger and online chat
- mobile phones
- pagers
- satellite phones
- teletext
- text messaging
- videoconferencing
- viewdata.

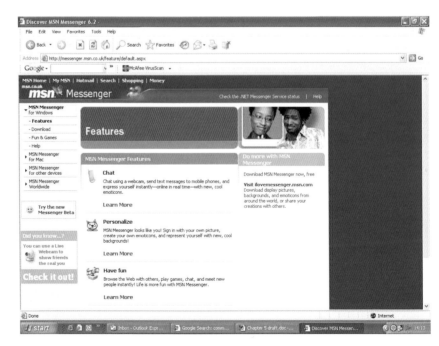

Figure 5.1 MSN messenger

Public networks such as the Internet, to which anyone can connect almost anywhere in the world, mean that millions of computers can be linked together. This means that users can:

- communicate with each other quickly, for example by e-mail
- share files
- use browser software to access web pages
- search for information.

The Internet

The Internet (**Inter**national **Net**work) is a large number of computer networks that are linked together worldwide via telecommunications systems. Messages and data are sent from the source computer, through a number of other computers until the destination computer is reached.

The **World Wide Web** (**WWW**) is a vast collection of pages of information in multimedia form held on the Internet. Pages can contain images, videos, animations and sounds. An organisation or individual can set up a website consisting of stored pages that are made available to other users. Much of the material on the WWW is freely available to anyone. Websites have a home page which provides links to other pages within the site.

Some pages are password protected and only available to subscribers. Businesses may password protect some of their information pages so that they are available to their employees but not to the general public.

Web pages are written in a language called **HTML** (**hypertext mark-up language**). Web pages can be created and websites built using web design software such as Microsoft FrontPage or Macromedia DreamWeaver or just written in HTML using a text editor such as Notepad. The user can create, edit or delete pages and set up or edit links between pages to allow easy navigation of the site.

Accessing the Internet

To access the internet, a home user would normally need:

- a computer
- a telephone line which provides the physical connection to a network
- a modem
- communication software, a browser and e-mail software.

A **modem** is a device for connecting a computer to a telephone line. It converts the digital signal used by the computer into the analogue signal used to transmit data down telephone wires for outgoing messages, and converts the analogue signal to a digital one for incoming messages.

A broadband modem also connects the computer to the telephone line. It uses ADSL (Asymmetric Digital Subscriber Line) modulation technology and special compression techniques to achieve much faster transmission rates.

A **browser program** is needed to view web pages written in HTML in human understandable form. There are several examples such as Microsoft Internet Explorer, Netscape Navigator and Mozilla Firebird.

The browser allows users to retrieve information from the WWW interactively over the Internet. It provides facilities for a user to store the addresses of commonly visited sites as **bookmarks** or **favourites.** It stores pages locally on the computer so that pages load quickly if they are revisited. (See Chapter 14.)

The user will need to subscribe to an **Internet Service Provider** (**ISP**) such as AOL, Tiscali or Wanadoo. The ISP will normally provide an e-mail address to enable the user to send and receive e-mail and a limited amount of web space so that the user can set up his/her own website. The ISP has a host computer that deals with communications and also stores data such as e-mail messages and web pages for the user.

An ISP provides a variety of services to the user, depending on cost. These include:

- dial-up access to a local (0845) phone number which allows access to the Internet for the cost of a local call
- dial-up access to a freephone (0800) telephone number to access the Internet if you pay a monthly subscription.
- ADSL broadband access to the Internet for the payment of a larger monthly subscription. Different speeds and maximum monthly downloads are available at different costs. ADSL broadband access allows the telephone line to be used for voice calls and to access the Internet at the same time.

Once set up, the software will make the connection to the Internet for the user at the click of a button.

Internet access and e-mail use have increased with the development of other devices which can also access these services such as palmtops, WAP mobile phones and digital televisions.

Services available

Once connected to the Internet the user can:

- access pages of information on the World Wide Web (WWW), including text, images, sound and occasionally video
- save these pages and images locally for later reference
- leave messages on 'bulletin boards' and join discussion forums
- send and receive e-mail which is stored on the ISP's computer.

The ISP may also provide:

- free web space to set up and edit your own web pages
- additional e-mail addresses for the user's family
- latest news, weather, TV and radio information
- its own search engine for searching the web
- its own Internet shopping facility
- bulletin boards for newsgroups (special storage space which is used for messages relating to a particular interest group, for example, Star Trek, old computers, coarse fishing or teaching ICT).

Figure 5.2 Tiscali is an internet service provider

Other ways of accessing the Internet

▶ Big organisations where a large number of users need to access the Internet are likely to find that the use of a modem and dial-up or even ADSL broadband facilities will not meet their needs.

The user's computers are likely to be organised into a local area network which is linked to the Internet via a terminal server. The organisation is likely to have a permanent link to the Internet via a fibre optic cable.

Televisions with digital capabilities, either digital TV or a normal TV with a conversion box, allow a user to access the Internet. Some Internet services can be accessed using WAP (Wireless Application Protocol) mobile phones or some BT phone boxes.

WAP mobile phones provide Internet access and e-mail facilities as well as standard phone activities. WAP is an Internet protocol that has been designed especially for mobile phones. A text based information service is provided and information is available to the user in the following areas:

- UK news headlines with details of some recent stories
- sports news
- entertainment news together with the facility to search for suitable venues such as clubs or restaurants
- up-to-date share prices
- TV guide
- weather information
- travel information.

Standard e-mail facilities such as reading, replying and forwarding messages are also provided.

The Internet and business ◀

▶ With hundreds of millions of people across the globe using the Internet, commercial interests have recognised the opportunities offered by this new technology.

The Internet offers businesses many opportunities. For example, they can:

- market their products to a world-wide audience with a website
- carry out research
- sell products directly over the Internet (e-commerce)
- use videoconferencing for virtual meetings
- use EDI (Electronic Data Interchange) to communicate with suppliers
- use Intranets and Extranets to get up-to the minute information
- use e-mail to communicate quickly.

Commercial web sites

Many businesses use websites to promote themselves. Some have found that not only is it much cheaper than conventional advertising but it reaches a much larger audience. They can also include animations and videos.

Before setting up a website, a business will need to register a **domain name**. This will be the URL (Uniform Resource Locator) or web address of the site. It is sensible to have a domain name that is similar to your company name e.g. http://www.kodak.com or http://www.cadbury.co.uk.

Domain names are unique so the business will have to make sure that nobody else is already using it.

Domain names should be easy to remember but they do not guarantee that the site is owned by who you think it might be. Visit http://www.brucespringsteen.com. This is not an official site but one run by a fan who registered the domain name first!

Companies may prefer to use a name linked to their business such as http://www.diy.com (B&Q). Some companies register the domain name first and then name the company after the URL, such as http://www.amazon.com or http://www.lastminute.com.

case study 1
▶ Domain name troubles

You might think that http://www.brucespringsteen.com is rock legend Bruce Springsteen's website. In fact it is an unauthorised Bruce Springsteen site.

Springsteen went to arbitration to try to win control of the domain name which was owned by Jeff Burgar, an Internet consultant from Alberta, Canada. However, Springsteen could not convince a United Nations arbitration panel that Burgar was using his name for profit or ill will. Burgar proved that he is using the site legitimately as a fanclub site.

Springsteen lost the case. 'It's the right decision,' says lawyer Marc E. Brown, a partner specialising in Internet law. He added it's often a case of 'who registers first, wins.'

Burgar might sound like the little guy fighting the rich rock star but he has registered 1,300 celebrity domain names, including variations on Carmen Electra, Mariah Carey, John Travolta, Tom Cruise, Melanie Griffith and the heavy metal band Guns N' Roses. The Canadian has also registered domain names corresponding with teams in the National Football League and National Basketball Association, as well as other sports franchises.

Geordie pop star Sting was denied ownership of Sting.com in a similar case. American Michael Urvan claimed to have been using the name Sting for eight years. Sting ended up buying the domain name from him.

Why buy and sell online?
It has been predicted that online shopping will account for a quarter of all sales by 2010. Why has e-shopping expanded so quickly? On the next page are some advantages and disadvantages.

Advantages of online shopping over conventional shopping for the customer

✓ Wide choice of items
✓ Can shop at any time, day or night
✓ Special websites compare prices at different sites and pick out the cheapest
✓ Saves travel, parking, pollution, etc

Disadvantages

✗ Can't see items
✗ You have to wait for it to arrive
✗ Possibility of fraud if your credit card details are intercepted
✗ Post and packing costs

Advantages of online shopping over conventional shopping for the store

✓ No need for expensive buildings, car parks, etc.

✓ Large customer base wherever you are based

✓ Data is entered into the computer for you (by the customer)
✓ You can set up in areas where it is cheap to operate, e.g. due to lower wages or taxes.

Disadvantages

✗ Dependent on the equipment – if it breaks down all business is lost
✗ Many people are reluctant to use online shopping as they are frightened of fraud
✗ As customers can't try out goods, e-tailers need to have a refund policy
✗ It may be unwise to send perishable and fragile items to customers by post

Advantages of online banking over conventional banking for the customer

✓ Available 24 hours a day, 7 days a week

✓ You can check balances without leaving home
✓ You can pay bills and set up direct debit online

✓ The bank does not have large overheads so can offer better interest rates

Disadvantages

✗ Dependent on the equipment – if it breaks down you can't use it
✗ Possibility of fraud

✗ There is no building to go to withdraw cash or pay bills – there has to be a link with other banks or the post office
✗ Lack of human touch – there is no bank manager to go and see

Promoting your site

Search engines such as Google and Lycos enable users to search the Internet using selected keywords. A search engine is a program that allows a user to enter a query and will search a very large database to find matching items. This is commonly known as **surfing the net**.

Google is the world's most popular search engine.

Figure 5.3 Google with the browser Mozilla Firebird

If you want to attract visitors to your site, it is a good idea to put keywords into the HTML script for a web page so that they are picked up by the search engines. You can also register with some search engines like Yahoo.

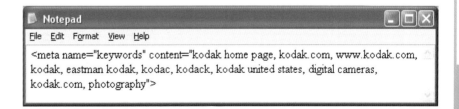

Figure 5.4 The keywords from the Kodak site

Activity 1

a) Go to a search engine like **Google**. Type in **diy online**. What do you get? Do you get a link to **www.diy.com**?

b) Visit a commercial site like http://www.cadbury.co.uk. Click on **View > Source**. Scroll down to the line beginning **<meta name="keywords"** Find the keywords for the site. Then go to a search engine and search on three of the keywords. Is the site listed?

E-commerce

E-commerce (Electronic commerce) is the conducting of business transactions over networks and through computers. It is usually used to describe buying and selling goods over the Internet but includes other electronic business transactions such as Electronic Data Interchange (EDI – see below), electronic money exchange and using point-of-sale (POS) terminals.

There seems no limit to what you can buy over the web. You can order clothes from catalogues or food and wine from supermarkets using your credit card. The volume of e-commerce sales in the UK is around £40 billion per year.

Videoconferencing

Videoconferencing, sometimes called teleconferencing, means being able to see and interact with people who are geographically apart. Two or more people can be connected to each other.

The equipment needed includes:

■ a high specification PC
■ a webcam usually positioned near the monitor
■ a headset consisting of a microphone and head phone.

A fast Internet connection is required to transmit the video images as well as videoconferencing software.

It is also possible to use dedicated videoconferencing equipment. These machines connect directly to each other using telecommunications links.

The use of videoconferencing enables business meetings and interviews to take place avoiding the expense and time of travel. The equipment can be expensive and at present the image quality is still not as good as on television or video but continues to develop as hardware improves.

Activity 2

See examples of videoconferencing at http://www.videoconferencing.com

Intranets and Extranets ◀

Intranets

An **intranet** is an internal network, for example, within a company, including information pages and electronic mail facilities. It uses the same browser software as the Internet and can also be connected to the Internet. A company could use this to provide employees with information – for example, schedules for the day, stock information or orders due for delivery, as well as internal e-mail.

The Bullring shopping centre in Birmingham is one of the most popular shopping centres in Europe.

The retailers share an intranet and each store can access information about the building, its services and facilities. The intranet gives the retailers easy access to site information when they need it, and helps to create community feeling among the shopkeepers.

Figure 5.5 The Bullring shopping centre in Birmingham

1. Explain the difference between an intranet and the Internet.
2. Explain how an intranet could be used by a school or college, and describe the information that could be stored on it.

Extranets

Companies can expand their corporate intranet systems into an extranet. This allows employees of another company, for example, a supplier, access to part of the first company's intranet. The supplier can access sales information for their products. Having this up-to-date information will help them plan their production schedules.

Extranet links can use either the Internet using **encryption** or private leased secure lines.

WHSmith News uses an extranet to allow its key customers such as Tesco, Asda and its own retail arm, WHSmith – to access sales data to improve their efficiency and help spot trends.

Richard Webb, business systems manager at WHSmith News, said the reports enable the company to react to sales trends and to help customers with their internal reporting to support decisions about production quantities.

'It also shows how we're performing. It's much more of a collaborative approach.'

WHSmith News saved £1 million in costs in its first year by using ICT to streamline its supply chain processes and reduce waste of the magazines it sends out to retailers.

Electronic Data Interchange (EDI)

▶ **EDI** is a means of transferring information such as invitations to tender, letters, orders and invoices electronically. It allows the computers in one organisation to 'talk' to the computers in their supplier's organisation, regardless of computer manufacturer or software type.

EDI cuts down the paper mountain. Although all large organisations and most smaller ones use computers, it is true that the vast majority are still essentially paper based.

For example, a simple order is raised on one computer, printed, mailed, then received by the supplier who rekeys the details into another computer. The process is expensive, time-consuming and prone to postal delays and errors. EDI changes all that. Acting as a giant, efficient electronic mailbox, it collects the orders directly from one company's computer and sends them to the supplier's computer. It cuts out printed mailings and removes rekeying, minimises the margin for error and saves days in the processing cycle.

case study 4
► EDI at Nissan

Nissan's Sunderland plant started production in 1986. Rapid increases in production levels meant that the paperwork generated soon reached large quantities with as many as 15,000 delivery notes each week.

The labour costs of dealing with all this paperwork and the associated mailing costs were excessive. There was also the potential for human error. Following an investigation Nissan decided to use EDI.

Almost immediately there were savings in labour and mailing costs, a shortening of the time for delivery information to reach suppliers and a reduction in the level of human errors. EDI is used to transmit delivery requirements to Nissan's logistics partner, Ryder Distribution Services, who in turn use EDI to send delivery data to Nissan. The volume of mail to suppliers was reduced by 90–95 per cent.

Electronic mail (E-mail) ◄

► With e-mail software it is very easy to send and receive electronic mail to or from any other person or organisation who has an e-mail address, known as a mailbox, anywhere in the world for the same cost as accessing the Internet. Most businesses now advertise their e-mail addresses. An e-mail address is usually of the form:

sally.miggins@computerland.co.uk

Addresses are in lower case letters. Words are separated by full stops. No spaces are allowed. The UK at the end is the only indication of the geographical location of this address.

E-mail software contains a text editor that allows a user to prepare a message. These messages are equivalent to traditional letters or memos that are delivered physically. E-mail does not have the facility for a one-to-one conversation as in a telephone conversation.

E-mails can include attachments – computer files that are sent with the e-mail. For example, it is possible to send word-processed documents and images as attachments. The person receiving the e-mail can then store and use these files in the normal way.

E-mails are stored on the Internet Service Provider's computer for the recipient and will be stored there whether or not the recipient's own computer is switched on. Users have to check their mailbox to see if they have any mail. If they forget to check, e-mail isn't very quick! E-mail can also be sent within an organisation on a local area network.

For dial-up connections e-mail software can be set up to check automatically for new mail every hour or so. However, always-on connections that receive e-mails straight away, are more common with the increase of broadband access.

Documents sent as e-mail attachments can be loaded by the receiver without the need to retype them. Journalists send copy to their newspapers by e-mail. The copy can then be imported into the newspaper's desktop publishing system.

E-mail software such as Microsoft Outlook Express enables users to:

- click on a Reply icon to reply to an e-mail without having to type in the recipient's e-mail address
- forward an e-mail to another e-mail address without retyping it
- set up an address book of e-mail addresses
- set up a group of several e-mail users to whom the same e-mail can be sent (See Case Study 5 below)
- set the priority for an e-mail
- store all e-mails sent and received.

case study 5
▶ Group e-mail

Charlie Moffat is the secretary of his local Civic Society. The society's executive committee meets four times a year. The committee has ten members. Whenever there was a meeting, Charlie used to type out an agenda, photocopy it ten times, place each copy of the agenda in an envelope, write a name and address on each envelope, stick on a stamp and post the letters.

Now Charlie sends out the agendas by e-mail. He has set up a *group* of all the committee members in his e-mail address book.

When Charlie writes to all the members of the committee, he creates a new e-mail. Then he only has to select the group name in his address book and the e-mail will be sent to all ten people.

- Describe three other features of e-mail.

Problems with the Internet ◀

▶ There is a vast amount of information available on the Internet and it is perhaps inevitable that problems arise. Some concerns include the following points:

✗ Material may not be factually correct – there is nobody to check or police content.

✗ A lot of information is out of date as site developers fail to update their sites regularly.

✗ Some sites contain pop-ups – annoying, unrequested advertisement pages that load automatically.

✗ It is possible to download software, videos and music from the Internet in breach of copyright laws.

✗ The Internet contains questionable material such as pornographic pictures, some of which may be illegal, such as child pornography.

✗ The text on some sites is offensive, for example, defamatory or racist literature.

✗ Viruses may be transmitted over the Internet. (See Chapter 7.)

✗ Fraud is common on the Internet. For example, sites claiming to sell items maybe totally fraudulent or because credit card numbers can be intercepted. According to the Association for Payment Clearing Services, this is estimated to be £138 million a year in the UK.

✗ Workers and students may simply waste time on the Internet. For example, visiting sites with games when they should be working. Surveys found that over 60 per cent of visits to pornographic sites were made during company time!

Where is a site based?

Internet sites are independent of their users' location. When you visit a site you cannot tell whether the server on which it is stored is in Britain or Bermuda. Internet companies can set up in areas that suit them, not areas close to their market.

For example, some betting companies set up websites in Gibraltar and the Channel Islands. This meant that gamblers using these sites did not have to pay the UK betting tax. Fearing a loss of trade, the British government scrapped betting tax.

Policing the Internet

The international nature of the Internet and the anonymous nature of the pages make policing very difficult. Some Internet Service Providers try to filter known offensive sites but millions of new pages are being created every year making the prevention of access difficult and prosecution practically impossible. Software can be installed that will filter out pages that contain any unacceptable words.

Different countries have different laws on such matters. If someone in country A publishes information that is legal in country A but illegal in country B, have they broken the law if someone in country B accesses their pages?

Despite the possible dangers, Internet access and e-commerce are growing rapidly.

Communications methods ◄

Fax

Fax is an alternative communications method. Like e-mail it arrives quickly and gives a hard copy.

Fax is short for facsimile transmission. A fax machine uses telephone lines to transmit copies of an original document. The fax machine scans the document, encodes the contents and transmits them to another fax machine that decodes and automatically prints a copy of the original.

The document is sent as a graphic and therefore takes longer to send than a text file. Obviously you can only send faxes to someone with a fax machine but fax machines are now extremely common in business.

Unlike e-mail which can only be received when the Internet connection is open, faxes arrive automatically. However, if information sent by fax has to be entered into a computer, it would have to be retyped, wasting time and introducing the possibility of errors.

Fax modems

In recent years, there has been a **convergence of technology** in the ICT industry. Computers can be used as televisions, video and DVD players, telephones, music players and fax machines. Fax modems can be used to send faxes as well as e-mails. However, the computer can only receive faxes if it is left turned on in receive mode.

E-mail or fax?

Sending a letter may be too slow. A phone call does not give a permanent record. An office in another time zone, for example, in Australia or the USA, may be closed. How can a business send a message? What are the advantages of using e-mail and fax?

Internal e-mail is suitable for memos within a business using an internal network. It is easy to use, involves no paper and costs nothing. However, in some offices it is replacing personal contact. Employees are sending e-mails to the next door office instead of going to see the recipient personally.

The telephone is still a very useful means of communication, particularly where personal contact is involved and an immediate answer is required.

	Fast?	Hard copy?	Who can receive it?	Can load directly into the computer?	Easy to use?	Cost?
E-mail	Yes, much faster than a letter. However, users must check their mailboxes regularly.	Yes but needs a printer	Only those with an e-mail address.	Yes, for example, a newspaper can place an article sent by e-mail directly into a desktop publishing program.	The recipient must log in to get it. It is possible to access e-mails from any computer with Internet access.	A subscription to an Internet Service Provider.
Fax	Yes but a fax sends a message as a picture. Therefore it takes longer than sending an e-mail which sends the message as text.	Yes	Only those with a fax machine or computer with fax/ modem.	No, a newspaper would normally have to re-type a faxed article.	Yes	Upwards of around £60 for the machine. Cost of call depends on distance.

Teletext

Teletext is an electronic information service which can be viewed on specially adapted televisions. The user will have to pay a little extra for a Teletext TV, which is operated using the TV's remote control. Teletext can be used to view information such as news, weather forecasts, TV schedules, traffic information and sports results provided by the television companies. Teletext is cheap and easy to use. 80 per cent of UK households have a teletext TV, with an average of 20 million people using the service each week. Each page is numbered and transmitted in sequence. When a particular page is requested the viewer must wait until the requested page is next transmitted.

Teletext services are offered by the BBC, ITV, Channel 4 and Channel 5. Viewers can access over 3,200 pages, with around 50,000 daily updates.

However, pages can be slow to load and restricted by the format of the page. Few colours are used and the graphics are poor.

Advantages and disadvantages of using Teletext as an information source

Advantages	Disadvantages
✓ Cheap to use; most households in the UK own a TV set. For a small extra cost teletext provides access to a range of information.	✗ Only a limited amount of information is available.
✓ No need to buy a computer.	✗ Changing from page to page can be slow.
✓ Easy to use; information can be accessed from an armchair using a remote control handset to enter the number of the page required.	✗ The information is only text based; only very poor graphics are displayed.
	✗ Limited interaction

Viewdata

Viewdata was a forerunner to the Internet enabling users to send e-mail and to access and send information. Examples of its use included home banking, home shopping or holiday booking by using a specially adapted television set and a telephone line. By today's standards it was very primitive and limited.

PRESTEL provided by British Telecom was the world's first public viewdata service, starting in 1979. PRESTEL was never very successful but a French equivalent Minitel still has millions of users.

Advantages and disadvantages of using Viewdata as an information source

Advantages	Disadvantages
✓ Interactive; can search databases, pay bills or order goods	✗ Need to use telephone line, so increased running costs compared to Teletext.
✓ No need to purchase a computer — use a TV.	✗ Has been totally superseded by the Internet.
✓ Can store large quantities of data	✗ Slow to operate
	✗ Low resolution graphics

Worked exam question

1 Students at a university are provided with free Internet access by the university.

   a) Describe one advantage to the university of providing this Internet access. (2)

   b) Describe one advantage (other than a financial one) to the students of having Internet access provided by the university. (2)

   c) Describe two disadvantages to the students of using the Internet for study. (4)

January 2004 ICT1

▶ **EXAMINER'S GUIDANCE** a) *This part says describe and has two marks. You will get one mark for stating the advantage and the second for giving a reason why it is an advantage. Remember an advantage must compare using the Internet with alternatives such as looking in books. The reason must be linked to the advantage:*

▶ **SAMPLE ANSWER** Students will have access to a huge amount of material for research. Students can conduct this research much more quickly than searching through books and other materials.

▶ **EXAMINER'S GUIDANCE** b) *This question is similar but must be from the student's point of view:*

▶ **SAMPLE ANSWER** Students can submit work by e-mail. This is much easier than submitting the work on paper.

▶ **EXAMPLES** c) *Examples of possible answers include:*

▶ **SAMPLE ANSWER** Information on the Internet may be inaccurate as the information may be out of date and there might not be a date of publication on the web page.

Students may experience health problems such as backache due to overuse of ICT.

SUMMARY

▶ **There are many communication methods that use Information technology. The most commonly used are:**
  ▶ **e-mail**
  ▶ **fax**
  ▶ **Internet**
  ▶ **mobile phones**
  ▶ **pagers**
  ▶ **satellite phones**
  ▶ **teletext**
  ▶ **text messaging**
  ▶ **videoconferencing.**

▶ **To access the internet, a home user would normally need:**
  ▶ **a computer**
  ▶ **a telephone line which provides the physical connection to a network**
  ▶ **a modem or a broadband modem**
  ▶ **communication software – a browser and e-mail software**
  ▶ **a subscription to an Internet Service Provider.**

▶ **An intranet is an internal network, giving employees access to the organisation's documents. It uses the same software as the Internet and can also be connected to the Internet.**

▶ **An extranet gives outside users, for example, suppliers or customers access to a specific part of a company's intranet.**

▶ **EDI (Electronic Data Interchange) means transferring documents, which traditionally have been sent in paper form, electronically.**

▶ **E-mail software allows a user to send e-mails to many recipients at once, to forward e-mails to a different recipient and to send computer files as attachments.**

Chapter 5 Questions

1. The use of e-mail has increased dramatically over the last five years. This has improved communications both internally within a company, and externally between companies and their suppliers and customers. Describe the facilities of an e-mail software package that you would use to carry out the following tasks efficiently.
   a) Pass on an e-mail message that you have received, in error, from a customer to the sales manager. (2)
   b) Inform a group of staff about the time and date of a meeting. (2)
   c) Send designs of a new product to the manufacturing department. (2)
   d) Send an important and urgent message to a supplier. (2)

   January 2001 ICT1

2. A British company has offices in California and New Zealand. Describe **three** ways in which the company can use the Internet to communicate with its offices abroad. (6)

3. A company that makes cricket bats intends to set up a website to advertise its range of products, and to take orders online.
   a) Describe **two** factors that the company should consider when deciding on a name for its website. (4)
   b) Having decided upon a name for the site, describe the next step that the company must take before it can use the name. (2)
   c) Describe **two** ways in which the company could use the facilities available on the Internet to encourage visitors to use their site. (4)

   June 2003 ICT1

4. You are using the Internet to research African history for an essay. You do not know of any suitable websites.
   a) Describe how you can use the Internet to find suitable websites to research African history. (2)
   b) Describe **one** concern that you may have about using this method of research. (2)

5. A company sales manager is working away from home and the office for a week.
   Describe **two** ways in which he can use ICT to send data to the office. (4)

   January 2003 ICT1

6. A local college has started running its courses online. Describe:
   a) **two** advantages to a learner of following an online course (4)
   b) **one** disadvantage to a learner of following an online course (2)
   c) **two** advantages to the course organisers at the college of providing a course online. (4)

   January 2003 ICT1

7. Many organisations have adopted e-mail as a method of communication only to find that it can have disadvantages. Describe **three** disadvantages of the use of e-mail, other than contracting viruses, for business communication. (6)

   June 2002 ICT1

8. You have just seen an advertisement for Internet banking on the television. Describe **three** concerns you might have about using this method of banking. (6)

9. A large clothing retailer has decided to set up an online store.
   a) Explain **two** advantages to the retailer of using this method of selling as opposed to selling from a high street shop. (4)
   b) Explain **one** advantage to the customer of using the online store rather than a high street shop. (2)
   c) State **one** disadvantage to the customer of using the online store rather than a high street shop. (1)
   d) Describe **two** ways in which the retailer could make use of the Internet to publicise its new service. (4)

   January 2002 ICT1

10. Mrs Jones has bought a book on gardening from a book company on the World Wide Web. She has now started to receive e-mails about garden furniture and is receiving plant catalogues through the post.
    a) Explain why Mrs Jones has started to receive the e-mails and the catalogues. (2)
    b) Some people are worried about ordering goods using credit cards over the Internet. Explain what can be done by the book company to prevent credit card details being misused. (2)

    June 2001 ICT1

11. Browsers and search engines are two items that are associated with the use of the Internet.

a) Explain what is meant by:

   i)   a browser   (2)

   ii) a search engine.   (2)

b) In order to use the Internet, the owner of a PC at home normally needs to register with an Internet Service Provider (ISP). State two services, in addition to e-mail, that an ISP could provide.   (2)

c) Changes in technology now mean that it is no longer necessary to have a PC to be able to use some Internet services. Give two devices that can be used instead.   (2)

d) Explain why it is possible to send e-mail successfully to someone who has not got his or her PC switched on.   (2)

June 2001 ICT1

There are many different jobs associated with ICT. Some jobs will involve using ICT only some of the time. Other jobs will involve using ICT most if not all of the time. These include development personnel such as systems analysts and programmers who produce new systems, and operational personnel such as operators and support staff who keep the system running and provide help for the users of the system.

There has been a blurring of definitions as some staff are responsible for development and support, as can be seen from the advertisements in figure 6.1. The Database Administrator post, for example, is involved in investigation, implementation and support.

The range of work in the ICT industry is huge and always changing. Each job will have specific skill and knowledge requirements. There are, however, personal qualities and general characteristics that are relevant to many fields of work within the ICT industry. It is often the possession of these, as much as specific ICT skills, that allows an individual to progress to a senior position.

PRODUCT DATA ANALYST

Intelligent? Efficient team player with attention to detail? Strong data analysis skills? Excel a must and Access DB a plus. Leading e-marketing company based in Leeds. Small team environment. Fun work culture. Excellent package.
Send CV to ICT@ICT.uk or fax 020 56789

WEB DEVELOPER
XHTML : PHP
CSS: MYSQL

Central London marketing agency working on creative projects. Salary on application.

Senior IT Support Person

Package 30K Plus Exciting role providing Pre and Post sales support to our customers. Visit www.itsupport.com to see our software solutions.

Based in Cumbria

We are also recruiting Sales People with experience in Technical Sales OTE 35K Plus
No agencies

IT Support

£24–28k + Bens

IT Security company is looking for a Support Engineer to provide internal/customer support. Solid expertise in Microsoft networking. Exp in following a plus: fw's, anti-virus, IDS, TCP/IP. Training provided.
Please send CV to jobs@jobs.com

Technical
Consultants

You will have a background of application design, specification and integration.

You will be able to research and analyse technical requirements at all levels and match these to the needs and constraints of the business.

You will have the capacity to produce creative and cost effective solutions within a complex customer environment. You will be confident with a consultative approach and be an effective communicator with business and technical people.

Figure 6.1 Job advertisements

Personal qualities and general characteristics

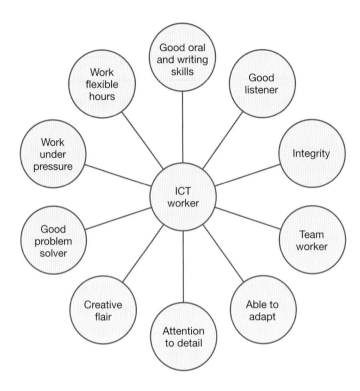

Figure 6.2 Personal characteristics

Good communications

The computer boffin, who rarely speaks to anyone but sits alone all day hunched over a computer screen, is a common public image of a person in the ICT industry. In fact there are few jobs that allow such isolation. Most require some communication with others – both oral and written. The jobs of three ICT professionals, Jeremy, Nathan and Sophie are described in case studies at the end of the chapter. In all three the importance of good communication skills is emphasised.

Written

At all stages of the system life cycle, written reports are produced. These may include feasibility studies, specifications, maintenance and end user guides as well as progress reports for management. The ICT professional will need to be competent in writing a variety of documents in good clear language, in a style, and using a level of technical detail that is appropriate for the audience.

A program developer needs to produce written documentation for his programs so that, when a program needs to be modified at a later date, other developers can gain a clear understanding of what the program actually does.

A software developer, when investigating an end user's requirements for a new ICT system, will need to be able to make clear notes of interviews and provide the user with clear documentation of the system to enable discussion. In Case Study 3, Sophie produces requirements specifications for her clients. To do this she writes a report that brings together the findings of all her discussions and observations. It lays out, in detail, what the new system is to do. It is important that Sophie writes the report in a clear, understandable way so that no confusion arises.

A member of a software company's help desk team would need to be able to document faults clearly and document solutions using technical terminology for the use of a fellow professional. They would also need the ability to provide written instructions suitable for non-technical system users. Such instructions would need to be written in clear, plain English avoiding technical terms and jargon.

Oral

When working with end users of a system, ICT professionals need to be able to discuss problems with users and provide solutions in a clear, jargon-free and friendly way. This will enable efficient and effective communication. Considerable time may be spent in face-to-face discussion with end users who have little knowledge of the technicalities of ICT systems. If an ICT support worker does not have good communication skills, he is likely to confuse a user when he tries to help them solve their problems. Care must be taken not to use language that will antagonise, patronise or confuse in such circumstances; jargon should be avoided.

A member of a help desk team will need to find out an end user's problem through careful questioning and then give instructions in a clear and understandable way. Case Study 1 describes how Jeremy has to feed back to a user the solution to a printer problem. He has to do this in a way that is clear and appropriate.

The ability to listen

An ICT professional investigating an end user's requirements will need to be a good listener by concentrating fully so that he obtains a clear understanding of what the user requires. Many new systems have proved to be unsatisfactory because the ICT specialist produced what he thought the user should want rather than what was actually needed. Sophie, in Case Study 3, is very careful to listen to the end user so that the system requirements that she produces fully meet the user's needs.

If a member of a help desk team does not listen very carefully to the end user then the user's wants can be misinterpreted or ignored and inappropriate instructions given. This can lead to frustration for the end user; he may decide not to ask for help again.

Integrity

An employee in the ICT industry must be trustworthy. An individual might have access to sensitive information and it is important that they can be relied upon not to misuse it.

A systems developer working with a client will obtain detailed information about the organisation that needs to be kept confidential.

Teamworking and getting on with a variety of people

The ability to work effectively in a team is essential for nearly all ICT practitioners as few work in isolation. A good team member is sensitive to the needs of other members, reliable, supportive and co-operative. In a strong team, ideas, views and information are freely shared and members build on the strengths of others.

ICT professionals are likely to need to interact with a range of people in an open and non-threatening way. When a member of an ICT support team goes to a user to help with a problem the user may be angry or frustrated. The support worker must display patience and act tactfully, politely and supportively. A software developer, when investigating the end user's requirements, needs to be approachable and gain the user's trust. If the user does not feel at ease it is unlikely that the developer will obtain all the information that he needs.

When a member of a help desk team is attempting to solve a problem for a user it is important that she keeps calm and prevents the end user from getting flustered.

Adaptability and the willingness to learn new skills

The one certainty in the ICT industry is that nothing stays the same! The rate of change in hardware and software performance has been very rapid in the last decade. Skills regularly need updating and old ways of doing things are often abandoned. A successful ICT practitioner must be able to adapt easily to new working methods. Much work is project based and an ICT worker is likely to move between teams. As projects overlap, it is not unusual to be a member of more than one team at the same time.

An openness to new ideas is essential. Sometimes courses are available for updating skills but the most effective employee is one who is able to acquire new skills in a variety of ways. Jeremy (Case Study 1) has to keep up to date with the regular developments that occur in the college network systems.

A help desk operator will need to keep up to date with changes in software.

Thoroughness and attention to detail

There are many ICT jobs that require precision and a detailed approach. For example, if a programmer does not follow the specification exactly then the resulting program may have unpredictable effects when implemented. A system tester must ensure that every test is carried out as specified and that results are accurately recorded. Those involved with entering data into a live computer system need to work with a high level of accuracy as incorrect data entry will lead to incorrect information.

Creative flair

The ability to think innovatively and come up with new ideas is needed in some ICT jobs. An outstanding programmer needs to have more than the necessary technical language skills. To solve some problems, an effective programmer will need to think of new ways of finding solutions. However, programmers are likely to have to stick exactly to a given specification and will be expected to work within tightly defined parameters. 'Creative flair' cannot be used as an excuse to implement a system in a way that appeals to the programmer but does not meet the needs of the user as laid out in the requirements specifications!

If a web designer is to create exciting and effective sites, she will need to possess a strong visual sense and spatial awareness as well as sound technical knowledge. Nathan, in Case Study 2, needs to show such flair if he is to come up with solutions to unusual problems.

Analytical approach to problem solving

An ability to approach problem solving in a systematic and logical way is essential for many ICT roles. Many organisations require new employees to take aptitude tests to demonstrate that they can take this approach.

A network manager may have to work out the cause and location of a fault in a network. To do so efficiently requires a systematic and logical approach. A member of a help desk team needs to consider alternatives and find solutions to end user problems. They need to stick at the problem and see it through until a solution is found.

When producing a requirements specification or designing a new system, an ICT professional needs to use an analytical approach to make sure that all factors are taken into account. Such an approach is necessary for Jeremy, Nathan and Sophie in each of their jobs. (See Case Studies 1, 2 and 3.)

Ability to work under pressure

There are likely to be many situations when an ICT professional is under pressure: a deadline could be looming, a program might not be performing as it should, a crucial hardware device could fail or a user could come up with unexpected and urgent demands. The pressures might mean that the employee has to work very long hours for a period of time.

The professional has to be able to take orders, be responsible for their own job and perhaps manage several different jobs at the same time. The ability to organise time and to prioritise tasks is vital. It is important that deadlines are met and work is not left to the last minute. This is apparent in Sophie's role (Case Study 3). She has to meet the demands of several projects as well as putting in many extra hours of work to ensure that deadlines are met.

Willingness to work flexible hours

In certain jobs it is essential that the employee is able to work flexible hours. Many systems for multi-national organisations are worldwide and different offices will be in very different time zones. An employee providing software support could be working in London, whilst the users are located in Los Angeles. When a new system is introduced it is likely that she will be required to work late into the night so that she is available to answer queries that occur during the Los Angeles working day.

An ICT support worker is often required to be available 'on call'. This means that for certain hours, when the employee is not in the office, she must be available to be contacted by pager to deal with queries. This could occur in the middle of the night. As an example, in Case Study 1, every fourth week Jeremy has to work until 8p.m. on week nights as well as Saturday to ensure that support is available to the users of the network.

When a network fault occurs a team member will need to find a solution as quickly as possible even if this means working past the official end of the day. New software may need to be installed at times when the usage of the network is low, perhaps an evening or at weekends.

Skills and knowledge ◀

> Each job will have its own technical skills requirements. These are not personal skills. (Remember to read exam questions carefully – do not include an answer about skills and knowledge if the question asks for personal characteristics.)

Skills requirements might relate to the characteristics of specific hardware, the use of a range of facilities offered by particular software, or perhaps the knowledge of a given programming language. Such skill requirements are not static and an ICT professional will need to regularly update their skills. A network manager will need to have a very detailed and specific technical knowledge of networking. A web developer will need to have a completely different set of knowledge and skills.

For ICT roles such as systems developers, a knowledge of general business practice is essential as well as a detailed understanding of the specific industry, such as banking, retail or education.

Activity 1

Imagine that you are preparing your CV to use in applications for jobs in the ICT industry.

1. Prepare a list of your ICT skills and knowledge.
2. Itemise the *personal* qualities that you possess which would show that you are suitable for employment. Back up each quality that you list with evidence to support your claim.

For example, you could be good at teamworking as you have successfully taken part in an expedition for a Duke of Edinburgh Award.

Activity 2

Use the Internet to search for job advertisements in the following fields:

Database administrator   Programmer
Data entry clerk   Systems analyst
Network administrator   User support
Web designer

Draw up a table with the following headings to display your findings:

Job title	Skills and experience	Personal qualities

case study 1
► Jeremy

Jeremy is the senior ICT technician in a FE college and has three technicians working to him. The normal working day is 8.30a.m. to 5p.m. but once every four weeks he has to stay until 8p.m. on Monday to Thursday as well as cover on the Saturday. The following week he has Monday off. Some tasks, such as adding a network printer to a classroom, which involves installing the printer driver in all 20 computers, can overrun at the end of the day. The task cannot be left as the computers will be needed by a class at 9a.m. the next day.

Jeremy's job is varied. When he gets to college his first task is to check that nothing has gone wrong overnight and that the backup procedures took place satisfactorily. Part of the day will be spent staffing the help desk. In between calls he will get on with other tasks such as monitoring the network usage, studying the documentation for new software, or preparing material for a staff training session.

At the help desk, all user problems are logged on a database and when a problem is solved the resolution is added. Often a problem will require Jeremy to go to the user to resolve the fault on site. There are over 300 members of staff with vastly differing ICT skills. Jeremy has to make sure that the explanation and help he gives are appropriate to that user and that he neither goes over their head on the one hand nor patronises them on the other. For example, it is important that someone who reports a printer fault is not made to feel stupid when it turns out that they failed to check that the mains lead was attached. On the other hand, they need to be made aware so that they won't call the help desk for the same problem again!

The software and hardware used in the college is regularly updated. Jeremy has to teach himself the details of the changes. Sometimes the manufacturer may run a course, but more often he will learn through help files available on the Internet and by reading articles in specialist magazines.

Much of Jeremy's time is spent on housekeeping and other network jobs. To enable him to do this he has full access rights to the entire network.

■ Describe the personal characteristics that Jeremy needs to be successful in his job and explain why each is needed.

Worked Answer

Jeremy has to be prepared to work flexible hours as jobs such as installing a printer driver may require him to work past the end of the working day. His work on the help desk requires excellent oral communication skills as he works directly with end users. He needs to provide them with solutions to their problems in a suitable and understandable manner. He needs to be a good listener so that he can correctly interpret what a user requires and must be patient when listening to users' problems. Jeremy must adopt an analytical approach when solving a user's problem that has not occurred before so that a solution can be found as quickly as possible.

case study 2
▶ Nathan

Nathan is a technical consultant for a business specialising in producing software for conducting e-business over the Internet and using wireless devices. He has to use his extensive technical knowledge to provide a detailed solution for a user's application and hardware. This requires a clear, logical approach to solving the problem, so that all factors are taken into account, combined with a creative flair that allows him to find ways to deal with unusual problems. He needs to present his solution in terms that the user will understand.

When Nathan first meets a customer, they can be in a state of panic, as he is often called in to resolve a live problem that is affecting current service. To reassure them that he can solve the problem, he needs to ask questions before the meeting and carry out some background research. He has to ask clear and concise questions and not get lost in too much detail. He needs to develop a rapport with the client and must establish some common ground and avoid disagreement.

Meeting with clients is only part of Nathan's job. He also has to oversee the development of new software, resolve performance issues, discuss hardware requirements and provide plans for the next release of software. Many of the tasks he needs to complete stretch over a number of weeks. Each week he has to decide how much attention is needed by each task. Sometimes he has to work long hours as several tasks may require attention at the same time. In general he works on his own with his client.

Nathan finds consulting an exciting and diverse career but does not enjoy the travelling that it involves. His daily travel varies from an hour on the train to two hours in a car, with the additional complication that his location from week to week, and sometimes day to day, is not known until the last minute.

■ Copy and complete the table below. The table should contain five personal qualities needed by Nathan in his job, together with a justification of each.

Personal Quality	Justification
Needs to be able to get on with a variety of people	Nathan's job involves him working closely with customers who have problems with their current systems. He needs to gain their confidence to make sure that he finds out the information he needs as quickly as possible.
Ability to work under pressure	
Adaptability	

case study 3
▶ Sophie

Sophie works as a project manager in the central ICT department of a high street bank.

After gathering user requirements, she designs the system solution and specifies the requirement for developers (programmers) on her team. She manages the implementation of the solution including the physical release of software. Knowledge of the business area and the system enables her to design the best solution for the users. She always has to consider the users' role and how she can best solve their problems. It is very important that she listens carefully to what the user says by concentrating carefully and asking questions to make sure that she understands what she has been told. The new system needs to be based on what is really needed, not just what Sophie herself thinks should be needed.

The initial stages of the projects involve requirements gathering and the writing of specifications documented in a form that is clear to the users and the system developers. This liaison will continue throughout the project, with informal meetings with the users during development and implementation.

In the banking world, work tends to be driven by deadlines. As a project nears the time when it needs to be delivered it is often necessary to undertake evening and weekend work. The system that Sophie works on has global coverage so different time zones often require late and early conference meetings. She currently travels to Paris and New York as her two main projects are based there.

Often new tasks arise that have not been planned for. (This happened recently when a new project had been prioritised by someone very senior in the bank.) This causes difficulties because she either has to manage to fit the additional tasks in or tell other users that their deadlines cannot be met.

Her team is currently providing post-implementation support for a completed project and providing handover to those responsible for day-to-day support. She is also managing two further projects in parallel which are at different stages in the project cycle, as well as assisting on two other projects for which her specific expertise is required.

■ Describe the personal characteristics that Sophie needs to be successful in her job and explain why each is needed.

Worked exam question

When producing a requirements specification for an ICT solution to a task, an IT professional needs to use certain personal skills. State two such personal skills and explain why each of them will benefit the IT professional when preparing the requirements specification. (4)

January 2004 ICT1

▶ EXAMINER'S GUIDANCE
There are many characteristics that you could choose from; make sure that you choose two that you can back up with a good justification. There have been many questions similar to this one. You must be very careful to look at the particular context (in this case someone is preparing a requirements specification) and make sure that your answer fits it – don't rush in with any general answer.

▶ SAMPLE ANSWER
In Case Study 3, Sophie has to prepare requirements specifications for her bank. She needs to have good written skills as she has to write 'specifications documented in a form that is clear to the users and the system developers'.

She needs to have good listening skills. To produce an accurate specification she must listen to what the 'user says by concentrating carefully and asking questions to make sure that she understands what she has been told. The new system needs to be based on what is really needed'.

▶ EXAMINER'S GUIDANCE
Other possible answers are given below. Produce your own justification for each based on the Case Study 3. You will need to refer to the main text.

- *Be approachable and gain the users' confidence*
- *Have good analytical skills*
- *Be able to communicate well orally*

SUMMARY ◀

As well as requiring specific ICT skills, professionals in the industry are likely to need some or all of the following personal qualities. It is important to be able relate the quality to the particular jobs as some attributes may not be appropriate.

▶ **Good written communication skills**

▶ **Good oral communication skills**

▶ **The ability to listen**

▶ **Integrity**

▶ **Teamworking and getting on with a variety of people**

▶ **Thoroughness and attention to detail**

▶ **Creative flair**

▶ **Analytical approach to problem solving**

▶ **Ability to manage pressure**

▶ **Willingness to work flexible hours**

▶ **Adaptability and the willingness to learn new skills**

Chapter 6 Questions

1. An important part of the development of an ICT solution is the production of documentation for its users.
Describe **two** personal skills that are needed by an ICT professional when producing user documentation. (4)

June 2004 ICT1

2. You have been asked to write a job description for a vacancy on a software company's help desk team.
State, giving a reason for each, **two** personal qualities that are relevant to the job which you would ask for in the description. (4)

January 2003 ICT1

3. Professionals involved with ICT systems often have to work with people who have little, or no, understanding of the ICT systems that they are using.
State **two** personal qualities that ICT professionals should have that will enable them to help such people effectively, and give an example of when each quality would be needed. (4)

June 2005 ICT1

4. A company is recruiting a new member of staff for its ICT support desk. The head of personnel has asked the manager of the support desk what personal qualities the new employee should have in order to be able to carry out the job effectively.
State, with reasons, **two** personal qualities that the manager would want a new employee on the help desk to have. (4)

January 2005 ICT1

What is computer crime? ◀

▶ Computer crime is any criminal act that has been committed using a computer as the principal tool. As the role of computers in society has increased, opportunities for crime have been created that never existed before.

Computer crime can take the form of:

- the theft of money (for example, the transfer of payments to the wrong accounts)
- the theft of information (for example, from files or databases)
- the theft of goods (by their diversion to the wrong destination) or
- malicious vandalism (for example, destruction of data or instroducing viruses).

Committing a crime breaks the law as passed by Parliament. Crimes are punished through the courts. Punishments are likely to take the form of a fine or, in severe cases, prison.

What is malpractice? ◀

▶ Malpractice is defined as negligent or improper professional behaviour. It occurs when employees, although not breaking the law, perform acts that go against their professional code of practice and, intentionally or unintentionally, cause harm to their organisation or clients. An employee who carelessly leaves his workstation logged on, or divulges his password to others, could be enabling unauthorised access to data.

Excessive use of a computer at work for personal use by an employee could be malpractice.

Malpractice is not breaking the law but breaking professional rules set by the employer or professional body. Punishment is likely to be a warning, downgrading, dismissal or expulsion from the professional body depending on severity.

Why is computer crime on the increase?

The rapid spread of personal computers, wide area networks and distributed processing, has made information held on computer more vulnerable. The arrival of ATMs (Automated

Teller Machines), the Internet and mobile phones has created new opportunities for illegal activity.

Every single one of the top 100 companies in the FTSE Index has been targeted or actually burgled by computer criminals. The British police have evidence of 70,000 cases where systems have been penetrated and information extracted. One enquiry revealed three hackers had been involved in making 15,000 extractions from systems.

case study 1
▶ 28 arrested in global web fraud sting

Robert Jaques, vnunet.com 29 October 2004

Police have arrested 28 individuals suspected of being part of a global Internet-based organised crime network dealing in identity theft, computer fraud, credit card fraud and conspiracy.

A 19-year-old British man from Camberley, Surrey, was arrested as part of the sting operation on Wednesday by National Hi-Tech Crime Unit (NHTCU) officers.

Led by the US Secret Service, investigators from nearly 30 US and foreign law enforcement agencies nabbed 27 others from seven countries suspected of being involved in the crime ring.

Criminals allegedly used three websites to traffic counterfeit credit cards and false identification information, and documents such as credit cards, driver's licences, domestic and foreign passports and birth certificates.

'We believe that the suspects have trafficked at least 1.7 million stolen credit card numbers, leading to losses by financial institutions running into the millions,' said acting detective chief superintendent Mick Deats, head of the NHTCU.

1. What is meant by identity theft?
2. Research other cases of Internet-based crime.

Banking security experts in the USA have estimated that an average bank robbery nets $1900 and the perpetrator gets prosecuted 82 per cent of the time. With a computer fraud, the proceeds are nearer to $250,000 and less than two per cent of the offenders get prosecuted.

Weak points within an IT system ◀

▷ The weak points within an IT system are associated with hardware, software and people. Particular threats include:

- data being wrongly entered into a system
- access to data stored online
- access to data stored offline such as on a floppy disk
- viruses
- data being transmitted using a network

- internal staff not following procedures
- people from outside trying to see/steal/alter data.

Data entry

Data can be fraudulently entered into the system with criminal intent. A corrupt data entry clerk could purposely enter the wrong account number for a transaction so that an unsuspecting account holder is debited. An employee, who was operating a system that photographed students and produced college identification cards, was caught accepting bribes from students to input false dates of birth to be printed on to the card.

case study 2
▶ Bank fraud

A woman, who opened a bank account using false information, saying that she expected to receive her divorce settlement shortly, carried out a more elaborate fraud. She later returned to the bank and surreptitiously removed all the paying-in slips (used by customers to pay money into their accounts) and replaced them with paying-in slips that she had had specially printed.

These paying-in slips were exactly the same except they had her account number printed at the bottom in MICR characters — just like the paying-in slips at the back of a chequebook.

When reading paying-in slips, the computer looks for the MICR numbers. If there are none, the operator has to type in the bank account number given. If there are MICR numbers, the information is automatically read and not checked.

Money paid in with the fake paying-in slips was paid directly into the woman's account. Customers did not notice any errors until they checked their bank statements. By this time the woman had withdrawn over $150,000 in cash from her 'divorce settlement', disappeared and was never seen again.

Data stored on computer

Users' personal computers are particularly vulnerable, especially if they are attached to a network. If unauthorised users can gain access to the system they could be able to retrieve, take a copy of or alter data. This could be achieved if a computer user were to leave her computer unattended whilst logged on to a system, with no form of protection.

The use of laptop and palmtop computers produces risks whenever sensitive data is being stored. Such devices are more easily stolen as the following article shows.

case study 3
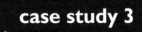
▶ MI5 laptop theft

John Leyden, vnunet.com 24 Mar 2000

A laptop computer containing sensitive information on Northern Ireland has been stolen from an MI5 intelligence agent, it emerged today as security experts warned that not all the information on the device was necessarily secure.

The £2,000 computer was snatched from the Security Service worker as he stopped to help a passer-by in the ticket hall at Paddington Underground station in central London.

■ State three things the MI5 agent could have done to reduce the risk of losing a computer with sensitive and valuable data.

Data stored offline

Data that is stored offline, for example, on a floppy disk, a CD-R or a memory stick, is vulnerable to loss or theft. Disk stores should be kept locked when left unattended. There should be formal clerical systems in place so that details are recorded whenever disks leave the store. The filing and recording system should be maintained rigorously to ensure that files stored on removable media are not mislaid.

Viruses

A virus is a program that is written with the sole purpose of infecting computer systems. Most viruses cause damage to files that are stored on the computer's hard disk. A virus on a hard disk of an infected computer can reproduce itself onto a floppy disk. When the floppy disk is used on a second computer, the virus copies itself on to this computer's hard disk. A type of virus program called a **worm** is a stand-alone executable program that exploits the facilities of the host computer to spread.

This spreading of the virus is hidden and automatic and the user is usually unaware of the existence of the virus until something goes wrong. Another form of virus is the **Trojan Horse**, a destructive program that passes itself off as an innocent program.

Thousands of viruses exist with their damage varying from the trivial to the disastrous. Some viruses have little effect. Others delete all your data.

A lot of viruses are distributed by e-mail. You may get an e-mail that says something like

Hi! I am looking for new friends.
My name is Jane, I am from Miami, FL.
See my homepage with my weblog and latest webcam photos!
See you!

If you open the attached file or click on the hyperlink, you will probably contract the virus. This sort of virus is very prevalent as the story below reveals.

case study 4
▶ Christmas card virus hits one in 10 e-mails

Robert Jaques, vnunet.com 16 December 2004

The Zafi-D worm (W32/Zafi-D), discovered earlier this week posing as a Christmas greeting, is spreading rapidly around the world.

IT security experts have reported that the virus is currently accounting for around three-quarters of all virus reports, with some estimates suggesting that the infection is present in as many as one in 10 e-mails.

Zafi-D, which is believed to originate from Hungary, spreads inside bogus Christmas greeting e-mails. The e-mails can use a variety of languages including English, French, Spanish and Hungarian.

■ Give three pieces of advice about how to avoid these viruses.

Find out about the latest virus threats at
http://us.mcafee.com/virusInfo/default.asp

Networks

Data being transmitted over a network is particularly vulnerable to external threat. The risk of unauthorised access increases when data is transferred over a WAN using public communication links. A line can be tapped to allow eavesdropping of the signal being transmitted along the link. This has been recognised as a real problem for Internet users.

Many people will not purchase goods via the Internet because they are concerned about the risk of their credit card details ending up in the wrong hands.

Internet

The rapid growth in the use of the Internet, for advertising, selling goods and for communication, has made many information systems vulnerable to attack.

Internal IT personnel

Security procedures are only as good as the people using and enforcing them. A high percentage of breaches of a company's security are made by its own employees. Sometimes this is due to laziness and not following procedures. Sometimes it is due to dishonesty.

Disgruntled, dishonest and greedy employees can pose a big threat to an organisation as they have easy access to the information system. They may be seeking personal gain and it is not unknown for employees to be bribed to provide information to a rival. Data may be altered or erased to sabotage the efforts of a company. Information about a business may be of great value to a competitor. Industrial espionage does exist in the cut-throat competitive world of big business.

External threats – hacking

Hacking means attempting to gain unauthorised access to a computer system – that is, use by a person who has not been given permission to do so. Anyone who gains unauthorised access is often called a hacker. Hacking is often achieved via telecommunications links. Many hackers have no specific fraudulent intent but enjoy the challenge of breaking into a system.

Although they may have considerable technical expertise, it is possible to find guides on hacking on the Internet. These allow less expert users to become hackers. In some instances the hacker's purpose in accessing the system could be to commit fraud, to steal commercially valuable data or even to cause damage to data that will have serious consequences for the company whose system it is.

case study 5
▶ Hackers

Gregory Herns, 21, from Oregon, USA and Joseph McElroy, 18, from East London might be regarded as typical hackers. They both hacked into computer systems not because they were malicious but because they wanted to store files that they had downloaded illegally.

Herns hacked into the network at the NASA Space Flight Centre to store some movie files. The attack caused NASA's systems to crash and cost $200,000 to fix. In court Herns admitted his guilt and apologised for the inconvenience he had caused. He was jailed for six months.

McElroy hacked into no less than 17 computers within the Fermi National Accelerator Laboratory in America. He used the computers that he hacked into to store hundreds of gigabytes of illegal games, music and movies to exchange with his friends.

New Scotland Yard's Computer Crime Unit traced McElroy's IP address, the unique identifier for computers connected to the Internet. He was sentenced to 200 hours community service for breaking the Computer Misuse Act, 1990.

More serious was the case of Daniel Baas. Baas, 25, from Ohio USA, hacked into several commercial computer systems including Acxiom, one of the world's largest credit card database users. Baas was apparently motivated by curiosity but stole about 300 computer passwords and data files from Acxiom.

Baas' actions cost Acxiom about $5.8 million in staff time and travel expenses, payments for security audits and new encryption software. Judge Dennis Helmick sentenced Baas to $2\frac{1}{2}$ years in jail.

Methods of protection ◀

Physical security

The most obvious way to protect access to data is to lock the door to any computer installation. The lock can be operated by a conventional key, a 'swipe' card or a code number typed into a keypad. Of course it is essential that any such code must be kept secret. Staff should not lend keys or swipe cards to anybody else. Locks activated by voice recognition or fingerprint comparison offer alternative, but expensive, stronger methods of security. (See section on Biometrics.)

Additional physical security measures include computer keyboard locks, closed circuit television cameras, security staff and alarm systems. Passive infrared alarm systems to detect body heat and movement are commonly used, as they are reliable and inexpensive.

Computer systems with terminals at remote sites are a weak link in any system as access to them could provide an intruder with access to the whole system. It is essential therefore that such terminals are fully protected. Computer workstations should be logged off whenever they are not in use, especially if the user is away from his desk. Disk and tape libraries also need to be protected, otherwise it would be possible for a thief to take file media to another computer with compatible hardware and software.

Staff and authorised visitors should wear identity cards, which cannot be copied and should contain a photograph. These are effective and cheap. These security methods are only effective if the supporting administrative procedures are properly adhered to, for example, doors must not be left unlocked and security staff should check identity cards and challenge anyone without one.

The security measures used by an organisation will reflect the value of the data stored and the consequences of data loss, alteration or theft. Financial institutions like banks need to have the very highest levels of security to prevent fraud.

Firewalls

A firewall is used to prevent unauthorised access to a computer system. The growth of always-on connections means that a firewall is now as necessary at home as in a business.

Firewalls can operate in two ways. A firewall machine is a dedicated computer that operates between a local area network file server and the external network such as the Internet. The firewall machine has built-in security precautions to prevent someone from outside accessing data without permission.

Firewall software such as McAfee Personal Firewall Plus can be installed on a home computer connected to the Internet. The firewall software will intercept any attempt to access locally stored data from outside.

The software can be set up automatically to allow access from authorised addresses or sites and to block access from other users.

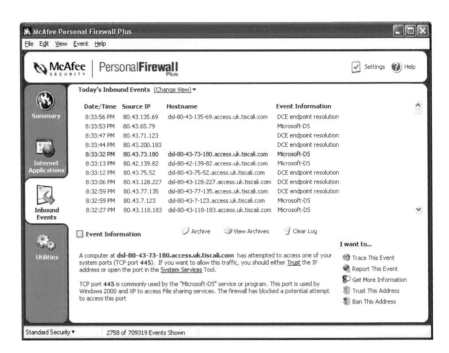

Figure 7.1 McAfee Personal Firewall

Activity 1

Learn about software like McAfee Personal Firewall Plus at
http://www.mcafee.com

Virus protection: prevention, detection and repair

The risk of getting a virus can be reduced by sensible procedures such as not opening e-mail attachments or using floppy disks if they are from an unknown source.

However, that does not guarantee that you will never be affected by a virus. Antivirus software such as McAfee VirusScan or Norton AntiVirus can detect viruses on your computer system and repair them.

This sort of software can also prevent viruses getting onto your computer by automatically scanning new files such as e-mail attachments.

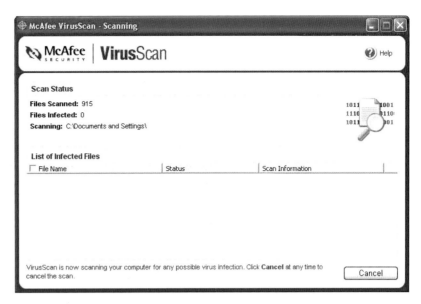

Figure 7.2 McAfee VirusScan

However, it is not enough to purchase and install antivirus software. New viruses are being discovered regularly and it is vital that antivirus software is up to date. You will need to register with the antivirus software company to receive updates which are published regularly. Normally you can receive these updates automatically via the Internet.

Identification of users

To make sure that unauthorised users do not access a networked system, all authorised users must be able to be recognised. The usual way to do this involves every user being allocated a unique user identification and secret password. Only when the identification number and password are keyed in, is the user able to access any of the software or data files.

The software and data that they are permitted to access will depend on the user's access level.

Levels of permitted access

Users can be given one of several different access rights to a system. The rights can be different for different parts of the system.

Possible access rights include:

Full rights	a user can carry out any action on the file or data
Read only	the data can be accessed to be viewed or printed, but not altered in any way
Read/write	the user can read or create new data records
Update	the user can change the data held in a record
Delete	the user can delete a whole record
Append	the user can add a record
No access	the user is barred from any form of access to the data

Student users of a school or college network have full rights to their own file space. They can read, create, amend and delete files in their area, possibly subject to a maximum file space. No other user, except the network manager, can access their area.

There may be shared areas to which teachers have full access rights but students have read-only access. Teachers can save (write) documents here for student use.

There may be other shared areas used by teachers to store data where the students have no access rights. These may be used for storing important documents such as schemes of work.

Some areas of the disk will be write-protected for everyone except the network manager. For example, only the network manager should be allowed to install new and delete old software or add new and delete users. To access very sensitive information, users will need to know several passwords.

case study 6
▶ The newsagents

Mr Blyth runs a shop in a chain of newsagents, FastNews. The in-shop system has two linked computers, one on the counter and one in the back office. The shop assistants use the counter computer to inform customers of the amount that is owed and enter details of any payments made.

Any details of changes in orders, cancellations due to holidays or closure of accounts are recorded in a black book. New customers fill in a form with details of their address and newspaper requirements.

Mr Blyth uses the computer in the back office to produce round lists for the paper girls and boys. Every night he uses the data from the black book to update the computer records as well as create records for the new customers. Once a month he runs a program that produces sales statistics that he sends to the head office of FastNews.

If any problems occur with the system, FastNews send their technician to the shop to sort it out.

■ Describe the user rights that are needed for each of the three categories of user: Mr Blyth, the shop assistants and the FastNews technician. You may need to consider different categories of data.

It is important that users follow strict procedures to maintain security. Network software can be set to

- only allow passwords that are between 6 and 12 characters
- not allow dictionary words or names to be used as passwords
- only allow passwords that are combinations of letters and numbers
- force each user to change his password after a set time has elapsed
- deny access to a workstation where an incorrect password has been entered three times in a row.

A network access log can be kept. This keeps a record of the usernames of all users of the network, which station they have used, the time they logged on, the time they logged off, which programs they have used and which files they have created or accessed.

The use of identification codes backed up by passwords can be vulnerable to hacking. Other, more secure, methods that identify a user are continually being developed. One method is to use biometrics.

Biometrics ◀

▶ Biometrics is the name given to techniques that convert a unique human characteristic such as a fingerprint or an iris scan into a digital form that can be stored in a computer or on a smart card.

Biometric data could also be stored about the shape of someone's face, the shape of their hand, their palm prints, their thumb prints or their voice.

Biometric data can be used in physical security such as opening doors, to access computer systems and even accessing cash machines. As this data is unique to the user, fraud and forgery are impossible in theory.

Biometric data identification can also be stored in documents such as passports and identity cards, so that the holder can prove who they are.

IBM has developed an experimental system, FastGate, which uses a hand, voice or fingerprint to ease business passengers through passport control. This system identifies passengers by comparing their fingerprints, voice patterns or palm prints with a digitised record stored on a central database.

Activity 2

Find out more about the application of biometrics at
http://www.biometricgroup.com/

case study 7
▶ Identity cards

The UK Government is planning to bring in identity cards (ID cards) by 2008 to 'strengthen national security and protect people from identity fraud'.

They believe the cards will tackle illegal working, stop people claiming free services to which they are not entitled and make it more difficult for criminals to have multiple identities.

Each card will contain personal information – the holder's name, address, sex, date of birth and a photograph. It will also incorporate a microchip that will hold biometric data – details of a person's fingerprints, facial dimensions and an iris scan – which are unique to every individual and are said to be difficult to forge.

Opponents are concerned about the cost, expected to be around £3 billion. They also warn that the Government's poor track record on implementing other IT projects suggests the scheme could be shambolic. There are also concerns about civil liberties if the ID cards are made compulsory.

■ Give two advantages and two disadvantages of the introduction of ID cards.

Encryption ◀

▶ Data encryption means scrambling or secretly coding data so that someone who intercepts it, for example, by tapping a telephone line, cannot understand or change the message.

Encryption methods are regularly used to protect important and confidential information when it is stored or being transmitted from one device to another.

An example of the use of encryption occurs in the banks' Electronic Funds Transfer (EFT) system. Banks and other financial institutions transfer very large amounts of money electronically. These transfers are protected by the use of data encryption techniques.

The simplest of all the methods of encrypting data uses a translation table. Each character is replaced by another character from a table.

However this method is relatively easy for code breakers to decipher. More sophisticated methods use two or more tables. An example of this method might use translation table 'A' on all of the even bytes and translation table 'B' on all of the odd bytes. The use of more than one translation table makes code-breaking relatively difficult.

Even more sophisticated methods exist based on patterns, random numbers and the use of a key to send data in a different order. Combinations of more than one encryption method make it even more difficult for code-breakers to determine how to decipher encrypted data.

Protecting against internal crime

▶ Employees working in sensitive areas must be totally reliable. They will often need to be vetted before appointment. Strict codes of practice exist for employees and anyone found to be in breach of these regulations is likely to be dismissed.

The use of an **audit trail** can enable irregular activities to be detected. An audit trail is an automatic record made of any transactions carried out by a computer system. Whenever a file is updated, or a record deleted, an entry will appear in the trail. The means that a record will be kept of any fraudulent or malicious transactions or deletions that are made.

If possible, the different stages involved in carrying out a transaction should be divided up so that no one person is responsible for the whole process. This method is also used when a program is being written: no one programmer will be allowed to write the whole program so that producing code that carries out fraudulent transactions will be very hard to achieve without the involvement of other programmers.

Internet malpractice

▶ With so many workers having a computer with Internet access on their desks, there is a growing concern about Internet misuse at work.

This could be through:

- wasting time surfing the net at work
- e-shopping
- sending and receiving personal e-mails during work time
- accessing inappropriate sites such as those displaying pornographic images
- visiting chat rooms.

There is a growing trend of sending e-mails with joke attachments. As well as posing a security risk, as these attachments can carry viruses, such messaging can be very time wasting. In many cases the 'funny' material may be seen as offensive.

IT departments can track the sites that a user accesses as well as read the contents of e-mail. Some organisations are using these facilities to monitor staff usage. Workers have complained about 'Big Brother' treatment. You can understand why employers want to do it.

- In Australia police officers were found to be sending offensive material and pornography through the internal e-mail system.

- In Britain both Nestle Rowntree and Camelot have introduced 'no e-mail Friday' policies to stop staff wasting time.
- In 2000 mobile phone company Orange sacked forty members of staff for the 'distribution of inappropriate material' in what is believed to be the biggest Internet sacking case in the UK.
- In a survey in the USA, a quarter of companies said that they had sacked an employee for violating Internet policies.

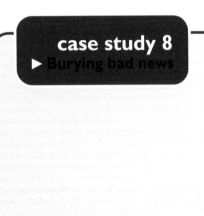

case study 8
► **Burying bad news**

A British government adviser sent an e-mail to a colleague on the afternoon of 11 September 2001 suggesting that it might be 'a good day to bury bad news.' The adviser, Jo Moore, said the Government could use the attack that day on the World Trade Center to distract attention from 'bad' news stories.

She had not reckoned with the fact that e-mails leave a permanent record. When her distasteful suggestion became public, she had to resign.

- Rumours about David Beckham's marriage spread after details of text messages that he had sent to his former personal assistant came to light. Why is it unwise to say something controversial in an e-mail or a text message rather than in a phone call?

Internet issues ◄

► The Internet has become such an important part of our life in the 21st century that those who do not have Internet access will be disadvantaged. There is a gap between the 'haves' and the 'have nots'. Provision of IT centres throughout the country and computers with free Internet access in public libraries have attempted to bridge this gap.

There are many other issues related to Internet access.

Censorship

There are many sites that hold offensive materials that may be racist, antisocial or pornographic. Illegal terrorist organisations can publish material that incites violence — for instance it is possible to access a site that holds information on how to produce a bomb at home.

The availability of newsgroups that allow users to share information also poses a problem as violent political extremists, paedophiles and pornographers can set up groups.

The need for some form of censorship on the web is constantly being debated. Many people argue that it is not acceptable that offensive materials such as pornography or articles that incite racial hatred, should be available on the net.

Others feel that the freedom of the Internet being available to anyone to set up a site is its very attraction. It is not bound by government restrictions and 'red tape' nor is it the property of big business. Censorship would only erode this freedom.

There are practical difficulties in imposing effective censorship on the Internet because of its global nature. There are different laws covering the publication of material in different countries. Although it may be illegal to store certain material in one country, citizens can access such material from a site based in another country where the material could have been stored legally.

Concerns of parents and schools and the desire to prevent children from viewing inappropriate material have resulted in the development of a range of software that prevents access to undesirable sites. This usually takes the form of a filter that prevents the display of pages from unsuitable sites. Often this works by blocking pages containing certain unacceptable words.

Activity 3

Net Nanny is software that aims to keep kids safe online. Find out about it at
http://www.net-nanny-software.com/

Security

As mentioned earlier in this chapter the use of the Internet provides a security problem as using it opens a computer system to attack from viruses, hacking and other fraudulent activities. The majority of viruses are passed via the Internet either directly through programs or other files that are downloaded or through e-mail attachments.

Very often an organisation will have access from a local area network to the Internet so that all workstations have rapid access. If one station on the network contracts a virus, it can quickly spread to all the other machines. A firewall and antivirus software are essential.

Ethics

The global nature of the Internet, which provides open access to millions of users worldwide, makes policing it very difficult. There is no regulatory body which determines who can publish material on the Internet. It is easy for anyone to set up a website and post material there, making any information they like easily available to millions of web users. There are no checks made on the data that is stored.

Many people tend to assume that because some information is on the web it must be correct. A vet has noticed an alarming trend of pet owners using information from the Internet to diagnose their pets' ailments for themselves. Owners are using sites where they can input the symptoms and get a diagnosis. Unfortunately the information is often wrong and potentially risks the health of the animal. The vet was contacted by an owner who had incorrectly diagnosed her cat as suffering from a thyroid problem. The treatment that the owner gave from the advice given on the web nearly cost the cat its life.

The information may not be impartial. Sites offering medical advice may in fact be trying to persuade you to buy medicine from them.

SUMMARY

▶ **Computer crime is any crime that has been committed using a computer as the principal tool.**

▶ **Malpractice is behaviour that is legal but goes against a professional code of practice.**

▶ **Weak points in the security of an IT system include:**

  ✗ **data being wrongly entered into a system**

  ✗ **access to data stored online**

  ✗ **access to data stored offline such as on a floppy disk**

  ✗ **viruses**

  ✗ **data being transmitted using a network**

  ✗ **internal staff not following procedures**

  ✗ **people from outside trying to see/steal/alter data.**

▶ **Weak points can be reduced by:**

  ✓ **physical security**

  ✓ **internal procedures and codes of conduct**

  ✓ **encrypting vital information**

  ✓ **user IDs and passwords**

  ✓ **access levels**

  ✓ **firewalls**

  ✓ **antivirus software**

  ✓ **biometric security**

  ✓ **vetting potential employees.**

Chapter 7 Questions

1. Explain, using examples, the differences between malpractice and crime as applied to Information Systems (4)

    June 2002 ICT1

2. John O'Neill takes his laptop computer home at weekends so that he can do some work at home and so that his son may use the computer for his homework. Describe **three** threats to the data stored on John's laptop caused by him taking the computer home at weekends. (6)

3. A company offering security services for ICT systems includes the following quotation in its advertisements 'You are protected against hackers, viruses and worms, but what about the staff in the sales department?' Describe **three** ways in which a company's own staff can be a weak point in its ICT systems. (6)

    January 2003 ICT1

4. Information systems need to be protected from both internal and external threats.

    a) Explain, using examples, the differences between an internal and an external threat to an information system. (4)

    b) For each of the following, describe a measure that a company can take to protect their information system from:
    i) internal threats (2)
    ii) external threats. (2)

    January 2002 ICT1

5. Explain, with reasons, **two** levels of access that could be given to different categories of users of an online stock control system. (4)

    June 2001 ICT1

> A number of laws have been passed over the last 20 years as the use of ICT has grown. These laws protect computer data and systems in various ways.

Computer Misuse Act 1990

> The Computer Misuse Act 1990 was introduced as a result of concerns about people misusing the data and programs held on computers. It allows 'unauthorised access' to be prosecuted and aims to discourage the misuse or modification of data or programs.
>
> The Act aims to protect computer users against malicious vandalism and information theft. Hacking and knowingly spreading viruses were made crimes under the Act.
>
> The Act has three sections:

- unauthorised access to computer material
- unauthorised access with intent to commit or facilitate commission of further offences
- unauthorised modification of computer material.

The penalty for each of the three categories is increasingly severe.

Section 1 – Unauthorised access to computer material

In this category, a person commits an offence if he tries to access any program or data held in any computer without permission and he knows at the time that this is the case.

The maximum penalty is six months in prison and a £5,000 fine.

This category applies to people who are 'just messing around', 'exploring the system', 'getting into the system just for the sake of it' and have no intention of doing anything to the programs or data once they have gained access.

It covers the act of guessing passwords to gain access to a system and have a look at the data that is stored. An authorised user of a system may still be in breach of this category of the act if she accesses files in the system that have a higher level of access than she has been allocated rights to. A student gaining access to a fellow student's area, or breaking into the college administrative system, is breaking this category of the act. It is an offence even if no files are deleted or changed.

Section 2 – Unauthorised access with intent to commit or facilitate commission of further offences

This category covers offenders who carry out unauthorised access with a more serious criminal intent. The access may be made with an intention to carry out fraud.

For example, breaking into a personnel or medical system with the intention of finding out details about a person that could be used for blackmail falls into this category. Another example of an offence would be breaking into a company's system with the intention of finding out secret financial information that could be used when carrying out stock market transactions. The information obtained in this way could be used by a rival company.

A further example of an offence in this category would be guessing or stealing a password, using it to access another person's online bank account and transferring their money to another account.

Persistent hacking is also included in this second category.

Prosecution under this category can lead to a maximum of five years in prison.

Section 3 – Unauthorised modification of computer material

This third category concerns the alteration of data or programs within a computer system rather than simply viewing or using the data or program. This could include deleting files or changing the desktop set-up. However, the deleting has to be done deliberately and not just by mistake. In this case the program code could be actually changed. This could stop a program from running or to act in an unexpected manner. This category also includes using a computer to damage other computers linked through a network even though the computer used to do the damage is not modified in any way.

Alternatively, data could be changed: the balance of a bank account altered, details of driving offences deleted or an examination mark altered.

This category includes the deliberate distribution of computer viruses.

Prosecution under this category can lead to up to five years in prison.

Why so few prosecutions?

Even though the Computer Misuse Act has now been in force for a considerable time, there have been relatively few prosecutions under the Act. Organisations are unwilling to make prosecutions, as they fear that such an action will result in a fall in the company reputation. A lack of confidence from their customers could result from any suggestion that the systems and data could be unsafe and vulnerable to misuse.

case study 1
▶ Computer Misuse Act cases

A temporary employee at British Telecom gained access to a computer database containing the telephone numbers and addresses of top secret government installations. The employee, who had worked at BT for two months, found passwords written down and left lying around offices and used them to call up information on a screen. The employee was guilty under section 1 of the Act as he accessed the data but made no use of it, nor did he tamper with it in any way.

Christopher Pile, who called himself the Black Baron, was the first person convicted under the Computer Misuse Act. Pile created two viruses named Pathogen and Queeg after characters in the BBC sci-fi comedy Red Dwarf. The viruses wiped data from a computer's hard drive and left a Red Dwarf joke on the screen which read 'Smoke me a kipper, I'll be back for breakfast ...unfortunately some of your data won't'. The Black Baron was guilty under section 3 of the Act as data was altered on a computer's hard disk.

Two 18 year-olds arrested in Wales were alleged to be computer hackers involved in a million dollar global Internet fraud that involved hacking into businesses around the world and stealing credit card details. The youths were arrested under the Computer Misuse Act 1990; a home PC computer was supposedly used for the crime. Apparently they had accessed the credit card databases of nine e-commerce companies, and had published the details of thousands of credit card accounts on the Internet. They were prosecuted under section 2 of the Act as they used the data they obtained to carry out fraud.

- For each of the cases described below, explain which category (or categories) of the Computer Misuse Act has been broken.

1. A student at a college plays around with the desktop settings of a computer in the IT Centre.

2. An employee, having used a computer to order some books over the Internet, leaves their credit card details, written on a piece of paper, next to the computer. Someone else finds the paper and uses the details to order some books for themselves, changing the delivery address.

3. In January 2003, Simon Vallor was jailed for two years having been convicted of writing and distributing three computer viruses. He apparently infected 27,000 PCs in 42 countries.

4. An 18-year-old man hacked into, and made changes to, a major newspaper's database which cost the newspaper £25,000.

5. In 2004, John Thornley pleaded guilty to four offences contrary to the Computer Misuse Act having mounted a hack attack on a rival site, and introducing a Trojan type virus to bring it down on several occasions.

The Copyright, Designs and Patents Act 1988

Copyright laws have long protected the intellectual rights of authors, composers, artists, etc. so that books, works of art and music cannot be copied without permission from the author or unless financial compensation is made. Copyright applies to all work, whatever the format it is produced in; material made available on the World Wide Web is covered by copyright. It is an offence to download music or video files without the permission of the copyright holder.

The copyright law also applies to computer software. The law makes the copying of software illegal and protects the producer by deterring copying, ensuring that he or she does not lose money.

The purpose of the Copyright, Designs and Patents Act 1988 is to make the copying of software illegal and so deter the activity. It aims to protect the producer, ensuring that he or she does not lose money.

The Act makes it illegal to undertake any of the following without permission:

- Copy (or pirate) software
- Sell or distribute copies of software
- Adapt software
- Transmit software.

When a person buys software he does not buy the program, only the right to use it under the terms of the licence. It is illegal to copy or use software without having obtained the appropriate licence. Criminal penalties can include unlimited fines and two years imprisonment or both.

A software copying and licensing agreement is a legal contract between the software producer and the user that sets out how the piece of software may be used.

It is very important for organisations to ensure that, in the workplace, all their employees are working within the law. If an employee is found using unlicensed software on the organisation's computer then the organisation can be held responsible and prosecuted. As a result the organisation could be fined. This would apply both if the software were related to work, perhaps an unlicensed copy of a desk top publishing package, or for recreational purposes such as a game.

Software licensing methods

Computer owners, particularly if they own more than one computer, for example a company with a network, must be aware of the terms of the licence agreement which comes with the software.

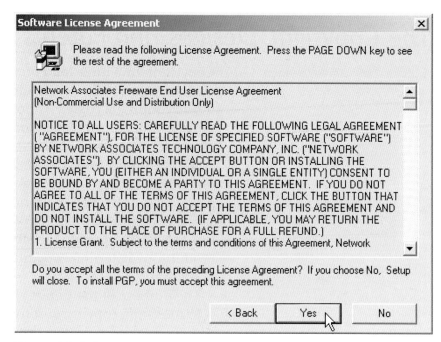

Figure 8.1 Software licence agreement

Some licences are bought outright and allow the purchaser to use the software for as long as they wish. Other licences are rental agreements which allow the purchaser to use the software for a year. If the software is needed after that time, a further fee must be paid. The rental option is often a very sensible one for business users. Software can have only a short, useful life before a newer and better version or product comes on the market.

A number of different licence agreements are normally available:

A **single-user** licence allows a copy of the software to be installed on a single machine. The software is usually supplied as a package consisting of the programs on disks (floppy or CD) together with user manuals. If the user wishes to install the software on an extra machine he must purchase another copy.

An organisation would purchase single-user licences for specialist software that is likely to be used by just a few users. For example, an accounts package would only be needed by a few employees in the Finance Department, so single-user would be the most suitable licensing arrangement.

If the agreement specifies that only one copy may be in use at one time, then the user is entitled to install the software on two computers – perhaps his desktop PC and a laptop – as long as at any given time the software package is only being used on one of the computers.

A **multi-user** licence allows an organisation to install the software package on an agreed number of computers. The programs would be copied onto the hard disk drives of each computer. This would normally cost less than purchasing the same number of single-user licences. A college that teaches Delphi programming to A level Computing students might purchase a multi-user licence for 20 copies which could be installed in one classroom.

A **site licence** allows a user to purchase a single copy of the software with permission to install the software on all the computers at a single location. This is a cheaper method than purchasing a single copy for each machine. An organisation would purchase a site licence for a generic software package, such as a word processor, that is likely to be used by nearly every user.

A method of licensing that is increasingly being used with networked systems is the **licence by use.** This allows the software to be installed on a large number of computers. However, only an agreed number of users are allowed to run the software at any given time. A 10-user licence of this type would allow the software to be installed on 50 computers as long as there were never more than 10 people using the package at once.

An equivalent licensing method for an organisation running a local area network is a **network licence**. One copy of a software package will be stored on the file server. If a 10-user network version of a package is bought, then only 10 people can use the package at any one time. There can be hundreds of computers on the network and the package will be available to any one of the computers. When an eleventh user tries to use the software package, access will be denied. This form of licensing is common in the education sector where students may need to be able to access specialist software in different locations around the campus.

Other forms of network licence allow the software to be used simultaneously at any number of computers.

Some software is made available without the restrictions of copyright. Such software is known as **public domain** software. These programs can be distributed, copied and used free of charge. Any users can alter the program code of such software. **Shareware** is software that is licensed to be used without charge for a trial period. After that time a fee must be paid if the user wishes to continue using the software. Most shareware is obtained by downloading from the Internet.

Freeware is software that is available under similar rules but, unlike public domain software, the code is not allowed to be altered. The program is copyrighted, but the author does not charge for it, allowing a user to copy and use it at will. **Open source** software consists of programs that are freely available and are distributed in a form that other programmers can readily modify. The purpose of such software is to allow programs to be developed and improved by many programmers.

Software piracy

Software piracy is the name given to the unauthorised copying of software. It applies whether the copying is carried out on a large scale, where copies are sold for financial gain, or by an individual user for personal use. A user is allowed to make copies of software for backup use only.

Software piracy is a very large problem. Many people do not seem to realise that whenever they take a copy of software from a friend to use on their own computer they are breaking the law.

The following types of software piracy have been identified:

- **Professional counterfeits**: professionally made copies of software including the media, packages, licences and even security holograms. They are made to resemble the genuine article as far as is possible.
- **Recordable CD-R**: pirates compile large amounts of software onto one recordable CD-R and make multiple copies of the CD-R. There is usually no attempt to pass these off as the genuine article. These recordable CD-Rs will then be sold to customers in different ways through mail order, 'under-the-counter' at retail outlets or at markets, and are even advertised on the Internet.
- **Hard disk loaders**: dealers or retail outlets who load infringing versions of software onto a computer system to encourage customers into buying their computer hardware. Customers will not have the appropriate licences, will not be entitled to technical support or upgrades, and may find the software on the computer to be incomplete or to contain viruses.
- **Internet piracy**: downloading or distribution of software on the Internet. Just because software is present at certain sites on the Internet does not necessarily mean it is free or legal for you to download. It may have been placed on the Internet without the copyright owners' consent.
- **Corporate overuse**: installation of software packages on more machines than there are licences for. For example, if a company purchases five single-user licences of a software program but installs the software on ten machines, then they will be using five infringing copies. Similarly, if a company is running a large network and more users have access to a software program than the company has licences for, there will be corporate overuse.

Preventing breach of copyright

Software companies are getting more and more sophisticated in their attempts to stop the software pirates. Some of the measures taken include:

- The licence agreement is clearly printed on the packaging.
- Some games are designed only to run if a code is typed in. This code changes each time the program is run and can be found by looking in the manual or using a special code-wheel which comes with the software.
- Some programs will only run if the CD-ROM disk is in the CD-ROM drive.
- Some programs will only run if a special piece of hardware called a dongle, sold with the software, is plugged into the back of the computer.

The **Federation Against Software Theft** (**FAST**) was founded in 1984 by the software industry. It is supported by over 1,200 companies. It is a not-for-profit organisation that aims to prevent pirate software and has a policy of prosecuting anyone found to be breaching copyright law.

FAST also works to educate the public about good software practice and legal requirements.

case study 2
▶ Software pirate jailed for two years

A software pirate was jailed for two years on nine counts as a direct result of investigations by FAST and Kingston trading standards officers.

The pirate first came to FAST's attention when he placed an advert in a trade magazine offering computer software at very low prices under a bogus company name.

When officers visited the pirate's address, they found two CD writers and over 500 pirated CDs containing pirate software. While on bail he started counterfeiting again and a further two CD writers, scanners and more CDs were seized. He was sentenced to a total of two years in prison.

1. Name the Act under which the software pirate was prosecuted.
2. Explain why the activity described is illegal.
3. What name would you give to the form of software piracy described?
4. Describe three other forms of software piracy.

Activity 1

1. Find out more about the fight against illegal software at the FAST website http://www.fast.org.uk/.
2. Produce a leaflet that outlines the kinds of activities that FAST is involved in.
3. Produce a poster for your classroom, a slide presentation or a series of web pages aimed at an audience of students in your school or college. You should make clear to them which of the activities a student might carry out are illegal under the Computer Misuse Act or Copyright Act.

The **Computer Misuse Act of 1990** makes the following illegal:

▶ accessing computer material without permission e.g. hacking

▶ unauthorised access to a computer to commit another crime

▶ editing computer data without permission e.g. spreading a virus.

The **Copyright, Designs and Patents Act 1988** makes copying software illegal and so deters the activity. It aims to protect the producer, ensuring that he or she does not lose money.

The Act makes it illegal to undertake any of the following without permission:

▶ copy (or pirate) software

▶ sell or distribute copies of software

▶ adapt software

▶ transmit software.

It requires all users of software to have a valid licence.

Computer owners must be aware of the terms of the licence agreement which comes with the software. A number of different licence agreements are normally available:

▶ **Single-user licence** – the software can only be used on one machine. Some licences state that software may be installed on more than one machine but that only one can be used at any given time.

▶ **Network licence** – may be for up to 15 or 20 stations on a network or every station on the network, depending on the licence – this licence is obviously much more expensive than single user licences. Some network licences state a maximum number of concurrent users – for example, only 20 users can have the software open at the same time.

▶ **Multi-user licence** – allows an organisation to install the software package on an agreed number of computers.

▶ **Site licence** – enables the software to be used on any computer on the site.

Chapter 8 Questions

1. As the use of ICT increases so does the need for legislation to control its use.
Explain, using an example for each one, what is covered by:

  a) the Data Protection Act   (3)

  b) the Computer Misuse Act   (3)

  c) copyright and licensing agreements.   (3)

June 2003 ICT1

2 a) Describe what is meant by a software copyright and licensing agreement.   (2)

  b) Explain why software copyright and licensing agreements are needed.   (2)

  c) Describe the possible consequences for a company of an employee using unlicensed software on a computer belonging to that company.   (2)

January 2004 ICT1

3. In 1990 an act was introduced to allow the prosecution of people who accessed computer systems without authorisation.

  a) Name the act.   (1)

  b) State, and give an example of, each of the three sections of the act.   (6)

  c) Few companies ever prosecute people under this act. Explain why this is so.   (2)

4. Describe **four** different types of software licence agreement that a company can make with a software company. For each one explain an appropriate example of use.   (8)

9 Data protection legislation

> 'Think before you give away personal information, you never know where it will end up!' (Advertising campaign slogan)

Why data protection laws were introduced ◀

> The development of information technology has meant that many organisations store details about you on computer. Examples include:

- Your school or college will store details of your courses, exam results and contact details.
- Your doctor will store details of your medical records.
- Your bank will store details of your account.
- If you have a part-time job, your employer will store your details.
- If you have a driving licence, your details will be stored at the DVLA.
- Stores may have details about you if you have a reward card or have bought products online.
- Your local council stores details of everyone who is 17 or over so that it can produce the electoral register.

These are all examples of personal data – data about living people.

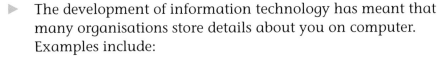

Activity 1

Make a list of all the organisations that you think store information about you.

The increase of personal data stored on computer has worried many people. Their main concerns are:

1. **Who will be able to access this data?** Will information about me be available remotely over a network and therefore vulnerable to being accessed by hackers for example? Can my medical records, for example, be examined by a potential employer?
2. **Is the data accurate?** If it is stored, processed and transmitted by computer, who will check that it is accurate? People often think it must be true if 'it says so on the computer'.

3. **Will the data be sold on to another company?** For example, could my health records be sold to a company where I have applied for a job? Can my school records, for example, be sold on to someone else? Could my personal details, collected by my employer, be used by a commercial company for targeting junk mail?
4. **How long will data be kept?** As it is very easy to store vast amounts of data, will data about me be stored even if it is not needed? For example, if I apply for a job but don't get it will the data be deleted?

What is personal data?

Personal data covers both facts and opinions about a living person. Facts such as name, address, date of birth, marital status or current bank balance. Results in examinations, details of driving offences, record of medications prescribed and financial credit rating are further examples of facts that could relate to an individual. Personal opinions such as political or religious views are also deemed to be personal data.

Data Protection Acts 1984 and 1998

It was due to these concerns about the use of personal data, that led to the Data Protection Act 1984. The 1984 Act set out regulations for storing personal data that was automatically processed.

The Data Protection Act 1998 strengthened the 1984 Act and enshrined the European Union directive on data protection into UK Law. This means that UK law is in line with the data protection laws in all the other countries in the European Union.

What the Data Protection Act 1998 says

The Data Protection Act 1998 sets rules for the electronic processing of personal information. The law also applies to paper records from 23 October 2007.

The law refers to:

- data subjects – people whose personal data is being processed
- data controllers – people or organisations who process personal data.

The law works in two ways:

- data subjects have certain rights
- data controllers must follow good information handling practices.

What the data controllers must do

Data controllers must follow the eight data protection principles.

Data controllers must register the fact that they are storing personal data with a government official called the Information Commissioner. The following must be registered:

- the data controller's name and address
- a description of the data being processed
- the purpose for which the information will be used
- from whom the information was obtained
- to whom the information will be disclosed and countries where the data may be transferred.

It is possible to use the Internet to find out whether a company has registered. Go to http://forms.informationcommissioner.gov.uk/search.html

The eight data protection principles

The data protection principles say that data must be:

1. fairly and lawfully processed
2. processed for registered purposes
3. adequate, relevant and not excessive
4. accurate and up to date
5. not kept for longer than is necessary
6. processed in line with your rights
7. secure
8. not transferred to countries without adequate protection.

Principle 1 means that you cannot collect data for one purpose and then use it for another purpose (even if the purpose is registered) without the permission of the data subject.

Principle 2 means that if a company intends to sell data on to another company it must register this with the Information Commissioner. (They will need the permission of the data subjects to do this.)

Principle 3 means that any irrelevant data should be deleted. Information about unsuccessful job applicants should not be kept.

Principle 4 means that the organisation must take steps to ensure that its data is accurate. Once a year a school, for example, may provide each pupil (the data subject) with a printout of their personal details for checking purposes.

Principle 6 means that data subjects have the right to inspect the information held on them, for payment of a small fee. They have the right to require that inaccurate data is corrected. They have the right to compensation for any distress caused if the Act has been broken.

Principle 7 means that appropriate technological security measures must be taken to prevent unauthorised access. This means information has to be kept safe from hackers and employees who don't have the right to see it. Your data can only be passed on to someone else with your permission. Backup copies should be taken so that data is also safeguarded against accidental loss.

Registration

Register with
Guardian Unlimited

Help with this page

1	Enter your email address:		We will send you an email to confirm your address.
2	Choose a password:		4-20 characters, case-sensitive, no spaces.
	Re-enter password:		
3	What country do you live in?	choose ⌄	
4	UK or US users only Postcode / Zipcode:		
5	☐	Tick this box if you'd like to be kept up to date with offers and developments from Guardian Newspapers Limited. You can change your preferences at any time on the My Details page.	
6	☐	Tick this box if you'd like to receive messages from organisations screened by Guardian Newspapers Limited.	

When you fill in this form to register with the Guardian Unlimited website, your details can be passed on if you tick the last box.

Principle 8 means that personal data cannot be transferred to countries outside the European Union unless the country provides an adequate level of protection.

Remembering the principles

P – registered **purposes** (2)
E – not transferred outside the **EU** (8)
R – **relevant** (3)
S – **secure** (7)
O – you can inspect your **own** records (6)
N – **not kept** for longer than is necessary (5)
A – **accurate** (4)
L – **lawfully** processed (1)

Activity 2

Test yourself. Close the book and try to name five of the principles.

Is your consent needed to process your data?

Suppose you apply for a supermarket loyalty card. The supermarket will need to store and process your personal details as part of their normal work. They do not need your consent to do this – you have agreed to this when you applied for the card.

However, the supermarket cannot pass your details on to another company without your consent. In practice this means that when you fill in the application form, you can tick a box to prevent your personal details being sold on to another company, for example, for direct marketing.

Note: If you cancel the card, your details are no longer needed and should be deleted by the supermarket. At any time you can write to an organisation that is sending you junk mail asking them to stop processing any data about you.

Exemptions from the Act

The following exemptions exist from the principles of the Data Protection Act:

- if the information is used to safeguard national security
- if the information is used for the prevention and detection of crime
- if the information is used for the collection of taxes
- personal data relating to someone's family or household affairs does not need to be registered.

What is the role of the Information Commissioner?

The Commissioner has the responsibility of ensuring that the data protection legislation is enforced.

The Information Commissioner keeps a public register of data controllers. Each register entry must include the name and address of the data controller as well as a description of the processing of personal data carried out under the control of the data controller. An individual can consult the register to find out what processing of personal data is being carried out by a particular data controller.

The Data Protection Act 1998 requires every data controller who is processing personal data to notify the commission unless one of the exemptions listed in the Act applies. At the commission office a complete copy of the public register is kept and it is updated weekly.

Other duties of the Commissioner include promoting good information handling. As well as keeping the register of data controllers, the Information Commissioner also gives advice on data protection issues, promotes good information handling practice and encourages data controllers to develop suitable codes of practice. He also acts as an Ombudsman.

Note: The Information Commissioner was previously called the Data Protection Registrar under the 1984 Act.

case study 1
▶ Is it legal?

A company registers the following use with the Information Commissioner:

Purpose:	The administration of prospective, current and past employees
Typical activities are:	Payment of wages, salaries, pensions and other benefits: training, assessment and career planning
Type of information:	Names, addresses, salary details and other information related to their work

The company wants to sell the names and addresses of their employees to another company for direct marketing. This is <u>illegal</u> as it is <u>not the registered purpose</u> so breaches Principle 2.

The police want the company to give them information about an employee in relation to a possible fraud. This would be <u>legal</u> as long as the police provided a certificate of exemption that this was <u>connected with detection of crime</u>.

case study 2
▶ Lack of security

Danny Hughes is an A level student who had a holiday job on the production line at Betta Biscuit plc. One lunchtime Danny decided to explore the factory and found his way into the computer room. There was no one about. Danny sat down at a terminal and typed in a few usernames with no luck. Then he noticed a birthday card on the desk; to Bob with love from Jane. Danny typed in the username BOB and was asked for a password. He typed in JANE and to his surprise it was accepted!

A menu appeared on the screen. Danny chose payroll. He could load up the payroll information of all the employees. Danny loaded the file of his friend Chris and cut his hourly pay by half. Two workers came in and saw Danny, but no one said anything. Danny logged off quietly and slipped out of the room undetected.

1. Suggest as many steps as you can that Betta Biscuit plc should take to improve their security.
2. Who has broken the law, Danny or Betta Biscuit or both of them?

Activity 3

You can find out more about the Data Protection Act and the Information Commissioner at http://www.dataprotection.gov.uk/ Explore the site and answer the following questions:

1. What are your rights in preventing junk mail?
2. What two laws does the Information Commissioner oversee and ensure compliance with?

case study 3
▶ **The DPA in the news**

Marks and Spencer admit breaking DPA for 15 years

In 1999 the High Street chain store Marks and Spencer had to change its procedures after learning it had been breaking the Data Protection Act for almost 15 years.

The company had been disclosing charge card account details to supplementary card holders – people who are authorised to charge goods to another person's account.

Lloyds TSB accused of breaking the DPA

In 2004 a customer alleged that Lloyds TSB had broken the Data Protection Act when it was transfering work to India. The bank was accused of sending its customers' personal financial data outside the European Union without their written consent.

Organ group president is fined

In 1996 Trevor Daniels, the president of the Association of Organ Enthusiasts, was fined £50 for keeping his membership list on his home computer without being registered.

Utility companies break DPA

In 1997 the then Information Commissioner reprimanded two utility companies for breaking the Data Protection Act. The companies stored names and addresses for sending bills to customers. They then used these details to send out direct mail advertisements to their customers.

1. Which data protection principle was Lloyds TSB accused of breaking?
2. Which data protection principle did Marks and Spencer break?
3. What did Mr Daniels do wrong?
4. Which data protection principle did the utility companies break?

Use the Internet to search for details of other breaches of the Data Protection Act. Use sites such as http://www.guardian.co.uk/ or http://www.independent.co.uk

Worked exam question

I When an organisation holds personal data, it should have procedures in place that allow the data subjects to view any data that it holds about them.

  a) State why it is necessary to have such procedures. (I)

  b) State **two** ways in which data subjects may request to view a copy of their data. (2)

June 2004 ICT I

▶ EXAMINER'S GUIDANCE *a) This part is very straightforward.*

▶ SAMPLE ANSWER It is necessary to have such procedures because the Data Protection Act says that you must allow data subjects to view any data that it holds about them.

▶ EXAMINER'S GUIDANCE *b) This is also a state question so a brief answer will suffice as long as you state two ways (one for each mark).*

▶ SAMPLE ANSWER One way would be to apply in writing.
Another way would be to apply in person. You may need to provide some ID.

SUMMARY

▶ **The Data Protection Act concerns the storage of personal data. Data controllers must:**

  ▶ **register with the Information Commissioner**

  ▶ **follow the eight data protection principles.**

▶ **The principles say that personal data must be kept secure and be accurate, up to date and only used for the registered purpose.**

▶ **Data subjects have various rights under the Act including the right to inspect data about themselves, have any errors corrected and claim compensation for any distress.**

▶ **Personal information involving national security matters, the detection of crime and the collection of taxes is exempt from the Data Protection Act.**

Chapter 9 Questions

I. a) With reference to the Data Protection Act of 1998, describe:

   i) the role of the Information Commissioner (2)

   ii) what is meant by a data subject. (2)

b) In addition to details about the company, state three items of data that a company must include in an entry on the Data Register. (3)

January 2005 ICT1

2. Appleton Office Supplies is a company that owns a garden centre. The company has built up a database of customers over the past five years. The company uses this database to send mailshots of their latest offers.

a) Kate Grey, a customer, asks the company if they have registered under the Data Protection Act. Does the company have to register? (1)

b) Kate says that as she has not bought any products from the office supplies company for four years, her data should be deleted from the database. Is she correct? (1)

c) Kate discovers that Appleton Office Supplies have passed her details on to another company without her permission. Has the law been broken? (1)

d) Who should Kate contact in this situation? (1)

3. An optician keeps records in a database of all its customers who have had eye tests. Eye test reminders are sent out to customers when they are due. Customers who do not make appointments after two reminders have been sent out have their details deleted from the database. Describe **two** possible reasons why these customer details are deleted from the database. (4)

January 2003 ICT1

4. The personnel department of a large company keeps records on all the employees of the company. These records contain personal data and details of the employees' position, training and medical history. The company is registered on the Data Protection Register and has to abide by the principles of the 1998 Data Protection Act. Three of these principles are:

■ 'Personal data shall be adequate, relevant and not excessive in relation to the purpose or purposes for which they are processed'

■ 'Personal data shall be accurate and, where necessary, kept up to date'

■ 'Appropriate technical and organisational measures shall be taken against unauthorised or unlawful processing of personal data and against accidental loss or destruction of, or damage to, personal data'

■ For each of the principles stated above, describe what the company must do to comply with them. (6)

June 2002 ICT1

5. Data protection legislation was introduced into the UK in 1984; it has since been superseded by the 1998 Act.

a) State why the legislation was originally introduced. (1)

b) State what type of data is the subject of the Data Protection Act 1998. (2)

c) A company wishes to collect data from order forms submitted by its customers to sell to other companies. State **two** actions that the company must take so that it can legally collect and sell that data. (2)

d) The Data Protection Act gives individuals the right to see what data is being held about them.

   i) State how an individual must ask to do this. (1)

   ii) Could an individual have to pay to receive a copy of his or her data? (1)

January 2002 ICT1

6. a) State why an organisation must apply for entry on to the Data Protection Register. (1)

b) State **three** items of information that must be provided by the data user about the data that is to be stored. (3)

June 2001 ICT1

7. When buying a new house through a large estate agency, customers are asked if they object to the data they are giving to the estate agent being passed on to other companies.

a) Explain why the estate agent must ask this question. (2)

b) State, with an example, what the estate agent could do with the customers' details if they give permission for them to be passed on. (2)

January 2001 ICT1

8. The Data Protection Act 1998 is an act designed to regulate the processing of personal data.

a) What is meant by personal data? (1)

b) With whom should companies register if they store personal data? (1)

c) What is meant by the term *data subject?* (1)

d) What rights to data subjects have if they think data is incorrect? (2)

Many computer users have blamed computers for various problems with their health. In some cases the effects can be long term and prevent the user from working in the future. Many of these problems are avoidable. The Health and Safety (Display Screen Equipment) Regulations of 1992 made it a legal requirement for employers to take various measures to protect the health of workers using computers.

Health problems associated with computers and preventing their occurrence

Repetitive Strain Injury (RSI)

It is widely accepted that prolonged work on a computer can cause repetitive strain injury. Using a keyboard which is positioned so that hands have to be held at an awkward angle can cause this injury. Squeezing the mouse over long periods can lead to stiffness. RSI affects the shoulders, fingers and particularly the wrists of those typing all the working day. The symptoms are stiffness, pain and swelling. Permanent injury can be caused preventing the employee from working. Case Study 1 (page 118) explores a case where an employee suffering from RSI was successful in a case against her employer.

A TUC report claims that young workers are more at risk from RSI than their older colleagues. The key factors that put them at risk include having to carry out repetitive tasks at speed, needing to use a good deal of force when working, not being able to choose or change the order of monotonous tasks and having to work in awkward positions. The TUC data shows that 78% of younger workers have jobs which involve a repetition of the same sequence of movements and more than half the UK's four million workers aged 16–24 are forced to work in awkward or tiring positions. A young graphic designer took her employers, Shell UK, to court and won. She claimed that she was never shown how to use a computer mouse. She was awarded £25,000 damages for RSI that she began to suffer two years after joining the firm at the age of 20.

The risk of RSI can be reduced by using specially designed, **'ergonomic' keyboards**. These should be tiltable and have well sprung keys. It can help to use wrist supports while typing.

Desks should have sufficient space on them to allow the user to rest his wrists when not typing.

Managers should ensure that work is varied during the day so that no user spends all the working day at the keyboard.

The user should take regular breaks from working with a computer; they should maintain a good posture and ensure that they do not press the keys too hard.

Eye strain

Looking at a screen for a long time can lead to eye strain, particularly if the screen is of a poor quality and flickers or has the wrong contrast setting. Problems also occur if the lighting in the room is at the wrong level, or the screen is poorly sited causing glare or reflection on the screen. The symptoms are headaches and sore eyes.

The risk of eye strain can be reduced by having suitable lighting, using non-flickering screens and fitting screen filters to prevent glare and reflection.

Appropriate blinds (rather than curtains) should be fitted to windows to reduce glare and prevent sunshine reflection. If necessary, appropriate spectacles should be worn when using a computer.

The eyeline should be approximately level with the top of the screen and the screen slightly tilted.

Employers are obliged to pay for any employee who works long hours in front of a computer screen to have a free eye test.

The user should take regular breaks from working with a computer and should refocus their eyes every ten minutes.

Back problems

Sitting in an uncomfortable position at a computer or bad posture can lead to serious back problems. This is likely to be the case if chairs are at the incorrect height. The symptoms are back pain or stiffness, possibly a stiff neck and shoulders and sore ankles.

The risk of back problems can be reduced by having an ergonomically designed, adjustable swivel chair that supports the lower back, and can be adjusted to the right height and tilt. Chairs should also have a five point base – that is more stable than just four legs. Screens that tilt and turn can be adjusted to the correct position so that the back is not twisted or bent. Document holders next to the screen can reduce the neck movement that would otherwise occur; frequent neck movement can create back problems.

The user should take regular breaks from working with a computer.

The use of a footrest can help prevent back damage.

Ozone irritation

Laser printers emit ozone which can act as an irritant. Inkjet or dot-matrix printers do not emit ozone. The symptoms are problems with breathing, headaches and nausea.

The risk of irritation can be reduced by locating laser printers at least one metre away from where someone is sitting to avoid the ozone emissions, and providing good ventilation.

Radiation

In the USA research has revealed that an unusually high percentage of pregnant computer users have abnormal pregnancies or have suffered miscarriages. This may be pure coincidence but it has been suggested that it is caused by electromagnetic radiation from monitors.

Low emission monitors give off less radiation.

Screen filters can also cut down radiation.

Epilepsy

It has long been suggested that flickering computer screens have contributed to the incidence of epileptic attacks in users.

Again the use of low emission monitors and screen filters is likely to reduce the risk of triggering an epileptic attack in users.

Stress

Using computers can be frustrating and repeated frustration can lead to stress. Frustration can occur if:

■ a user has inadequate training in the use of a piece of software
■ the response time is very slow
■ the human computer interface is inappropriate – perhaps too cluttered
■ there are too many stages or keystrokes required to carry out a simple task
■ hardware failure is a common occurrence – for example, the printer gets jammed or the computer crashes several times a day.

Remove frustration by providing users with adequate support and training, choose well designed software that has an interface that is appropriate for the user and install hardware that is capable of meeting the demands of the tasks.

How big is the problem?

As computer use has increased the incidence of RSI has risen. In 1995 the US Occupational Safety and Health Administration said that of all the illnesses reported to them, 56 per cent were RSI cases, compared with 28 per cent in 1984 and 18 per cent in 1981. Among the generally accepted causes of these cases were poorly designed workstations, ill-fitting chairs, stressful conditions and extended hours of typing.

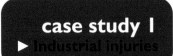

case study 1
▶ Industrial injuries

At a recent tribunal a city council employee won her case and claimed £250,000 in compensation for office injuries.

The employee, an accountant, is suffering from a form of RSI called tenosynovitis, an inflammation of the tendon sheaths of the wrist, caused by, among another things, excessive use of keyboards. Tenosynovitis is commonly found among data inputters and journalists.

Tenosynovitis is the best known form of RSI because it is a glaring medical condition and was the first type to be recognised by the courts. The employee's illness began when her employer computerised the office.

She was issued with a chair that was so high her feet didn't reach the floor. She got into the habit of leaning forward to compensate, which aggravated a latent back complaint. When she started to take time off sick, she was expected to clear the backlog on her return, which meant more time in her chair, and so on. Conditions were aggravated by cramped working conditions and the stress of having to report to two different managers. She was refused a new chair.

She won her case on the grounds that she had been discriminated against as a disabled person. Recently, the ceiling on compensation for such claims was removed, hence the huge potential damages.

■ Produce a report outlining the steps that her employers could have taken to prevent her from suffering from RSI.

What the law says ◀

▶ In 1992 the European Union introduced regulations to try to prevent health problems associated with computer equipment.

The regulations were called the Health and Safety (Display Screen Equipment) Regulations 1992.

Employers must:

1. provide adjustable chairs
2. provide tiltable screens
3. provide anti-glare screen filters
4. ensure workstations are not cramped
5. ensure room lighting is suitable
6. plan work at a computer so that there are breaks
7. provide information on health hazards and training for computer users
8. on request, arrange for appropriate eye and eye sight tests for computer users
9. provide special spectacles if they are needed and normal ones cannot be used.

Note: These regulations apply only to offices and not to students in schools or colleges.

Activity 1

Find out more about health hazards and ICT at the Health and Safety Executive's web site: http://www.hse.gov.uk/

List the services that the site provides for a) an employer b) an employee.

The Trades Union Congress (TUC) health and safety newsletter site, http://www.hazards.org/ is worth exploring too.

Activity 2

Produce an induction booklet for new employees that provides them with guidelines in how to use the computer equipment safely. You should include a description of the organisation's responsibilities to them.

Designing software to minimise hazards ◀

▶ Software should be designed to reduce health risks. Software designers must be aware that bright colours can cause eye strain, annoying use of sound can lead to headaches and the use of flashing images (e.g. in games) can lead to epileptic attacks.
Designers must ensure the following:

- Screen layouts are clear so that eye strain is minimised.
- Colour schemes are not too bright and have good contrast otherwise eye strain could occur.
- Text is a suitable size, minimising the chance of eye strain.
- Sufficient instructions and help facilities to enable learning are included otherwise the user could feel stressed. Clear and helpful error messages will allow users to put their mistakes right for themselves.
- Menu systems are well structured so that the number of keystrokes or mouse clicks is minimised. Lengthy navigation could be stressful.
- Annoying sounds and flashing images are used sparingly to reduce the possibility of an epileptic attack and reduce eye strain and stress.
- Software is compatible with other packages otherwise slow use could lead to stress.
- Pre-coding and the use of drop down lists can reduce data entry and help prevent RSI.
- Logically ordered fields are used to make data entry easier and reduce stress; the fields on the screen should be in the same order as on the written document from which they are being copied as it can be annoying and time consuming to have to scan the written document for the required data.

Worked exam question

I Describe three features of poorly designed software that can cause stress or other health problems to a user. (6)

January 2001 ICT 1

▶ EXAMINER'S GUIDANCE

As this question allocates 6 marks for 3 features you will need to gain 2 points for each feature, so just listing 3 features will not be enough. You will need to identify a feature and then explain why it would cause stress.

There are many features that you could choose from; don't choose the first ones that come into your head but rather choose features that you can write enough about!

The information in the preceding section itemises features that developers should include for good software design; this question is asking for the opposite, so you will need to turn things around a bit. One point that is made 'colour schemes are not too bright and have good contrast otherwise eye strain could occur' could be turned around to:

▶ SAMPLE ANSWER

'Screen designs that have very brightly coloured backgrounds with text displayed in a poorly contrasting colour can cause eye strain'

Now add three examples of your own.

Activity 3

Copy and complete the table below. (some ideas have been included)

	Associated health issues	Preventable steps that can be taken
Keyboard		tiltable keyboard
Chair		
Software packages		
Computer desk and surroundings		
Office and surroundings		
Monitor	Glare can cause eye strain	
Printer		

Regular use of ICT equipment over a long period of time may lead to health problems, particularly:

▶ RSI (Repetitive Strain Injury), often stiffness and swelling in the wrists

▶ eye strain

▶ back problems

▶ irritation due to ozone.

These problems can be reduced by taking sensible precautions: not using equipment for too long; introducing adjustable chairs and screens; using wrist supports and screen filters.

New regulations have been introduced throughout the European Union setting standards for using ICT equipment in offices. Employers have duties to:

▶ provide adjustable chairs

▶ provide adjustable screens

▶ provide anti-glare screen filters

▶ pay for appropriate eye and eyesight tests

▶ plan work so that there are breaks from the screen

▶ provide information and training for ICT users.

Display screen equipment users are entitled to regular checks by an optician or doctor, and to special spectacles if they are needed and normal ones cannot be used. It is the employer's responsibility to provide tests, and special spectacles if needed.

Software should be designed to minimise health risks by taking great care over the design of screen layout.

Chapter 10 Questions

1. Name the following:

a) legislation used to protect companies and individuals producing software (1)

b) an Act introduced to protect personal details about individuals (1)

c) an Act designed to allow companies to prosecute anyone accessing their information systems without authorisation (1)

d) legislation to protect employees working with ICT systems. (1)

June 2004 ICT1

2. If software is not designed properly, it can cause stress in a user. For example, if a data entry screen is cluttered with multi-coloured and unnecessary images the user can become confused and disoriented.

Describe **three** other features in the design of a software package that could cause stress in a user (6)

3. An ICT professional within a company has been asked to produce health and safety guidelines for employees working with ICT. The guidelines will be stored on the company's intranet so that all employees can access them at all times.

State **four** guidelines that you would include and explain the reason for each. (8)

4. Mr Hadawi is setting up a new office for his car hire business. He needs to equip the office with a computer that will be used all day by his employee. Mr Hadawi wishes to ensure the health and safety of his employee.

Describe **two** features that Mr Hadawi should consider when buying and installing each of the following:

a) the screen

b) the chair

c) the keyboard

d) the desk and surroundings. (8)

5. A clerk working in the accounts department of a large company spends all day entering employee timesheet data into the company's payroll system. The clerk uses a terminal linked to the company's main computer. To ensure the health and safety of the clerk, state, with reasons:

a) **two** work practice procedures that the company could introduce (4)

b) **two** design features that the workstation the clerk uses should have (4)

c) **two** design features that the software the clerk uses should have. (4)

June 2005 ICT1

▶ Data capture is entering data into a computer. This may be done automatically, as in scanning a bar code on a library book, or manually, as in a new student at a college filling in an application form that is then used as a source document for entering the data at a keyboard.

Automated data capture, such as scanning the bar code, removes the need to key in data and allows large quantities of data to be read quickly. It has an additional advantage of reducing the occurrence of errors, as humans are prone to error.

A range of data capture methods have been developed, each suited to a different range of applications and circumstances.

Data capture methods ◀

▶ The volume of data to be captured will play a major part in determining the method used. A flatbed laser bar code scanner would be a sensible choice for entering the details of products sold in a large, busy supermarket. However the expense of purchase and installation would not make it a sensible choice for a small boutique.

The method of capture chosen will also be influenced by other factors such as speed and accuracy. The table below outlines the factors to be considered when choosing an appropriate method for a specific system.

The purpose of all methods of data entry into a computer system is to convert the data from the form in which it exists in the real world into a computer readable form. Examples of the form in which the data is stored before entry include letters on a page, pencil marks on a document, black and white stripes in a bar code or sound waves.

As all data held within the computer has to be stored in binary code (made up of 0s and 1s), the devices described below all convert the real world data into binary codes which can then be processed by the computer software. This process is known as the encoding of data.

Factors influencing the choice of data capture method

Volume of data	If the volume of data is large, then automatic data capture equipment is appropriate. The cost of installation, maintenance and staff training can be justified.
	With a high volume of data, manual data entry would not be able to cope within a reasonable time.
Speed	Speed can be an important factor in data entry. A flatbed bar code scanner can be used at higher speeds at a busy supermarket checkout than a hand-held scanner.
	Automated data entry methods, such as OCR and OMR, can produce very fast data entry.
Nature of system	A particular system may have a specialised data capture method associated with it. For example, the need for security against fraud means that Magnetic Ink Character Recognition (MICR) is the chosen method for entering data from cheques.
	In a dirty or dangerous environment such as a factory, the use of a keyboard may not be appropriate. Stock and goods may be identified by bar code. The use of magnetic media may be impractical due to magnetic fields.
Ease of use	The conditions under which data is to be entered, together with the range of skills of the users may influence the choice of data capture method.
Technological development	The choice of data capture method for a particular system may have been different a few years ago and may be different again in a few years' time. New methods are being developed all the time. However, it is important that methods are reliable and have the confidence of the users.
Cost	The cost of installing a particular method of data capture will be a major factor in any decision. Cost could relate to staffing, or hardware, as well as the cost of changing from the old system to the new. The greater the volume of data the more likely that a higher cost method can be justified.

Optical Character Recognition (OCR)

Optical Character Recognition is a method of data capture where the device recognises characters by light sensing methods. These characters are usually typed or computer printed, but increasingly devices are able to recognise handwritten characters.

Traditionally, OCR has been used for many years to input large volumes of data by commercial organisations such as utility companies.

OCR is now common using a flat bed scanner connected to a PC. Originally these scanners were only used for scanning images which could then be stored in a variety of formats such as **jpg** and **gif**.

Now scanners are usually sold with OCR scanning software as well. The system uses a two-stage process. First a page of text is scanned and the data is encoded as a graphical image. Then the OCR software scans the image using special pattern recognition software where groups of dots are matched against stored templates. A character is selected when a sufficiently close match is found.

The text can then be edited using word processing software. Accuracy rates can be as high as 99 per cent, depending on the quality of the original. If text is all the same size and in a simple font, the OCR is more likely to be accurate. OCR software still has difficulty distinguishing between similar letters: **rn** is often mistaken for **m**.

OCR provides a fast way of entering text to be stored in editable form without the need to retype.

Activity 1

On the Internet perform a search on *OCR scanner accuracy rate*. Can you find out how accurate OCR scanners are?

case study 1
▶ OCR on the roads

A version of OCR called Automatic Number Plate Recognition (ANPR) is used by the police to read car registration numbers picked up by CCTV or speed cameras.

As a vehicle approaches the camera the software takes a series of 'snapshots' and stores them in a file. When the number plate is of sufficient size for the OCR software the frame is scanned and the registration number is read and stored.

A similar system is used in London in the congestion charge zone. Motorists entering this zone have to pay a charge which was initially £5 per day. The system cost £200 million to implement but the scheme paid for itself within 30 months.

There are 230 cameras on 8-metre poles. The cameras capture the registration numbers of 98% of the cars in the charging zone.

The police use ANPR to check for stolen cars and to catch speeding motorists. As a vehicle passes, the ANPR equipment reads the number plate and the software checks it against the Police National Computer databases. If the number plate is matched, for example, with a stolen car, the ANPR equipment will sound an alert so that the car can be stopped.

Optical Mark Recognition (OMR)

Optical Mark Recognition is a form of mark sensing where preprinted documents are used. These documents contain boxes where marks can be made to indicate choices or a series of letters or numbers that can be selected to indicate choices. The reading device detects the written marks on the page by shining a light and recording the amount of light detected from different parts of the form. The dark marks reflect less light. The OMR reader transmits the data about each of the preprogrammed areas of the form where marks can be expected. The forms are printed with a light ink which is not detected.

Multiple choice exam papers use a special OMR answer sheet. Each student is given a mark sheet and they put a mark with a pencil through their choice for each answer (usually represented by a letter) on a grid. All answer sheets are gathered together and read by an OMR reader. Appropriate software is used to check the marks against the expected ones for the correct answers and the students' scores can be calculated.

The National Lottery and football pools coupons use a similar system. In some hospitals patients can select meals from a menu printed on OMR cards. The cards are fed into a computer system that produces accurate information quickly to be used by the catering services. OMR is a popular method for collecting questionnaire data.

OMR avoids human keyboard entry, which is prone to mistakes. OMR allows for fast data entry of a high volume of data.

Forms have to be carefully designed and filled in as marks that are entered in the wrong place will either be ignored or cause the form to be rejected. Care needs to be taken to keep the forms uncreased, as bent or damaged cards are likely to be rejected by the reader.

Figure 11.1 Lottery payslip

Magnetic Ink Character Recognition (MICR)

Magnetic Ink Character Recognition is another fast and reliable method of entering data. Documents are preprinted with character data in special ink that can be magnetised. The print appears very black. The shape of the characters is recognised by detecting the magnetisation of the ink. MICR is almost exclusively used to read cheques. The bank sort code and customer account number are printed in magnetic ink. The banks' clearing house computers can read these numbers. It is used instead of OCR to help minimise fraud. The hardware is expensive, so MICR is only used in situations when security is important.

Figure 11.2 Cheque showing MICR characters

Bar code readers (wands and scanners)

Bar codes are used as a means of identification and the pattern of the black and white stripes usually represents a code. Bar codes are attached to objects and have a wide variety of uses. The codes are read from the bars by detecting patterns of reflected light and encoded into computer-readable form using some form of scanner. These devices can be hand held (wand), where the reader is moved over the bar code, or fixed (scanner) where the object is moved across the reader. The bar code has separate right and left sides and can be read in either direction.

Laser scanners are frequently used in supermarkets to read the bar code which identifies the product. Each number in the bar code is represented by four stripes (two black and two white). The bar code is read very quickly with very few mistakes. An article number is a unique number given to a particular product. It is often printed beneath the bar-coded representation of the code. If, for some reason, the bar code reader fails to read the bar code, the operator can key in the code for the product.

Two common numbering systems are the European Article Number (EAN) and the Universal Product Code (UPC). These numbers are structured so that each part of the code has a particular meaning. For example, an EAN product code consists of 13 digits. The first two stand for the country of origin, the next five a manufacturer's number and a further six identify a specific product. (The last of these six is a check digit.)

Figure 11.3 A bar code

Magnetic stripe card

A magnetic stripe card has a strip of magnetic material on the back of a card that is usually made of plastic. Encoded information stored on the magnetic strip on the back of cash, credit and debit cards can be automatically read into a computer when the card is 'swiped' through a reader. The pattern of magnetisation is detected and converted into encoded binary form for computer use. This process is much quicker than typing in the card number and is accurate, not being susceptible to human error. The stripe can be damaged if the card is exposed to a strong magnet as the magnetic pattern would be altered and so render the card unreadable.

Magnetic stripe cards are now widely used on train tickets. The stripe will hold data concerning the proposed journey. On the London Underground tickets are read when a passenger arrives at, or leaves, a station. As well as being used to confirm the validity of the ticket, data is collected on all the journeys made. This can be used to produce information on passenger patterns and flows that can be used when planning services.

As an alternative, passengers can now use an Oyster card to get through the barriers at underground stations. The Oyster card is a smart card – a plastic card with a microprocessor sealed inside it. The microprocessor stores season ticket and Travelcard details. The passenger just has to touch the Oyster card on to a yellow reader at the station. This is another data capture method. Find out more at http://www.oystercard.com

When parking a car at Heathrow airport, drivers are issued with a ticket that has a magnetic strip on the reverse side. At the time of issue the date and time of arrival are encoded on to the strip. When leaving the airport building to return to the car park, the driver inserts the card into a large payment machine. The machine has a magnetic stripe reader that reads the data from the card. The charge, based on the length of stay, is calculated and displayed on a small screen. After the driver has made the payment, using cash, credit or debit card, details of the payment are recorded on to the strip on the card which is then returned to the driver. When the driver leaves the car park in his car he inserts the updated ticket into a machine controlling the barrier.

Touch-tone telephones

A method which is being increasingly used for limited data capture is a touch-tone telephone. Banking systems allow the user to enter her account number using the keys on the telephone handset, in response to voice commands. The user can also choose the type of transaction required by pressing a specific key.

The following dialogue could occur:

Computer system: Thank you for calling the ... Bank. Please enter your account number followed by #
User enters 21978433#
Computer system: Thank you. Please enter your sort code followed by #
User enters 189345#
Computer system: Thank you. Please enter your four digit security code followed by #
2989# *And so on...*

Speech recognition

Speech recognition is a growing area of computer input. As computers get faster and memory increases, reliable speech recognition has become cheaper. Already mobile phones can recognise the name of the person the user wants to call. Soon we will be able to use speech technology to access information without the need for a keyboard or a mouse.

There are two main uses made of speech recognition systems. They are used to enable large quantities of text data to be input as words into a computer so that they can be used in a software package such as a word processor. Alternatively, speech recognition systems can be used to input simple control instructions to manipulate data or control software. This is particularly appropriate when the environment makes the use of keyboard or mouse unsuitable, such as in a factory. Users of such systems can create and modify documents in a word processor. They can enter data into a variety of packages including form filling. The user can surf the Web or send e-mails simply by speaking.

Speech recognition systems provide users who have a limited ability to type, possibly due to repetitive strain injury or other disabilities, with a manageable way of interacting with a computer system.

Speech recognition systems are used to enter large volumes of text and are particularly useful for professionals who are not skilled in keyboard data entry. In the past such users would have dictated to a secretary or used a Dictaphone so that a typist could later audio type the text. The use of speech recognition software allows the user to input the text directly without the need for a typist. This removes any time delay and provides the user with control.

Advantages of using a speech recognition system

- Users who are not trained typists can achieve faster data entry than through keyboard use.
- Leaves hands free for other purposes.
- Enables users with disabilities to enter data.
- Can be used in areas where a keyboard is impractical.

Limitations of speech recognition in practice

- The user must speak each word separately leaving clear gaps between the words. This is not how they would speak naturally.
- The software needs to be trained to recognise an individual voice.
- Excessive background noise can interfere with interpretation of speech.
- Homophones (words which sound the same but are spelt differently) can be confused (such as their, they're or there).
- Many cheaper systems only recognise a small number of words.

case study 2
► Dragon Naturally Speaking®8

Dragon NaturallySpeaking 8 claims to be the best selling speech recognition software in the world.

It claims to work at speeds up to 160 words per minute – about three times faster than typing – with accuracy rates as high as 99%.

It allows the user to dictate directly into popular software such as Microsoft Word, Microsoft Outlook Express, Microsoft Excel and Corel WordPerfect.

Activity 2

Find out more at http://www.scansoft.com/naturallyspeaking/

- What does the website say are the advantages of using NaturallySpeaking?

Key-to-disk entry

Where large volumes of data have to be entered, offline key-to disk systems may be used. In these systems the data entry clerks type in the data, which is stored straight away on disk. This method would be used in batch processing (see Chapter 16), where large batches of data are entered before being processed. (As the entry is offline, it does not affect the performance of the main computer.) Key-to-disk data entry involves the transcription of data that has earlier been captured on paper.

Direct Data Entry (DDE) using a keyboard

Direct Data Entry is the input of data directly into a computer system for processing immediately. Here the data could have originally been captured on paper, or could be based on verbal data from a customer or over the telephone. DDE is a very widely used method of data entry. However, the speed and accuracy of the data that is input depends upon the skill of the operator.

There are a number of factors that must be considered when choosing a method of data capture for a particular system. These include:

- the volume of the data
- the speed that it has to be input
- the nature of the system
- the necessary ease of use
- the state of current technological development
- the cost.

Data capture is the process of encoding data in machine-readable form. Data capture methods include:

- OCR
- OMR
- MICR
- bar code scanning
- magnetic stripe card
- touch-tone telephone
- speech recognition
- key-to-disk
- DDE.

Chapter 11 Questions

1. A village store has just installed an electronic point of sale (EPOS) system including a bar code reader.

   a) Describe **two** advantages that the store gains from using the EPOS system. (4)

   b) Describe **one** disadvantage to the store of the EPOS system. (2)

   January 2005 ICT2

2. Pictures are scanned onto a computer and stored in files. Describe two types of files that can be used to store pictures on a computer. (4)

3. A friend has told you that she has bought a scanner with OCR software and software that can convert photos to JPEG. However, she does not know what these terms mean.

   a) What does the term OCR mean? (1)

   b) What does the term JPEG mean? (1)

4. A company has offices on five different sites. Each office has between ten and twenty members of staff working in it. Internal e-mail is used as a means of communicating between the staff. It has been suggested that speech recognition input and voice output might be used for the e-mail system.

   a) State the extra input and output devices each PC would need to support speech recognition input and voice output. (2)

   b) State **two** advantages to the staff of using a speech recognition system. (2)

   c) State **three** reasons why the speech recognition system may not be effective. (3)

   d) State **two** disadvantages of the voice output system. (2)

   January 2002 ICT2

5. The local council wishes to store the contents of documents on a computer system. The documents consist of handwritten and typed text. The documents will be scanned and OCR (optical character recognition) software will be used to interpret the text and export it to files that can be read by word-processing software.

   a) i) Describe **two** problems that could occur when scanning and interpreting the text. (4)

   ii) Describe **two** advantages to be gained by using OCR software. (4)

   June 2001 ICT2

Errors ◀

Why are errors a problem?

Some errors in data can lead to catastrophic results, whilst others can affect the acceptability of a computer system. As businesses and other organisations are dependent on information from computers, it is essential to try to reduce the occurrence of data errors and so ensure that the information is as accurate as possible.

Results of errors

There are many examples in newspapers of the results of errors occurring in computer systems. These include pensioners receiving gas bills for millions of pounds, others who are sent letters threatening legal action unless an outstanding payment of £000.00 is received within ten days. An error in a program caused a newly developed fighter plane to turn upside down when it crossed the equator. (Luckily this was detected during simulation testing.)

When errors can occur

Errors can occur at several stages in a system:

■ when the data is captured
■ when data, initially collected on paper, is transcribed (copied), usually via a keyboard, and entered into a computer
■ when data is transmitted within a computer system, particularly over a network link
■ when data is being processed by software.

Errors in data capture and entry

The majority of errors are introduced at data entry. Consequently automated methods are used whenever possible. Most of the methods of data capture described in Chapter 11 are reliable and automatic. For example, by using bar code readers at a supermarket checkout, no data needs to be typed in, thus saving time and removing the chance of transcription errors. However, no method of data entry can guarantee to be error free.

It is not always possible to use automated data entry methods. As stated above, at a supermarket checkout, the use of bar-coded product codes which can be read by a scanner removes the need to key in data. However, in many supermarkets fresh products such as vegetables are weighed at the checkout and the appropriate code is keyed in. If the operator wrongly identifies the vegetable or mistypes the code, then incorrect data is input. In some systems the operator often is given the facility to enter a number for multiple items rather than scan each item separately. Miskeying could result in a customer being charged for 50 tins of baked beans instead of 5!

Many errors occur when data is originally captured. The data for many systems originates on paper. Application forms of many types, mail order requests, census forms and details of car repairs undertaken are all examples where data is often first captured on paper. Errors can be recorded at this stage. A common mistake is to enter a date of birth with the current year. Forms that do not clearly indicate what is required will lead to errors.

Transcription errors

Whenever data is manually copied there is a chance that errors will be made. These copying errors are known as transcription errors. They can occur when the person involved misreads what is written or mishears what is said. Poor handwriting and unclear speech over the telephone are both likely to lead to transcription errors. Long codes made up of numbers or letters that have no particular meaning to the person keying in the data are particularly vulnerable to error. The skill and accuracy of the typing of the data inputter will have a major effect on the number of transcription errors made.

A common form of transcription error is a **transpositional** error where the order of two characters is mistakenly swapped. A code number 134638 could easily be mistyped as 136438. It is likely that this code number is being used to identify something such as a bank account, a hospital patient or a product. Entering the wrong code could have serious consequences, resulting in the wrong person's bank account being debited, the wrong patient's notes being updated with a drug prescription or the wrong product being ordered for a customer.

Activity 1

For each of the transcription errors below explain what is wrong and why the error is likely to have been made:

SO23 5RT entered as S023 SRT

Leeming entered as Lemming

419863 entered as 419683

2000000 entered 200000

Hatherley Road entered as Haverly Road

238.591 entered as 2385.91

23/5/89 entered as 23/5/01

199503 entered as 195503

Reducing data capture and transcription error

The use of automatic data entry, where there is no need for the keying in of data, removes the possibility of transcription errors. In a computerised system for a lending library, a hand-held scanner is used to read the borrower's identification number from a barcode on their membership card as well as the accession number which is held on a barcode in the book.

Methods of recording the current meter reading of a householder's electricity have developed through the following systems:

- A form filled in by the reader that was later transcribed using key-to-disk.
- A pre-printed OMR card where appropriate boxes were shaded to represent the digits.
- A hand-held computer with data relating to the customer's account so that data can be entered and checked at the house.

A **turnaround document** is a document that is produced as output from one computerised system and at a later time used as an input to another system. It can be read in using an OCR reader thereby minimising the amount of data that has to be keyed in.

As a transpositional error is a very common form of typing error, it is crucial that it is avoided as far as possible. Paper forms need to be designed with great care so that the chances of errors being made are kept to a minimum.

A data entry screen should be designed to follow the layout of data on the paper form. Mistakes are more likely to be made if the eye has to jump around the page to find an appropriate data field.

The greater the number of characters that need to be keyed in, the greater is the chance of error. Wherever possible codes should be used.

To ensure that only valid choices can be entered, options can be given for the user to choose, either in the form of tick boxes or drop-down lists.

Human errors such as transcription errors can be detected using two techniques – validation and verification.

For each of the following systems, suggest how a method of data capture could remove the need for data transcription.

1. In a school library, the name and class of pupils together with the book accession number and return date are keyed in whenever a pupil borrows a book

2. Lists of the marks that pupils were awarded in their AS level course work are sent in to the examination board from centres. On receipt of these lists the marks are keyed in by administrative assistants.

3. Employees in an office write down the time of their arrival and departure in a book. These figures are keyed in using DDE (Direct Data Entry) at the end of the week so that overtime pay can be calculated.

4. Members of a postal book club can order books by telephone. A clerk takes details of members' account numbers and the codes of the books required then keys in the data using a DDE system.

Verification ◄

▷ **Verification** is used to check that no changes are made to the data as it is entered. The most common method of verification involves typing data into the computer twice. The computer automatically compares the two versions and tells the user if they're not the same. When network users change their password, they have to type in the new password twice to verify it. The key-to-disk method, where data is entered and stored on to a magnetic disk offline before it is entered into the system as a batch, can allow the data to be entered twice for verification.

Validation ◄

▷ Validation is computerised checking that detects any data that is not reasonable or is incomplete; the data must obey preset rules. There are many different validation techniques that can be included in a program; one or more might be included for a particular data item. The most common techniques are listed below:

- **Presence check**. This checks that an entry has been made for the field. For example, the Surname field in an order form cannot be left blank.
- **Range check**. This checks a value to be within a certain range of values. For example, the month of a year must be between 1 and 12. Numbers less than 1 or greater than 12 would be rejected. In the same way, a mark gained in a test could be checked to be between 0 and 50.

- **Length check**. This checks that the right number of characters has been entered.
- **Type check**. This checks whether data is text or numeric etc.
- **Format check** (or picture check). This checks that data is of the right format, that it is made up of the correct combination of alphabetic and numeric characters. The format of a National Insurance number must be of the form XX 99 99 99 X. The first two and the last characters must be letters. The other six characters are numbers. Any other format is rejected. A format check is commonly used with a date field.
- **Cross-field check.** This checks that data in two fields corresponds. For example, if someone's gender is stored as Female, their title cannot be Mr. If the month in a date is 04, the day cannot be 31 as there are only 30 days in April.
- **Look-up list**. This checks that the data is one of the entries in the list of acceptable values. For example, the day of the week must be from the list Monday, Tuesday and so on.
- **Check digit**. This is used to check the validity of code numbers used for identification, for example, product codes in a supermarket or bank account numbers. These numbers are long and prone to data entry errors. It is crucial that such numbers are entered correctly so that the right record in the file or database is identified. A check digit is an extra digit added to the end of the original code. The value of the check digit is determined by the value and positioning of the other digits: for any given code there is only one possible check digit. When the code has been entered, the check digit is recalculated and compared to the entered value. If the two digits do not match, an error is reported.

Check digits are only used with codes that are used for identification purposes such as a bank account number, a credit card number or a student identification number.

Activity 3

What could be a consequence of making an error when entering:

1. the wrong examination number for a student's exam result
2. the wrong patient number in a hospital
3. the wrong product code when ordering an item of clothing online
4. the wrong account number when making a bank transfer.

case study 1
▶ Validation of meter readings

An electricity company reads the meters in individual houses. Figure 12.1 shows the device that is usually used to enter the data that is collected. These readings will be validated by a range check to make sure that they are within a sensible range. The records are fed into the computer.

The computer can check that the details for every house have been entered by checking that a control total, the number of houses, is correct. Of course, one house may have been omitted and another entered twice. This can be checked by making sure that no customer number is repeated.

When the bill is calculated it should be validated by another range check to make sure that it is not ridiculously high or low.

1. List three validation checks that could be made on the customer number. Explain the purpose of each test.
2. Another field that has data entered into it is the date that the reading is taken. Give three validation checks that could be made on the date. Explain the purpose of each test.

Figure 12.1 A handheld device to record meter readings

Activity 4

Generic software packages such as spreadsheets and database management systems have the facility to add data validation checks.

Set up a spreadsheet that allows the user to enter the data shown in the table below. The validation checks shown should be added. Suitable error messages for invalid data entry should be displayed. Figure 12.2 shows a dialogue box used in Microsoft Excel to set validation checks.

Data Item	Validation checks
Name	Maximum 25 characters
Team	One of: Basingstoke Bashers, Andover Athletic, Salisbury Stars, Winchester Wanderers, Southampton Swifts.
Position played	Whole number between 1 and 12

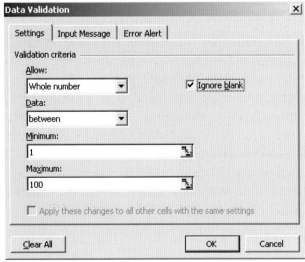

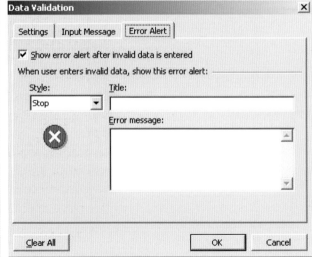

Figure 12.2 Excel data validation option

Accuracy versus validity

Validation checks can ensure that the data entered is reasonable and sensible, that it obeys set rules. Such checks, however, cannot ensure that the data entered accurately represents the source data.

It is possible that data entered could be **valid** but **inaccurate**. A temperature sensor recording the temperature in a furnace may give valid data, a number within a certain range, but the data may not accurately reflect the temperature if the sensor is not set up correctly. If '25 The Glebe', the address of a customer, is entered as '52 The Glebe' or even '61 Brockhampton Road', no validation error would be detected as both are reasonable addresses. However, neither is an accurate address for the customer. A man's date of birth entered as 25/03/1975 is a valid date but would be inaccurate if the man had been born in April.

Activity 5

State which of the following errors could be detected using validation checks. For those that could be detected, suggest a suitable check.

1. A car registration of 234 B 65
2. A date of birth for a 6th form college student of 12/4/1999
3. An entry of a quantity of 20 tins of dog food instead of 2
4. A name of 'Lian' instead of 'Liam'
5. An entry of a quantity of 2000 tins of dog food instead of 2
6. A date of admission to hospital of 31/04/2005
7. A shoe size of 5½ instead of 6½
8. A UMS score of 650 for A level ICT

Transmission errors ◄

▷ Data that has been entered correctly in a system can become corrupted when it is transmitted within a computer or when sent from one computer to another. This may be due to a poor connection or 'noise' on the line. All data is held within a computer and transmitted in binary coded form: everything is represented by a string of ones and zeros. Data corruption will result in one or more zeros being written as ones, or ones being written as zeros. It is likely that the resulting string of bits would be interpreted as another character or graphic etc.

For example, if just 3 bits were corrupted when transmitting the characters ICT in ASCII the result could become HGV.

1001001 (I) 1000011 (C) 1010100 (T)

1001000 (H) 1000111 (G) 1010110 (V)

Transmission error checking

Transmission errors can be avoided by the receiving computer sending the same message back to the original sender. If the two messages are the same, the data will be correct. The use of parity checks is a method that enables the detection of errors that can occur when data is being transmitted or stored.

A parity bit is an extra bit that is added on to a group of bits. The parity bit is solely used to check that the other bits have not been corrupted. There are two types of parity – even and odd. When even parity is used the parity bit is chosen to be 0 or 1 so that the total number of transmitted bits set to 1 (including the parity bit) is even.

Processing errors ◀

Errors occur due to incorrectly written software. Experience shows that programmers produce 30–100 faults in every 1,000 lines of code. Calculations could be worked out incorrectly, the wrong record could be updated in a file or certain types of transaction could be ignored.

Errors can also occur due to omissions in the specification (the document that lays out what a new system is to do), where certain situations are not considered when the system is designed. Designers must always assume that an operator can make errors.

One computer system tried to raise the temperature in a chemical process to 800 degrees when the operator had meant to enter 80, with the result that a poisonous chemical was released into the atmosphere.

A fatal error occurred when a patient received a lethal dose of radiation treatment for a cancerous tumour. The computer-controlled equipment had previously been used hundreds of times without causing an error. On this particular occasion the operator had altered the data entered by using the cursor keys in a particular way that had not been anticipated.

Other types of error can occur when the computer system is not operated correctly. For example, the name of an incorrect file can be entered and an out-of-date set of records used. A batch of data could be lost or forgotten so that a number of transactions fail to be entered into the system. Hardware failure, such as a disk corruption can cause some data to be lost.

Activity 6

Discuss possible causes of the following (there may be a number of possibilities) and suggest solutions:

1. A tenant is sent a letter that states that rent is overdue when in fact it has been paid in full.
2. An electricity bill demanding a payment of 2p is sent out.
3. A customer receives a copy of 'Madagascar' instead of 'Hitch Hikers' Guide to the Galaxy' from HOME VIDEO, a mail order company.
4. A doctor looks at a new patient's record before the patient attends surgery. She is expecting a 5-month-old baby, when in walks a 15 year-old.

Discuss the possible consequences of the following errors:

1. The wrong patient identification number is entered when entering the results of a blood test.
2. An electricity meter reading is wrongly entered.
3. 37 is entered instead of 73 as a student's mark in an ICT module exam.

Errors in processing: testing

Processing errors caused by incorrect coding should be spotted at the system's testing stage. Testing should not just include simple test data but should include extreme (boundary) data, the range limits and incorrect data. For example, a data field for an exam mark in the range 0 to 100 could be tested with the following field values:

25, 82 (valid data)

0, 100, 101 (extreme (boundary) data)

A, 200, –5 (invalid data)

Testing results should be compared carefully with the expected results, which should be calculated before the test is carried out. Incorrect data should be rejected. Testing may need to be performed on different hardware platforms and with different operating systems to make sure it works on all machines.

Errors in processing: specification, analysis and design

A very detailed and rigorous specification and analysis is required to ensure that all possible situations are taken into account. If this is not done, the programs that are produced will not take into account all combinations of data entry and will therefore produce errors under certain circumstances. There is a range of techniques that can be used to help to produce a specification that is clear and unambiguous. It is most important that the design and subsequent implementation follows the specification absolutely.

Particular care should be taken if software is being adapted to a new situation. When the Air Traffic Control system at

Heathrow was updated some years ago, software that had been developed for airports in the US was installed. Very soon some strange effects were noted – planes on the screen seemed to flip over! After investigation, the cause of the error was found to relate to the Greenwich Meridian. No account had been made in the software for the fact that part of the UK lies west of the meridian and part east. All locations in the US have values between 65° and 170° west. Leicester and Norwich lie at a similar latitude but Leicester has a longitude near to 1° west while Norwich lies near to 1° east. As the software did not distinguish between east and west values the two locations were taken to be the same. Fortunately the fault was detected during testing.

File totals

In batch processing, transaction and master files are read from start to end. An extra record is usually stored at the end of such a file and is used to check that data has not been corrupted.

As records are written to a file, running totals of certain fields are built up. These are called **control totals**. At the end of the file an extra record that contains the control totals is written. When the file is re-read in a later process the running totals are built up as the records are read. When the final record is read the running totals are compared with the control totals. If they are not identical an error has occurred and the software needs to take appropriate action.

Examples of fields that could be used as control totals:

- total number of records in the file
- total of current stock created by adding up the stock level field for each item
- total value of deposits in a transaction file for a banking system.

Sometimes totals are kept that have no meaning but are included only for error checking purposes. Such totals are called **hash totals**. An example for a suitable field for a hash total would be a product identification code field.

Record locking

In a transaction processing system records are updated as a transaction occurs. In a shared system, where there is more than one user, the situation could arise when two users were updating the same record simultaneously.

For example, imagine that two travel agents from different offices were trying to book passengers on to the same flight at the same time. Both would read the record for the flight – which indicates that four seats remain. Travel agent A carries out a transaction to book two seats for her clients and the updated record is written back, with two seats now available. Immediately afterwards travel agent B rewrites the record (which showed four seats available) and carries out a transaction to book three seats for the new clients. When the updated record is written back it overwrites the record that travel agent A updated and her transaction is lost.

To ensure that such errors cannot occur the software will be written in a way that prevents two users accessing the same record simultaneously. This is usually done by locking a record until a transaction is complete.

Backup (see Chapter 19)

It is not sufficient to find out that an error has occurred – it is necessary to recover from that error. An effective and thorough backup regime is vital to ensure that, if a file is corrupted or lost, it can be recreated in its original, correct form.

File version checks

Errors could occur if the wrong version of a master or transaction file were to be used by mistake. Consider a system in use by a credit card company. The system maintains a master file that holds details of the state of each customer's account. A transaction file made up of records each of which hold the details of a debit to an account is used to update the current amount owed field in the master file record. If, by mistake, yesterday's transactions were used instead of today's, the same debits would be made twice from an account. Data files will contain a header record that will contain data items such as version number and date created. These would be checked at run time to ensure that the correct version of a file was being used.

Report generation

Further checking should take place when reports are to be generated to ensure that the information is sensible. Regular utility bills such as gas, electricity or telephone can be checked against previous bills for the same customer and any major discrepancies highlighted. The total owing on bills can be checked to be within acceptable limits to ensure that bills for very large or very small or even negative amounts are not sent out to customers.

It is important that the date and in some cases the time is included on all reports so that the information is not wrongly interpreted.

Activity 7

Study the application form for Newtown 6th Form College shown in figure 12.3.

Determine the validation checks that would be necessary for each field so that as many errors as possible can be

Newtown 6th Form College
Application Form 2006

Please complete the form in black ink using BLOCK CAPITALS

Surname	
Forename(s)	
Home Address	

Telephone number	Post Code
Date of Birth	Age on 1/9/2006 yrs mths
Previous School	

Ethnic origin (please tick)

White	☐	Black Caribbean	☐	Black African	☐	Black Other	☐	Indian	☐
Pakistani	☐	Bangladeshi	☐	Chinese	☐	Other	☐	Info refused	☐

Provisional Course for September 2006

Please indicate which courses you are interested in. Please list, in order of preference, the subject name and the level (AS, A2, AVCE, GCSE, GNVQ Intermediate or Foundation).

Subject	Level

Current Courses of Study

Please list the GCSE subjects that you are currently studying, or have already taken, indicating which level paper you are being entered for (higher intermediate or foundation). Please ask your school to add your predicted (or actual) grades.

Subject	Level	Predicted Grade

Figure 12.3 Application form for Newtown 6th Form College

The information produced by a system is only as good as the quality of the data that is input.

Errors in data can have far-reaching effects.

Errors can occur when data is:

▶ captured

▶ transcribed

▶ transmitted

▶ processed.

Errors can be reduced in a variety of ways including:

▶ using automatic data capture methods such as **OCR** or **OMR** that remove the need for transcription

▶ verification checks

▶ validation checks such as: presence check, range check, format check, cross-field check, look-up list, use of a check digit

▶ a thorough analysis and specification that takes into account all possible circumstances

▶ thorough testing.

Data that is valid may not be accurate or correct.

Chapter 12 Questions

1. A company sells books over the Internet. Customers pay by using credit or debit card. The company collect details of the card from the customer using an online data entry form.

    a) List 3 fields that should appear on this form.   (3)

    b) For each of these fields describe a suitable validation check that could be applied.   (6)

2. When a candidate's AS module script has been marked, an examination board clerk enters the total marks allocated into a computer using a data entry form. For each candidate the candidate number, module number and mark obtained are entered.

    a) Explain why the data that is entered should be validated.   (2)

    b) For each of the fields given below, state an appropriate validation check and explain why it is appropriate.

        i)   Candidate number

        ii) Module number

        iii) Mark obtained   (6)

3. Describe, using examples, **two** types of validation check that could be used by a piece of software to ensure that a date is reasonable.   (6)

June 2004 ICT2

4. Read Case Study 2.

    a) What is it about producing bills using computer systems that increases the likelihood of a bill containing errors?   (2)

    b) What could Elf Business Energy do to prevent such errors?   (2)

5. Validation checks are used to ensure that data entered is reasonable. For **each** of the following describe **two** suitable validation checks. The four checks should all be different.

    a) A mail order for a company selling clothing   (4)

    b) A gas meter reading   (4)

case study 2
▶ The Canterbury Arms gas bill

In 2004 the landlord of the Canterbury Arms in Neath got a gas bill for more than £8,000.

Not only was this an extremely large gas bill for a pub, but the bill came from Elf Business Energy. The Canterbury Arms gets all its gas from British Gas.

And the bills kept on coming. It turned out that the Canterbury Arms was receiving a bill for another building in the same street. Elf Business Energy wanted the pub to pay for someone else's gas!

Getting the wrong bill is a serious problem. Jocelyn Kernick of Energywatch said 'Here in Wales we received over 3,000 complaints that related to billing issues last year and an awful lot of those cases involved address or name mix-ups.'

www.bbc.co.uk 28 June 2004

Flat files

▶ Traditionally computer systems stored data in files like this one:

Forename	Surname	Exam	Teacher	Result
Aisha	Ambreen	French	Miss Knight	E
Aisha	Ambreen	Art	Mr Hill	C
Gareth	Davis	Physics	Mrs Edwards	A
Gareth	Davis	French	Miss Knight	B
Fay	Hunt	French	Miss Knight	B
Fay	Hunt	Art	Mr Hall	C
Fay	Hunt	English	Ms Cornwell	B
Fay	Hunt	History	Mr Galloway	D
Jamie	Smith	Art	Mr Hill	E

This flat file stores examination results in a school. It consists of a number of records.

Each record in the file stores the details of a separate exam result and contains five fields; Forename, Surname, Exam, Teacher and Result.

A flat file system like this would work but it is not efficient for the following reasons:

- Data is duplicated. We can see that Fay Hunt has been entered for four exams. Each time a new exam result is received, her name has to be entered again.
- This repeated data is called **redundant** data. It wastes time typing the repeated data in. It can also waste space on the disk as the file is bigger than necessary. If the file is larger, it will take longer to load and save.
- Data can be **inconsistent**. Three students have exam results for the Art examination. In one the Art teacher is *Mr Hall*. In the other two it is *Mr Hill*. We don't know if this is the same teacher. If so, how do we know which name is correct?

  If the same data is entered several times, mistakes like this are more likely to occur.

With flat files it is difficult to add an extra field. For example, if an exam mark field is added to the file above every program accessing the file will need to be modified.

Organisations often used several flat files, some of which stored the same data. For example, a personnel file might store the following details about employees: Works Number, Forename, Surname, Home Address and National Insurance Number. The payroll file might also store Works Number, Forename, Surname and National Insurance Number.

Data has been duplicated. Any changes made to one file would need to be made to the other file, e.g. if a female employee changes her name on getting married.

Database Management Systems (DBMS) ◀

▶ More complex database systems have been developed that separate the data from the application programs. Using a relational database allows data to be stored only once in the system, avoiding redundant and inconsistent data.

Relational databases

A relational database stores data in a number of tables that are related to each other.

Relational database management software, which allows the user to manipulate data in a relational database, is now very common. Microsoft Access is the most popular example but there are alternatives such as Filemaker Pro or Lotus Approach.

Relational database management software allows the user to:

- set up **tables**
- set up **relationships** between tables using foreign keys
- set up **queries** to search the database using data from more than one table
- set up queries in a user-friendly manner using **Query by Example** (QBE)
- set up **on-screen forms** for data entry
- set up **reports** to present information
- set up **macros** to automate and customise the DBMS to suit the user.

How would it work for the exam results file?

Normally a database can have one or more tables; a relational database needs to have two or more tables that relate to each other. Commonly there are at least three tables.

The first table is usually a table storing data about people such as students, patients, customers, members, etc.

In this case there would need to be a student table. This would store details of every student such as their first name, their surname and probably other information such as date of birth, address and telephone number. Each student would only appear in this table once.

As there may be two students with the name Jamie Smith, each student is given a unique number. This number is used to identify them and is called the **primary key** field.

Part of the student table might look like this:

Student ID	Forename	Surname
...		
S015	Aisha	Ambreen
S016	Nicola	Carter
S017	Simon	Coates
S018	Gareth	Davis
S019	Fay	Hunt
S020	Lisa	Redwood
S021	Jamie	Smith
...		

The second table is usually a table storing services available for people identified in the first table. These could include lessons, doctors, items for sale, videos for hire, exams, etc.

In this case there would need to be a subject table like this:

Subject ID	Subject	Teacher
A001	Art	Mr Hill
A002	English	Ms Cornwell
A003	French	Miss Knight
A004	History	Mr Galloway
A005	Physics	Mrs Edwards
...		

There is then a third table that links the two other tables.

The only student data needed in this table is the Student ID as from this number we can look up all the other student data in the student table.

The only subject data needed in this table is the Subject ID as from this number we can look up all the other subject data in the subject table.

The third table would be called the exam result table. This would link the other two tables together and would look like the table on page 150.

Student ID	Subject ID	Result
S015	A003	E
S015	A001	C
S018	A005	A
S018	A003	B
S019	A003	B
S019	A001	C
S019	A002	B
S019	A004	D
S021	A001	E

This record shows that student S018 (Gareth Davis) got a grade B in subject A003 (French with Miss Knight).

Linked to the key field in the student table

Linked to the key field in the subject table

The relationships between the tables can be illustrated like this:

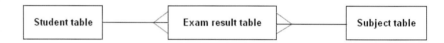

Figure 13.1 Entity Relationship flowchart

Each table is shown and the related fields joined. The 'crows feet' show that the relationship between the student table and the exam result table is one to many. The student can only appear once in the student table but many times in the exam result table.

Similarly the exam result table to subject table is a many to one relationship.

There are two fields in the exam result table that are the primary key field in another table. These are the Student ID and the Subject ID and are used to link the tables. When a field is the key field in a different table, it is called a **foreign key**.

The power of queries

The query feature in a DBMS is very powerful.

A query can be used to:

- search for information in one table
- search for information in related tables
- combine the information from related tables into a new table
- choose which fields are to be shown in the new table

- specify criteria for searching on; for example, find the names of all students with an exam result today.
- perform calculations on numeric or currency fields.

A **parameter query** is a query that lets the user enter the search criteria when the query is run. For example, suppose we wanted to see all the exam results for the student Fay Hunt.

When the parameter query is run, a dialogue box is displayed that prompts the user to type in the surname of the student. When Hunt is entered this will display all the exam results for students called Hunt.

Why would it be better here to search using the Student ID field?

Meaningful information

Information from a relational database is presented in a report. A report can be based on one table like the one in figure 13.2 showing a list of exam results for all students.

Exam results

Student ID	Subject ID	Result
S015	A003	E
S015	A001	C
S018	A005	A
S018	A003	B
S019	A003	B
S019	A001	C
S019	A002	B
S019	A004	D
S021	A001	E

Figure 13.2 Student results based on one database table

This isn't much use unless you know which student ID refers to which student and which subject ID refers to which subject. It would be more meaningful if the exam result list presented the student's name and not their student ID. This can be achieved using a query. A query can retrieve data from more than one table. A report can be based on that query.

The report would look like figure 13.3.

Exam results

Surname	Forename	Subject	Teacher	Result
Ambreen	Aisha	French	Miss Knight	E
Ambreen	Aisha	Art	Mr Hill	C
Davis	Gareth	Physics	Mrs Edwards	A
Davis	Gareth	French	Miss Knight	B
Hunt	Fay	History	Mr Galloway	D
Hunt	Fay	French	Miss Knight	B
Hunt	Fay	English	Ms Cornwell	B
Hunt	Fay	Art	Mr Hill	C
Smith	Jamie	Art	Mr Hill	E

Figure 13.3 Student results using data from more than one database table

Choosing fields

When storing information about people, 'name' is not normally stored as one field. 'Surname', 'Forename' and 'Title' are usually stored as separate fields. This enables the data to be sorted into alphabetical order by surname. (It is unusual to sort by forename.)

It also allows the name to be put together in different ways for different uses.

<Title> <Forename> <Surname> on an envelope will look like: Mr Patrick McGowan

Dear <Forename> at the start of the letter will look like: Dear Patrick

Addresses are usually stored as a number of different fields that can be output on different lines.

It is usually more appropriate to store date of birth rather than age, as date of birth, unlike age, does not change.

For each field in a table, the designer will need to specify data type, length and other properties. The choice of data type will allow the DBMS to store the data in the most efficient way and prevent the user from entering the wrong type of data into a field.

Data types

The data types available in most DBMS are:

Text   A group of characters. Text is used to store letters and numbers when calculations are not to be carried out. For example, text is the most appropriate data type to store a telephone number, customer number or house number. If a telephone number 02089945643 were stored as a number, the leading 0 would be lost. The designer can specify a size for a text field up to a maximum of 255 characters.

Numeric   A number. The number of decimal places stored can be specified.

Date/time   A number of different date and/or time formats can be chosen such as 25/03/06, 25/3/2006, 03/25/06 or 25 March 2006

Currency   Is used whenever money fields are to be stored. It can be set to 2 decimal places or no decimal places.

Boolean   Can hold only two values: True or False.

An optional default value can be selected for each field. A default value is a value that will be inserted into a field at data entry if the user does not enter one. An example of a default value could be the date of an order will be set to today's date: in most situations the user will not need to change this value, thus saving time at data entry.

Validation checks can be selected for a field. For example:

■ an item number must be on a list of item numbers
■ a surname cannot be more than 25 characters.

Sample exam question

1 A flat file system is used to store orders taken by an electrical retailer. Examples of records from the file are shown below.

Customer	Address	Order no	Date of order	Item no	Description	Price	Phone no	Sales staff no	Sales person
Paul Smith	38 Beech Road	2345	4/11/2001	456	Steam Iron	£35.45	01234 665577	78	Sue Sneath
Anne Chu	27 Ash Square	2359	4/11/2001	764	Toaster	£19.99	01234 897645	62	Bert Jones
Anne Chu	27 Ash Square	2359	4/11/2001	798	Kettle	£19.99	01234 897645	62	Bert Jones
Sean Page	19 Elm Lane	2361	5/11/2001	461	Microwave Oven	£125.00	01234 567483	78	Mrs Sneath
Joan Patel	16 Oak Close	2362	5/11/2001	764	Toaster New	£19.99	01234 1922837	78	Sue Sneath

a) Referring to the examples above, describe the problems that have occurred by storing the data in a single flat file. (6)

b) The flat file system is to be replaced by a relational database. What structures would be needed in this database to allow for the effective updating and retrieval of data? (4)

June 2002 ICT2

▶ **SAMPLE ANSWER**

There is redundant data: e.g. Anne Chu's name, address and phone number appear twice, Bert Jones' staff number and name appear twice, Sue Sneath's staff number and name appear three times.

There is inconsistent data: e.g. Sue Sneath also appears as Mrs Sneath, Toaster also appears as Toaster New.

b) The structures that would be needed in a relational database would be:

- There need to be a series of related tables. In this case there would be four tables.
- The tables would be
  customer table – a table of customers such as Anne Chu
  staff table – a table of sales staff such as Bert Jones
  stock table – a table of items for sale such as Steam Iron
  order table – a table linking the other three tables
- Each table would need a primary key, e.g. customer number, item number, staff number and order number.
- The tables would be linked by relationships

▶ **EXAMINER'S GUIDANCE**

You could answer part (b) by drawing the relationship diagram to illustrate the structure required. It would look something like this:

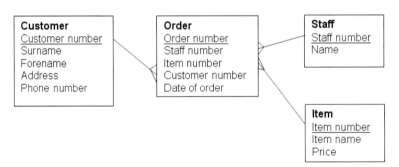

Figure 13.4 Entity Relationship flowchart

Table names are in bold. Primary key fields in each table are underlined.

Activity 1

Using Microsoft Access or another relational DBMS package, set up a database for the school exam results.

You need to carry out the following stages:

- Set up the Student table and the Subject table, using the fields given in the chapter. Add some more of your own as appropriate. Select the appropriate data type, field length and properties for each field.
- Set up the Exam result table.
- Create the relationships between the tables.
- Design forms for data entry for each table.
- Enter details of about 5 subjects.
- Enter details of about 10 students.
- Enter details of about 20 exam results entering the student ID and the subject ID.
- Write queries to:
  a) produce a list of the names of all the students
  b) produce a list of all the exam results including the name of the student (not the student ID) and the name of the subject (not the subject ID)
  c) produce a query to find the exam results for a student who has forgotten their student ID. (The user will have to enter the student's surname.)

Activity 2

For each of the following scenarios a database is required. For each one draw a relationship diagram showing the tables and fields. Underline the primary key fields and show how a foreign key acts as the link between the tables.

a) A conference has been organised for students of ICT A level in a large city and students are coming from a number of schools. The organisers wish to store data about individual students and the schools involved. (Two tables)

b) A holiday company stores details of hotels in a number of resorts. (Two tables)

c) An art dealer sells the paintings and other works of art produced by a number of artists. (Two tables)

d) The organisers of an arts festival wish to store data about venues where events are held and the artists who are taking part. (This requires three tables.)

Activity 3

Why should a games rental shop use a database? Could a manual system be better than a database system? Both systems record details of members and who has hired which game. (This could easily be done in a paper-based system by using a list of all games and the name of the hirer written next to it.)

A manual system is cheaper, unlikely to break down and requires little training. However, the computerised system will probably be better for the following reasons:

- Management information is automatically gathered. For example, details of each hiring, financial details, how many times a customer has hired a game, how many times a particular game has been hired, which customers have not hired a game recently and which games have not been borrowed in the

▶

past month or so. These figures can be used in preparation of accounts or to analyse which games are most popular.

■ Better service to customers. Using a bar code reader to enter the game code and the member code is very quick. Queues at the counter will be shorter.

■ Details of members and games can be found and printed quickly.

■ The names and addresses of members can be used for advertising purposes in a direct mail shot. The database can be queried to produce a list of people who haven't hired a game for six months. A letter can then be printed offering them a discount if they hire a game within a week of receiving the letter. The letter can be personalised using the mail merge from a word processing package.

■ Similarly automatic reminders can be sent out to members who have not returned a game by the due date.

■ The database can be extended to include the member's date of birth. The computer can be used to ensure that a member is old enough to hire, say, a particular category of game.

Describe in a similar form to the example given above, the advantages of implementing a database system for:

a) appointments at a hospital

b) booking at a leisure centre

c) orders at a knitwear business.

A simple guide to the advantages of relational databases and how to implement them can be found at

http://www.dti.gov.uk/bestpractice/assets/relational.txt

case study 1
▶ Relational database – Yellow Pages

Yellow Pages print and distribute over 27 million copies of its directories every year across the UK. Around 374,000 advertisers place over three quarters of a million advertisements in Yellow Pages every year. All businesses are contacted to establish in which classification and under what description they wish to appear in Yellow Pages.

Yellow Pages stored data about advertisers in 27 flat files. When Yellow Pages started to expand into other areas such as Talking Pages, Business Pages, The Business Database and Yell.com, they needed a more efficient and flexible data structure.

A relational database system resulted in a cost saving of approximately £300,000 per annum. The new system performed so well that Yellow Pages can use the system online for an extra three hours a day. It previously had to close down at 6p.m. in order to give enough time to update files – the new system closes at 9p.m., giving extra productivity.

The term flat file is used to refer to a single file that is like a two-dimensional table.

The use of flat file systems can produce data duplication where the same data item is stored in two or more different files.

Unnecessary data duplication is known as data redundancy.

Redundancy often leads to data inconsistency where the same item of data is stored differently in different places.

A database is a store of data that can be linked together in different ways. The software package that allows a user to set up and access a database is called a database management system (DBMS).

A relational database is made up of:

▶ tables that contain the data, each column representing one attribute (or field) of the data

▶ relationships or links between the tables

▶ forms that are used for data entry

▶ reports that are used to present data

▶ queries that are used to select data from one or more tables of the database

A primary key is a unique field or group of fields chosen to identify a record.

A foreign key is a field in a table that is identical to the primary key of another table and is used to provide a link between the two tables.

Advantages of a relational database over a set of flat files include:

▶ the reduction of data redundancy

▶ the reduction of data inconsistency

▶ there being a centralised pool of data that can be used for many applications

▶ data being independent of the applications

▶ the possibility of different users being allocated different access rights to different parts of the database.

Disadvantages of a relational database over a set of flat files include:

▶ the system being more complex to set up

▶ greater security and confidentiality issues arising if the data is used for a range of applications

▶ users needing to be trained to use the system.

Chapter 13 Questions

1. Give **four** advantages of using a relational database over a flat file information storage and retrieval system. (4)

January 2005 ICT2

2. A horse-riding school is setting up a database to store details of students and the times of their riding lessons. They have designed a student file part of which is shown below.

Student ID	First Name	Surname	Address 1	Address 2	Address 3	Age
004	Laura	Holden	29 Long Street	Oakton	OA8 9PG	13
005	Jenna	Jones	12 High Grove	Oakton	OA8 6BN	12
006	Claire	Lees	3 Cedar Road	Oakton	OA7 7VE	14

They have a lesson file which looks like this:

Lesson ID	Date	Time	Student ID	First name	Surname
056	18/03/06	9:30	004	Laura	Holden
057	18/03/06	10:00	005	Jenna	Jones
058	19/03/06	10:00	006	Claire	Lees

a) Which field is the key field in the lesson file? (1)

b) Which fields will be linked by a relationship? (1)

c) Suggest an improvement to the design of the student file and explain why it is an improvement. (2)

d) The database contains redundant data.

   i) What changes would be needed to the structure of this database to remove redundant data? (2)

   ii) Explain why these fields are redundant. (2)

3. A library stores details of books loaned in a flat file, part of which is shown in the table below.

Date	First Name	Surname	Address	Phone no	Book
17/03/06	Laura	Holden	29 Long Street	(01945) 889933	Wuthering Heights
18/03/06	Jenna	Jones	12 High Grove	(01945) 604599	Oliver Twist
18/03/06	Jenna	Jones	12 High Grove	(01945) 604959	Decline and Fall

Using examples from the table, explain **two** problems with using flat files. (6)

▶ Software is the name given to computer programs. Programs are made up of thousands of instructions that actually make the computer do what is required. Without software, computer hardware is no use. Programs are needed to control the hardware, the physical components of the computer, such as printer, processor or disk drive. There are two main types of software:

■ systems software
■ applications software

and each can be divided into subcategories.

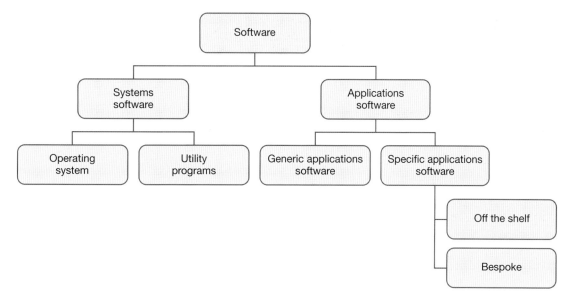

Figure 14.1 Types of software

Systems software is the name given to the programs which help the user to control and make the best use of the computer hardware. The operating system and utility programs are types of systems software.

Applications software is a term used to describe programs that have been written to help the user carry out a specific task, such as paying wages, designing a newsletter or storing details of payments. This task is usually something that would need to be done even if a computer was not used. A spreadsheet package and a booking system program written for a dental surgery are examples of applications software.

Systems software ◄

Operating systems

An operating system is software that is needed to run a computer. It controls and supervises the computer's hardware and supports all other software. It hides the complexity of the hardware from the user and provides an interface between the user and applications, and the computer's hardware. This means that the user does not have to bother about the details of the hardware. An operating system manages the computer's resources: memory, storage, processor time, files and users.

Some specific tasks carried out by an operating system are:

- memory management: allocating internal memory (RAM) – this is particularly important if the computer is apparently running more than one program at the same time
- managing all other programs – if more than one program is running, it schedules (allocates running time) according to pre-set priorities
- transferring programs and data between disk and RAM
- controlling input and output from attached hardware devices
- managing the user communication with the computer
- checking and controlling user access to prevent unauthorised access
- logging of errors.

An operating system may allow more than one program apparently to run at the same time. The programs are not actually running at the same time, as the operating system decides which program to run and switches from one to the other. This usually happens so quickly that the user thinks that the programs are running at the same time. The operating system is managing the use of processor time to make the very best use of it. When one program is tied up sending data to a printer the operating system can allocate the processor to another program. An operating system may allow more than one input device. The operating system checks which input devices are present and decides which should have priority.

The operating system manages the memory. It loads the program into RAM from disk and decides how much RAM to allocate to the program, how much to allocate to data and how much is needed for its own use. If there is not enough memory available, the operating system will give the user an error message. When several programs are running at the same time the operating system will need to keep track of where each one is stored and make sure that programs don't get mixed up.

An operating system also manages files stored on backing storage, for example, on a hard disk. The user does not need to know where each file is physically stored; he can simply refer to the file by a name. It is the operating system that matches the file name to the actual data on disk.

Network operating system

A special operating system is needed when a network is in operation. A network operating system is very complex. It has to monitor the network traffic. It deals with the checking of user names and passwords, restricts access to forbidden areas of the disk and manages the use of the computer's memory. If a network has a shared peripheral, such as a printer, then the operating system has to control a queue of documents which different users have sent to the printer, so that the documents are printed in turn.

Utility programs

Another category of systems software is utility programs. These are also known as housekeeping programs as they allow the user to carry out tasks that make the use of the computer easier such as tidying up the storage of files on a hard disk.

Utility programs are tools to help the user make more effective use of a computer. Although utility programs are not part of an operating system, they are often provided with operating system software. Examples of utilities include:

- **virus checking**: programs that will scan a computer's storage devices for the presence of known viruses.
- **file conversion**: converting files from one format to another. For example, a document file produced by Word will be stored with formatting codes that are specific to Word. For the document to be read by WordPerfect, a different word processing package with different formatting codes, a file conversion utility must be used.
- **disk formatter**: when a new disk is to be used it needs to be set up so that the computer's operating system can access it. Disk formatting was a common occurrence for users when floppy disks were the main form of transferable backing storage.
- **file compression** (sometimes referred to as zipping): many files, particularly graphics files, are very large. Compression is a technique used to reduce the size of the file. This is done to reduce the amount of backing storage space needed. Smaller files are quicker to send over the Internet.
- **file management**: files held on a backing storage device can be deleted, renamed or moved from one folder to another; copies may be made within different folders on the same device or on a different medium for back-up or transfer purposes; new folders (directories) can be created.

- **backing up a file**: making a copy of a file for security purposes.
- **garbage collection** and **defragmentation**: this involves removing unwanted data and files from a disk and closing up any gaps left on the disk so that all the free space is together. This will make more room to store new files.

Interfacing with peripherals

Software has a crucial role to play in the linking together of peripheral (input, output, storage and communication) devices to a computer. It is possible to use a range of devices with different specifications, made by different manufacturers, on the same computer. Software provides the interface so that the operating system can send and receive messages to a device that allows it to function.

Today it is very common to want to be able to add additional input, output or storage devices to a computer. For example, you may wish to add a scanner, a joystick, a printer or a CD-writer. Whenever hardware is added, the operating system must be set up to accept the new device. This is called configuring the system. Software is needed to interface with all peripherals: storages devices, input and output and display devices. This software needs to enable the processor to recognise and communicate with the devices.

Modern computers using an advanced operating system can immediately cope with a new device being plugged in. For example, if the user of a laptop which has a mouse pad plugs in a conventional mouse through a USB port whilst using a word processing package, the mouse is immediately active and can be used.

Peripheral device drivers

The most common way of configuring hardware is using special software called a peripheral device driver. For example, different printers operate at different speeds, using slightly different sizes for lines and numbers of lines on a page. When you buy a printer, it is supplied with a program called a **printer driver**. Installing the printer driver formats the computer's output for the particular printer.

A peripheral device driver provides communication between the operating system and the peripheral. A printer driver translates formatting and highlighting information into a form that the printer can understand. It performs size control and enables error messages sent from the printer to be understandable to the operating system (such as 'out of paper').

It could occur that a user who has installed a new piece of software on a stand-alone PC finds that a document printed on the attached printer does not replicate the image seen on the screen. This could have occurred because the software could have been written to communicate directly with the printer and is failing to transmit the appropriate codes.

A driver for a scanner translates the scanned images into a form that the software can understand. It will generate signals that can be interpreted by the operating system if the scanner is not ready.

A PC needs a device driver for every peripheral connected to it. Different screens will have different characteristics such as resolution and disk drives will operate at different speeds. The driver provides an interface between the operating system and the device.

Applications software ◀

▷ Applications software is software that has been written for a user task, such as producing invoices, cropping a photographic image or booking a flight. Applications software can be **package** (or **'off the shelf'**) **software**, which is software that is developed and sold to a number of users. Such software is usually supported with a range of manuals or guides. This type of software can be bought in a shop, from websites, through trade magazines or direct from the supplier. Package software falls into two categories: generic and specific.

Generic application software

The most common form of software is generic or general purpose application software. Generic application software is an applications package that is appropriate to many users. Many such programs are pre-installed on a computer when it is sold and can be used in many ways. You will use this type of software for your coursework.

Many generic software packages can be used to create customised applications for a user. The use of macros, buttons and customised toolbars enable this to be done. Data can often be imported from one type of package to another. (See Chapter 15 for a more detailed discussion.)

Word processing, database management, spreadsheet and presentation packages are examples of generic applications software. Integrated packages combine several distinct applications.

Word processing packages

Word processing packages are used to produce documents such as letters and reports. Text can be formatted in a variety of ways to improve the look of a document. Features can be added that make parts, such as headings, stand out by using different fonts, text sizes, bold or italics. Bullet points can usefully highlight important points. Text can be edited using facilities such as copy and paste, find and replace, insert or delete a word, line or paragraph or through the use of spell check.

A variety of objects such as symbols, graphics or other files can be inserted in a document.

Faster processing speeds and increased computer memory have allowed modern packages to include many extra features such as mail merge, text wrapping around imported graphics, e-mail, spelling and grammar checks and displaying text in tables and columns.

Text written by one person can be reviewed by another and comments can be added. This book is written by two authors. When one completed a chapter he sent it to the other, as an e-mail attachment, for checking and commenting. The word-processing package has the facility to show all edited changes made by the reviewer. Deleted text is highlighted and added text displayed in another colour. Comments can be added as well. When the reviewed chapter is returned to the author he can accept or reject each change (see figure 14.2).

Text written by ~~someone~~ <u>one person</u> can be reviewed by another and comments can be added. This book is written by two authors. When one author completed a chapter he[IS1] sent it to the other, for checking and commenting. The word-processing package has the facility to show all edited changes made by the reviewer. Deleted text is highlighted and added text displayed in another colour[IS2]. When the reviewed chapter is returned to the author he can accept or reject each change.

Figure 14.2 Using a word processor's reviewing facility

Activity I

Listed below are a number of advanced features of a word processor. Check that you can use each of these features on your word processor, using the online help if you need to.

Feature	Example of use
Use of headers and footers	Customised text that is added to appear at the top or bottom of every page in a document. Can include page numbers, date and/or time. The word processor automatically keeps track of page numbers so that the correct number appears on each page. (In a large document, such as a book, a different header could be used for each chapter.)
Create an automatic table of contents	Page numbers for chapter and sections can be inserted automatically into a table of contents.
Create an index	An alphabetic list of technical terms linked to all references in a text can be created automatically.
Import a graphic and wrapping around text	Embedding a graphical image into a document, positioning it and setting the text to flow around it.
Use of templates	A template is a document in which the standard opening and closing parts are already filled in. An example could be for a memo where the title and headings are provided in the template. The data specific to the message can then be filled in.
Outlining: create a document with consistent headings using style sheets	A style sheet is a file that defines the layout of a document. Parameters such as page size, fonts and margins are specified. Specific fonts can be allocated to different levels of heading and subheading.
Use mail merge	Merges text from one file into another file. This is particularly useful for generating many files that have the same format but different data. For example, a standard letter can be created with a number of merge fields, such as the recipient's name which are copied from the other file. Each letter will have a different name added to it.
Insert footnotes and endnotes	Automates the numbering and placement of footnotes to enable easy cross-referencing.
Create own customised dictionary for use in spell checking	A spell checker is a utility within the word processor that allows the checking of the spelling of words. It highlights any words that it does not recognise. It is possible to create an additional dictionary with extra words that are commonly included by the user.
Search and replace	The word processor can search for a particular word or phrase. The user can direct the word processor to replace the word with another, everywhere that the first word appears.
Use the thesaurus	A built-in thesaurus that allows the user to search for synonyms.

Worked exam question

Software packages contain many advanced features that are often only used by certain people. Explain, with the use of examples, two advanced features of a word processing package that would be useful to an author writing an ICT textbook.

June 2003 ICT 2 (6)

▶ **EXAMINER'S GUIDANCE**   *The question carries six possible marks, three for each feature. As with many ICT exam questions, it is quite easy to get one or even two of the three marks but is harder to write an answer that will be awarded full marks.*

You will probably be likely to come up with more than two features; you therefore need to decide the ones for which you can provide the fullest answers. How will the marks be awarded? Only one mark is likely to be given for naming the feature. It is important that you relate your answer to the scenario given in the question – don't just give any two features of a word processor. Advanced features were asked for so basic features such as formatting text as bold would not gain any credit.

First you need to think a bit more about what is needed in a textbook. It consists of text, organised into chapters and sections which have standard headings. Graphical images are included in the layout. The book has a table of contents at the start and an index at the end.

Some of the advanced features of a word processor that are likely to be used would include: use of a customised dictionary, importing graphics, producing an automatic table of contents, producing an index, reviewing comments made by editor, use of a style sheet and using headers and footers.

Now to turn two of these into full answers:

▶ **SAMPLE ANSWER**   An additional, customised dictionary could be built up (1) where technical ICT terms such as EFTPOS can be stored (1). This is accessed when the spellchecker utility is used to check for incorrectly spelt words so that the terms are not highlighted for being incorrect. (1)

A table of contents can be created automatically (1) so that it controls page references to chapters and sections (1). This ensures that the author does not have to enter the page references himself, nor change them whenever the text is altered (1).

▶ **EXAMINER'S GUIDANCE**   If you had chosen to write about the ability to import graphics you would need to think about the ways in which a word processor can deal with graphical images. You would need to discuss word wrap.

▶ **SAMPLE ANSWER**   Now write full answers for the following features, making sure that you link your answer to the ICT textbook author. (The first few features have some hints to help you.)

- Use of headers and footers (What would you have in a header/footer in a book?)
- Creating an index (See the definition in the table in Activity 1. Why is an index needed in a textbook?)
- Reviewing editing comments (See word processing packages)
- Use of outlining
- Use of style sheets
- Use of columns.

Activity 2

Describe three advanced features of a word processor that would be useful to a solicitor's secretary explaining in your answer how the feature would be used (9).

Database management packages

Database management packages are used for information storage and retrieval. These packages allow users to enter data and store it, to sort and query a set of records, and output information from the database in reports. More sophisticated packages will include wizards to help the user set up the database, import data from other packages and customise the database to hide the workings of the package from an inexperienced user.

A college would use a database management package to set up and access details of students and courses at the college. The package could be used to link students to courses. The data could be sorted so that class lists could be produced in alphabetical order. The information relating to an individual student could be retrieved through the use of a query.

Spreadsheet packages

Spreadsheet packages are computer programs that allow the user to create and manipulate electronically tables of values (in cells) arranged in rows and columns. The contents of any cell can be given a defined relationship (called a formula) with the content of other cells. Once the user has defined the cells and the formula for linking them together the data can be entered. If the contents of one cell is changed the contents of other, related cells are changed automatically.

Spreadsheets are ideal for storing, calculating and displaying financial information such as cash-flow forecasts, balance sheets and accounts. Today's spreadsheet users can set up several different types of graphs, perform many different mathematical functions and carry out 'what if' functions.

A small business is likely to make considerable use of a spreadsheet package.

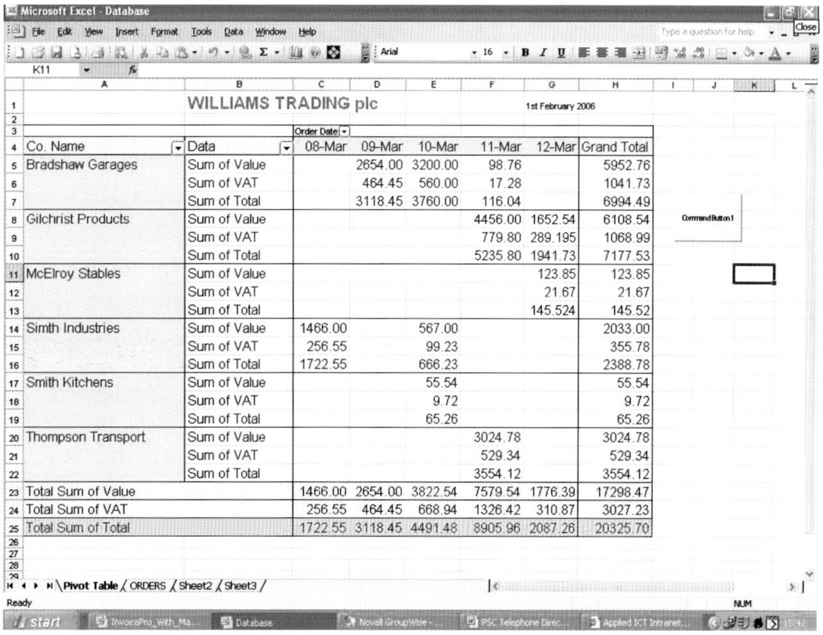

Co. Name	Data	08-Mar	09-Mar	10-Mar	11-Mar	12-Mar	Grand Total
Bradshaw Garages	Sum of Value		2654.00	3200.00	98.76		5952.76
	Sum of VAT		464.45	560.00	17.28		1041.73
	Sum of Total		3118.45	3760.00	116.04		6994.49
Gilchrist Products	Sum of Value				4456.00	1652.54	6108.54
	Sum of VAT				779.80	289.195	1068.99
	Sum of Total				5235.80	1941.73	7177.53
McElroy Stables	Sum of Value					123.85	123.85
	Sum of VAT					21.67	21.67
	Sum of Total					145.524	145.52
Simth Industries	Sum of Value	1466.00		567.00			2033.00
	Sum of VAT	256.55		99.23			355.78
	Sum of Total	1722.55		666.23			2388.78
Smith Kitchens	Sum of Value			55.54			55.54
	Sum of VAT			9.72			9.72
	Sum of Total			65.26			65.26
Thompson Transport	Sum of Value				3024.78		3024.78
	Sum of VAT				529.34		529.34
	Sum of Total				3554.12		3554.12
Total Sum of Value		1466.00	2654.00	3822.54	7579.54	1776.39	17298.47
Total Sum of VAT		256.55	464.45	668.94	1326.42	310.87	3027.23
Total Sum of Total		1722.55	3118.45	4491.48	8905.96	2087.26	20325.70

Figure 14.3 A spreadsheet demonstrating the use of a pivot table

Activity 3

Find out about each of the following features commonly found in a spreadsheet package and give an example of the use of each one:

Feature	Example of Use
The use of charts	Numeric data from the spreadsheet cells can be represented in many different graph or chart formats so that the data is easier to interpret.
Specialist functions such as IF, VLOOKUP	The IF function will check the logical condition of a statement and return one value if true and a different value if false. The syntax is =IF (condition, value-if-true, value-if-false)
Pivot table	A pivot table is a feature that allows the numeric data in selected columns and rows to be reorganised and summarised to obtain a desired report. It is especially useful with large amounts of data. For example, a shop owner might list monthly sales totals for a large number of products in a spreadsheet. If he wished to know which products sold better in a given time period, instead of looking through pages of figures to find the information, a pivot table could be used. This would allow him to reorganise the data very quickly and create a summary for each product for the given period.
Linked multiple sheets	A spreadsheet can be created with a number of different sheets each set up with the same formatting and formulae, but with different data in each sheet. For example, in a college where there are a number of classes for the same subject, the Head of Department could maintain a spreadsheet that acts as a mark book with a sheet for each class.
What-If modelling	A process of changing the value in a certain cell to see what will happen to the contents of another cell that contains a formula that refers to the original cell.

Presentation software (for more detail on the use of presentation software, see Chapter 17)

Presentation software such as Microsoft PowerPoint has become increasingly common with the development of the data projector. These devices can project a computer display onto a large screen and are ideal for a presentation to an audience, usually replacing the old OHP (Overhead Projector).

Presentations in PowerPoint can include text and graphics, displays can be animated to attract the audience's attention and only display part of a page at a time. Sound files can be added for extra effect.

Presentation software might be used by the head of a sales team who wishes to present information during talks that he has arranged to give to groups of salesmen in different parts of the country before the launch of a new range of products.

Using a presentation software package has advantages over traditional methods such as the use of an overhead projector and acetate slides. A presentation can be automated and require no physical intervention as would be required for slides. The package allows the use of video or animation which can improve impact. It also allows for the importing of live information from other packages. For example, the sales presentation could import graphs of projected sales taken from a spreadsheet.

Integrated packages

An integrated package consists of a number of distinct applications such as a spreadsheet and a word processor. Data can easily be transferred from one to another. Each part of the integrated package, such as the word processor, typically has fewer functions than a full package of the same type. Integrated packages are usually easy to use as all the applications have a common interface and many operations are the same, so skills are transferable. Naïve users require less training and can quickly build up confidence. Data can easily be transferred from application to application. Integrated packages offer sufficient functions to satisfy the occasional or inexperienced user.

Object Linking and Embedding (OLE)

Object linking and embedding provides a means of linking or sharing information between different programs such as a spreadsheet and a word processor. When using a word processor to produce a document that is to be a report on sales, a manager may wish to include extracts from data held in a spreadsheet together with some charts.

This can be done in two ways. The first uses an embedded object that is a selected part of the spreadsheet included as part of the document file. The document now actually contains all the data that makes up the object. The original spreadsheet can be modified or even deleted but the embedded object will remain unchanged. Using a number of embedded objects can result in a high storage requirement.

Using a linked object does not involve any storing of data in the document. Instead, a link is created to the spreadsheet file. If the data is changed in the spreadsheet the updates will be shown when the document is displayed. If the spreadsheet file were to be deleted then the link would be lost. Using linked objects allows reports to be kept up to date as data in other files is changed. Using linked files will minimise storage requirements as the spreadsheet data is only stored once.

Data standards

Most modern generic applications packages allow the user to store data files in a range of formats as well as the package's own format. This allows files to be imported and used in other packages.

A PC version of a word processing package allows many possible formats including:

Microsoft Word (*.doc)	Web page (*.html)	Rich text (*.rtf)
Text only (*.txt) – ASCII	WordPerfect format	Works (*.wps)

Specific applications software

Specific applications software is designed to carry out a particular end-user task, usually for a particular industry. It is of little use in other situations. The user will normally require knowledge of the subject area involved. A payroll application program would be an example of specific applications software; it is designed to be used exclusively for payroll activities and could not be used for any other tasks.

Specific applications software is available for wide-ranging areas such as engineering and scientific work, which include a range of specialist design tools including specialist Computer-Aided Design (CAD) packages and sophisticated mathematical software.

Simple graphics software such as Paint, which comes free with Windows, stores graphics files in **bitmap form**. This stores the colour of each pixel (dot) in the picture. As a result, bitmaps are large files and when they are resized, the image tends to be distorted.

Sophisticated graphics packages, like CorelDraw, store graphics files in **vector graphic form**. This means it stores pictures as a series of objects such as lines, arcs, text, etc. Facilities in the software allow individual objects to be resized, rotated and have fill colour and line characteristics changed. When storing a line, it will store the co-ordinates of the start and finish of the line, its width and colour. Not only does this save space, it means that the line can be moved, deleted or changed in colour or width without affecting the rest of the picture.

CAD programs are used for designing, for example, in engineering or architecture. Users can draw accurate straight lines and arcs of different types and thickness. By zooming in, designs can be produced more accurately. Designs can be produced in layers to show different information, for example, one layer might show electrical wiring, another gas pipes and so on. Special purpose CAD packages are available for many areas of design such as kitchen or garden design.

Software designed for use in doctors' or dentists' surgeries and booking systems for leisure centres or cinemas are all available.

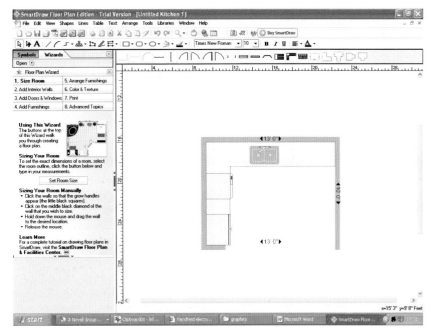

Figure 14.4 Example of a CAD package

Bespoke software

Application software can be bought **'off the shelf'** or can be written especially for a user. Specially written software is called bespoke or tailor-made software.

Bespoke software can either be developed in-house, by the programmers employed by the user's company, or by using an outside agency.

Since bespoke software is developed for a particular organisation, it can take the specific user needs into account and provide a system that exactly meets those needs.

Bespoke software is usually more expensive as the development costs must be borne by one organisation and not spread over a much larger number of users.

Development time is also a consideration as bespoke software will need to be designed, the programs written and tested before the system can be installed. 'Off the shelf' software, on the other hand should not take long to configure and install.

There are situations where an organisation has no choice but to develop bespoke software; if no software currently exists that can do the required job. Many businesses will want to develop new software to maintain a competitive advantage over their rivals.

When the BBC needed to train staff to use their outside broadcast presentation equipment, which was very expensive, they decided to use a simulation of the system for staff training as the equipment was in use nearly all the time.

As no such simulation software was available, a bespoke solution was the only option. The BBC commissioned a software company to develop and produce the software which would simulate the outside broadcast equipment. Now training can take place without the need for expensive equipment.

Californian software giant i2 produces bespoke software for clients. They have developed real-time order management systems with customers, such as Siemens, K-Mart and Caterpillar. The software, which needs to be tailored to the demands of the customer, helps them manage their suppliers, plan orders and make production more efficient.

Advantages of using pre-written software	Advantages of bespoke software
Ready to use immediately	Designed to meet the exact needs of the user
The user can be confident that it has been fully tested	May be the only way of solving the problem
Broad base of other users to call upon for help	May provide competitive advantage
Should be support from publishers; could be published user manuals	

Activity 4 – Off the Shelf or Bespoke?

For each of the following, state whether it would be more appropriate to use off the shelf or bespoke software. Justify your answers.

1. An international bank wishes to install a new system to allow customers a greater range of online banking features in controlling accounts.
2. A small charity wishes to install software to allow it to record details of donors and donations.
3. London introduced congestion charging and required an ICT system to ensure that charges are paid.
4. A company wishes to introduce a computerised payroll system.
5. A leisure centre needs to install a booking system for its facilities.

Software to access the Internet

Web browsers such as Microsoft Internet Explorer or Netscape Navigator allow users to access the Internet and view web pages. They provide a number of functions for the user which include:

- the ability to display the web page for a page selected by the user by typing in the page's URL (Uniform Resource Locator) – the unique address
- the ability to store the addresses of 'favourite' pages so that they can be accessed when required without the user having to remember the URL.
- a 'history' folder where details of pages visited are stored
- the ability to save pages for viewing offline

- allowing a user to go back to previously viewed pages – pages loaded previously are cached locally, i.e. stored on the hard drive to reduce loading time if the user decides to go back to a recently viewed page
- displaying animated sequences written in JavaScript and attached to a web page – these can make the web pages more lively and eye catching
- usually providing a link to a search engine.

SUMMARY

Software is the name given to computer programs without which no computer hardware can function. There are two main types of software:

▶ **Systems software** – programs which help the computer run more smoothly. **Utility programs** and **operating systems** are types of systems software

   ▶ An **operating system** hides the complexities of the hardware from the user. Its tasks include allocating internal memory (**RAM**), transferring programs and data between disk and **RAM**, checking user access and logging of errors.

   ▶ Examples of **utilities** include programs to delete, rename or copy files, format disks and compress files.

   ▶ Software has a crucial role to play in interfacing with peripheral devices. **Peripheral device drivers**, for example, printer drivers, are programs that allow a specific device model to communicate with the processor.

▶ **Applications software** – programs that carry out an end-user task, such as calculating staff wages. Applications software can be:

   ▶ **generic** – programs that can be used by many users in a variety of ways. Word processing, spreadsheets and database packages are examples.

   ▶ **special purpose** – software written to meet a particular need such as a booking system or a design package.

Software can be '**off the shelf**' or **bespoke**. Off the shelf software is developed and tested before selling to a number of users whilst bespoke software is developed solely for the specific end-user.

Browser software allows a user to access the information stored on the Internet.

Chapter 14 Questions

1. State **three** formatting facilities that are offered by word processing software.
   (One word answers are acceptable for this question.) (3)
   June 2005 ICT2

2. A new scanner is supplied with a set of drivers. These drivers are provided on a CD-ROM, together with optical character recognition (OCR) software for use with the scanner.
   a) State **three** functions of a scanner driver. (3)
   b) Give one reason why the drivers are not provided on a floppy disk. (1)
   c) Give one other method of providing the scanner drivers. (1)
   d) Describe one advantage of using OCR software. (2)
   June 2005 ICT2

3. Word processing software offers editing and formatting facilities.
   a) Explain the differences between formatting and editing. (2)
   b) Describe **three** editing facilities that are offered by word processing software. (6)
   c) Describe **three** formatting facilities that are offered by word processing software. (6)

4. Describe **four** functions of an operating system. (8)

5. A scanner is to be purchased for use with a personal computer.
   a) State one item of software that should be supplied with the scanner and why it is needed. (2)
   b) A map has been scanned and its image saved in a file. State **three** ways in which the image of the map could be manipulated before it is printed. (3)
   (The use of brand names will not gain credit.)
   January 2003 ICT2

6. The two terms generic package and integrated package are often confused.
   a) Describe, giving an example, what is meant by a generic package. (2)
   b) Describe, giving an example, what is meant by an integrated package. (2)
   January 2004 ICT2

7. Personal computer systems are usually supplied with some system software already installed.
   Explain, using examples, the purpose of system software. (4)
   June 2003 ICT2

8. Software packages contain many advanced features that are often used by certain people. Explain, with the use of examples:
   a) **two** advanced features of a word processing package that would be useful to an author writing an ICT textbook (6)
   b) **two** advanced features of a spreadsheet package that would be useful to an accountant preparing a financial report. (6)
   June 2003 ICT2

9. A company has 12 hotels in locations in the north of England. It has decided to upgrade its ICT systems and has decided to install new hardware and software.
   Name and describe **four** items of software that the hotel could buy. Explain why each each item would be required. (12)

10. A new computer system is sold with a printer, scanner and software. The software includes an operating system, drivers for the printer and the scanner, and an integrated package.
    a) State **four** functions of the operating system. (4)
    b) Explain why the peripheral drivers are also needed. (2)
    c) State **three** advantages of using an integrated package rather than separate applications packages. (3)
    June 2004 ICT2

15 Capabilities and limitations of software

Features of generic software

▶ Generic software is general purpose software that can be used for a variety of uses by a variety of users. Examples of generic software include word processors, spreadsheet software, database management software and presentation software. These are discussed in Chapter 14.

Software features

Generic software includes many of the following features that are often required and should be looked for when choosing a suitable package.

Links to other packages (See Data portability page 178)

This allows for the embedding or importing of data from other packages. (See Chapter 14). Files can be saved in the format of another package.

For example, Microsoft Word can open files in a variety of formats such as HTML, RTF (Rich Text Format) and TXT (text) as well as files in Word format (doc files).

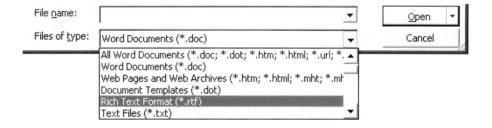

Figure 15.1

Files can also be saved in these formats.

Backwards compatibility (See Compatibility page 180)

Software must be able to read files set up in an earlier version of the program.

Search facilities

Search facilities allow the user to move quickly to the desired data. Search facilities are of course a feature of database packages, but the ability to search for words or phrases using **Edit**, **Find** is valuable in other packages such as word processors or spreadsheets.

Figure 15.2 Edit, Find in Microsoft Internet Explorer can find a particular word in a web page

Macro capabilities

A sequence of keystrokes and menu choices can be saved as a macro and then repeated simply by running the macro. Macros can speed up common operations by automating them such as using one keystroke instead of many or by customising a package for a particular use. They also allow a complex operation to be set up by an experienced user and used by less experienced ones.

For example, in an office a macro can be used in a word processing package that allows the user to select an icon from a tool bar (or an entry from a menu) that calls up the template for a particular type of document. The macro can move the cursor to different positions in the document where data needs to be entered.

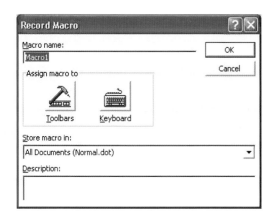

Figure 15.3 Recording a macro in Microsoft Word

Applications generators

Applications generators are software packages that allow the user to specify the interface required and the functions required, then automatically generate the code to produce the customised application.

This facility allows users to customise generic software packages, to perform a specific task or set of tasks without specialist programming knowledge, by describing the input, output and functionality required.

For example, it will typically allow menu systems, data capture forms and reports to be produced without the need for extensive programming code. Microsoft Access, for example, has several wizards that allow the user to customise the database management system so that it can be used by an inexperienced user.

Formatting capabilities

Software packages allow users to format text to suit their purpose. These features can be found on the **Format** menu in most software packages. Formatting text includes being able to change the fonts, colour, size and background colours as well as setting the text to bold, italics or underline. Paragraphs can be formatted with numbers, bullet points, hanging paragraphs and different line spacing.

Editing capabilities

Modern software packages allow the user to move around a document or sheet using the mouse or cursor keys, delete and insert data in the appropriate place with ease. Facilities to 'cut and paste' and 'find and replace' are standard. Some packages allow the editing to be carried out by another person; suggested changes are highlighted and the author can then accept or reject the changes as she wishes.

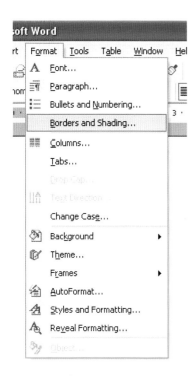

Figure 15.4 The Format menu in Microsoft Word

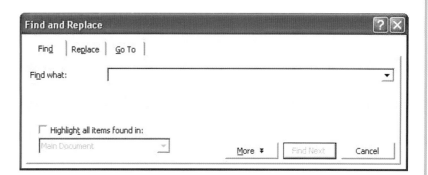

Figure 15.5 Edit, Find and Replace is a feature of most software

Ability to change or extend data and record structures

Flexible database management software allows for fields to be added or deleted when data is already recorded. Suitable safeguards are usually included to ensure that data is not lost unintentionally.

Short access times

Packages need to be able to retrieve data as quickly as possible. Speed of access can be a major factor in software selection.

Report generators

Report generators can take data from a database and turn it into a report. This report can then be distributed either electronically or as a hard copy independently of the database. The format of the report and its wording can be defined by the user and customised to suit the application.

The report may be in graph, tabular or text form. Data can be added to give totals and subtotals as required. The advantage of this sort of software is that once the report has been specified with this year's figures (say), when next year's figures are available, the report can be prepared automatically.

Appointments Report

03 February

Betty   Brown

Time	End Time	Customer ID	Forename	Surname	Style
12:00	14:00	23	Debra	Hudson	Highlights
15:00	16:00	34	Maggie	Crame	Perm
16:00	17:00	14	Jenny	Ashley	Perm

Yvonne   Black

Time	End Time	Customer ID	Forename	Surname	Style
09:00	11:00	56	Sally	Wicks	Highlights

Sally   White

Time	End Time	Customer ID	Forename	Surname	Style
09:00	09:15	2	John	Baker	Cut

04 February

Betty   Brown

Time	End Time	Customer ID	Forename	Surname	Style

Figure 15.6 Microsoft Access has a report wizard that allows the user to set up reports easily

Data portability

The ability to transfer data to or from another package or hardware platform is a feature that is an important requirement for users. This means data does not have to be typed in again, which would waste time and could lead to errors.

Data is said to be **portable** if it can be transferred from one application to another in electronic form. (Portability has a specialist meaning here – it doesn't mean 'you can put a floppy disk in your pocket and carry it around'!) It is very common to need to transfer data produced in one package to another package. Different packages have different functions, many of which are used by businesses today.

A user may have different packages, or versions of the same package, available at home and at work and will need to be able to transfer data. The growth in the use of networks has increased the need for portable data files. Portability ensures that documents produced on one package can be accessed by other similar packages, or by the same package on different hardware platforms.

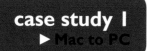

case study 1
▶ Mac to PC

In the 1990s the Windows PC dominated sales of personal computers. However, the Apple Macintosh had a significant share of the market. Commercial pressures had meant that these two types of computer had developed separately and data could not be transferred easily between the two platforms.

However, commercial pressures also meant that if the Apple Mac could not read PC data, sales may be reduced. Apple developed an operating system to be able to read data from a PC. Microsoft Office, previously only available for Windows, became available for the Mac.

Files could now easily be transferred between the two platforms. Peripherals such as the iPod or Palmtops could link to both the Apple Mac and the PC.

Portability and Microsoft Windows

Microsoft Windows offers portability – the ability to take data from one program to another. By using **Edit**, **Copy**, you can copy data from one program into the Clipboard. You can then use **Edit**, **Paste** in another program.

Microsoft Windows programs usually allow you to import data from and export data to another program. Many Windows programs are published by the same company, Microsoft, for example, Microsoft Word, Microsoft Publisher, Microsoft Excel and Microsoft Access. You can import into Word or Access from Excel, into Publisher from Word and into Excel or Word from Access.

Many software suppliers provide **filters** that allow documents developed in other companies' packages to be converted into a suitable format for input. Microsoft Word XP can import from WordPerfect 5.*, or WordPerfect 6.*. A WordPerfect user could buy Word XP and not lose previous work.

There are several different types of picture format, for example, gif, bmp and jpg. Word XP can import from at least 20 different formats of picture.

Activity 1

Using a computer magazine or the Internet, find advertisements for the following types of software package:
- word processor
- spreadsheet
- web design.

List the file formats that the package can support.

Upgradability of software

▶ Every few years a new version of the same program is produced. New versions called upgrades take advantage of increased speed, memory and processing power of later computers to offer new functions.

Reasons to upgrade

Software producers regularly produce new versions of their products. They mainly do this to:

1. add new features
2. increase sales
3. provide a version that will work with a new operating system or on a new platform.

To distinguish different versions, they have a number such as Microsoft Internet Explorer 6 or Microsoft Word 2003 or a name like Microsoft Excel XP. Major upgrades are usually numbered as '.0' versions (e.g. 4.0, 5.0). Minor changes are numbered as .1 or .2 or even .01 versions.

The new features take advantage of faster computers with increased memory. Sometimes they are very useful; sometimes less so.

- Microsoft Word 95 added an automatic spell check to the previous version, underlining a mistake as you type.
- The next version, Microsoft Word 97, added the function to save a file as a web page. Word could be used as a web editor.
- The next version, Microsoft Word 2000, added the ability to include frames in your web page.
- The next version Microsoft Word XP gives users the ability to hide white space in print layout view.

Figure 15.7 This version of Mozilla Firebird is version 0.6.1

Compatibility

When upgrading your software, e.g. from Microsoft Office 2000 to Office 2003, you will still want to be able to load your old Office 2000 files. It is essential that software upgrades are backwards compatible. For example, Microsoft Access XP can load files in Access 2000 format. It also contains a utility to convert Access 97 files to Access 2000 format and open them.

It is often not true the other way round. Software packages are not always forwards compatible. For example, files saved in Access 2000 cannot be opened in Access 97. If you want to use an Access 2000 file in Access 97, it is necessary to use the utility in later versions of Access to convert the file to Access 97 format.

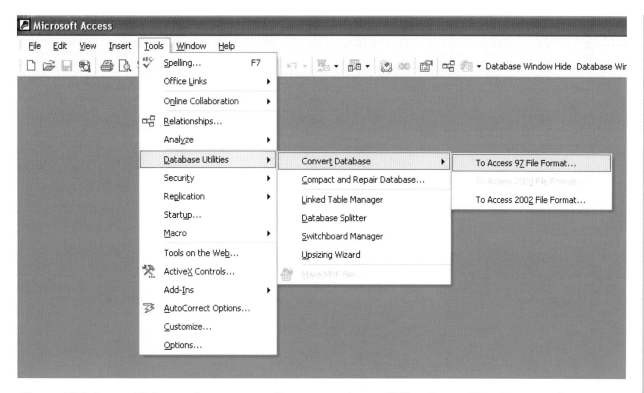

Figure 15.8 Access XP has a utility to convert files set up in Access 2000 to Access 97 or Access XP formats

---

Activity 2

Investigate which of these software products are forward compatible and which are not.
- Microsoft Excel
- Microsoft PowerPoint
- Microsoft Publisher

Remember

In the exam you must <u>not</u> use brand names such as Microsoft Word. You must use the general name for that type of software such as Word Processor.

Worked exam question

Part of a question on the January 2005 ICT2 paper asked candidates to:
Give **three** different examples of generic package software. (3)

► **THREE SAMPLE ANSWERS WITH EXAMINER'S GUIDANCE**

1 Three examples of generic package software are Microsoft Word, Microsoft Excel and Microsoft Access.

   This would get <u>no</u> marks. Although these packages are generic, brand names and not the type of software have been given.

2 An example of generic package software is a database.

   This would get <u>no</u> marks as the package is not a database but database management software.

► SAMPLE ANSWER

3 Three examples of generic package software are a word processor, a spreadsheet package and database management software.

► EXAMINER'S GUIDANCE

This would get full marks.

Characteristics of software upgrades

Software upgrades should be sufficiently similar to the previous version so that users are immediately comfortable with the new version. The increased processing power of recent computers means that upgraded software can be even more user-friendly.

When a new program is brought out it is important that:

- it has additional new features which make it attractive to the buyer
- a user can load work done in the previous version of the program (backwards compatibility)
- it looks similar enough to the old version so that users can start straight away.

Reasons not to upgrade

New versions of software may have more features and be more efficient than earlier versions.

However, users may not want to upgrade to the latest software for some of the following reasons:

- The current hardware specification may not be suitable for the new software, for example, the processor speed may be too slow or the memory inadequate.
- The cost of the new software may be prohibitive.
- The new features offered may not be required.
- Users may be reluctant to discard software that they know very well for a program that they have never used before.
- Training may be needed for the new software.
- Installation of the new software may mean that the equipment is out of action for a time.

---

case study 2
► **Cranmer Estates**

Cranmer Estates is a firm of estate agents with around ten branches in the north of England. They started using PCs which did not run Windows. They ran a DOS version of the word processing program WordPerfect 4.1 to produce details of houses for sale and to type letters.

Owner Derek Cranmer decided to invest in new equipment because he wanted to store details of houses for sale in a database, use a spreadsheet to keep accounts and to be able to send house details from one branch to another by e-mail. He decided to buy new Windows PCs with e-mail facilities running a word processing package, a database package and a spreadsheet package.

Derek considered many packages such as Microsoft Office Professional, Corel Office Professional (which included the latest version of WordPerfect) and Lotus Smart Suite. His priorities in deciding were:

1. Portability. It was essential to be able to import old WordPerfect files as he did not want his staff to have to type data in again.
2. Links to other packages. He also wanted to be able to take data about houses from the database into the word processor.
3. Training. He wanted to use a package where training was available. Derek found out that his local college ran courses in Microsoft Word, Excel and Access – all part of Microsoft Office.

The need for training persuaded Derek to choose Microsoft Office, which could also import from WordPerfect. After a pilot project at one branch was successful, Derek introduced the new system into all his branches.

Reliability of software

We all want software that is error free and will not crash while we are using it. However software faults that cause errors are not uncommon.

To produce 100 per cent error-free software is a near impossibility. A program will contain hundreds of thousands of lines of program code with millions of different pathways through it and this requires very rigorous testing.

In the software industry there are strong commercial pressures to produce software before the competition and to keep development costs down. Often software is published without being fully tested.

Errors often only come to light when the software is used on a particular specification of PC or in an unplanned situation. Producers may need to distribute program 'patches', which repair errors that have been discovered. Upgraded .1 or .2 versions of software may be distributed free or at a considerable discount to existing users of the .0 version.

Testing is a vital part of software development. Programs should be tested by colleagues who have not been involved with the actual production themselves. Then they will be given to selected users to try out in real situations and report errors before the official release date. This means that they can be tested on different hardware platforms, with different memory sizes and processor speeds that may operate differently.

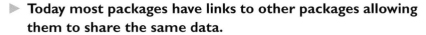

▶ Today most packages have links to other packages allowing them to share the same data.

▶ Data is said to be portable if it can be transferred from one application or platform to another.

▶ Windows software offers portability.

▶ New versions of software are similar to the previous version so that users can use the new version straight away.

▶ The new version should be able to load files saved in the previous version (backwards compatible). Old versions are not always able to load files from later versions (forwards compatible).

▶ New software must be tested thoroughly before being released commercially. However, time and financial pressures, and the number of different paths and platforms means that software may still have errors when it is sold.

Chapter 15 Questions

1. A friend tells you that they have bought a word processing package with macro facilities and search facilities. Explain what is meant in this context by:
   a) Macro facilities (1)
   b) Search facilities (1)
   c) Give **one** example where a macro might be useful in a word processing package. (2)
   d) Give **one** example where a search facility might be useful in a word processing package. (2)

2. a) Explain what is meant by the term generic package software. (3)
   b) Give **three** different examples of generic package software. (3)
   January 2005 ICT2

3. A large mail order company has decided to upgrade the software used to process customer orders.
   a) Explain possible technical implications of changing the software. (4)
   b) Explain possible human implications of changing the software. (4)
   January 2004 ICT2

4. Charles has two computers: a desktop computer and an older laptop computer. The desktop computer is running the latest version of a database management package but the laptop is running an older version.
   a) Explain why Charles might encounter problems when transferring files from the desktop computer to the laptop computer. (2)
   b) Explain how Charles might avoid these problems. (2)

5. Having purchased a new software package for her computer, Jackie finds that it does not work. Explain **two** reasons why the package may not work. (4)

6. A freelance reporter who regularly contributes articles to various newspapers and magazines is considering which word processing package she should purchase. A friend has said that most modern application packages enable users to produce files which are portable.
   a) Explain what portability means in this context. (4)
   b) Explain why portability is important. (4)

16 Characteristics of processing data

Modes of operation

▶ All computers work on a basis of

Input   Process   Output

Different computer systems require different modes of
operation that determine how the computer is used.
Sometimes it is appropriate or necessary to process each
occurrence of data as it presents itself, whilst in other
situations it is more appropriate, efficient and cheaper to
collect a large amount of data before processing it all together.

For example, if you go to a bank's Automatic Teller Machine
(ATM or 'hole in the wall') to find out the current balance of
your account, you want a response there and then, within a
few seconds. You would not be happy to wait for 50 other
people to make a similar request before yours was dealt with!

A computer system may control a chemical process by
inputting data on factors such as temperature from sensors
and make necessary changes such as turning off a heater.
Anything but a very fast response could prove disastrous as
the substances could overheat and cause an explosion.

On the other hand, the most efficient way to enter the
responses to a survey involving several hundred people is to
collect them together and read them automatically, by using
an input device such as OMR or OCR (see Chapter 11).

The four modes of operation to be considered are:

■ real-time
■ batch
■ transaction (or pseudo real-time)
■ interactive.

There is some overlap between these four; most transaction
processing applications are also interactive.

A number of factors will determine the mode of operation
for a particular system. These include hardware availability,
the volume of data, the required response time as well as the
nature of the system.

Before investigating these in more detail it is necessary to
define some of the terms that will be used.

Master file	A main file of records relating to a system. The data in this type of file does not change very frequently. For example, a banking system would have a master file of account details, such as name and address, with one record for each account; a stock control system for a retailing business would have a stock master file where each record held details relating to one item of stock.
Transaction	A single change to a record held in a master file. The record of a deposit or withdrawal of an amount of money into or from a bank account would be a transaction.
Transaction file	A collection of transaction records built up over time and used to update a master file with changes.

Real-time processing

A system running in the real-time mode of operation is one that can react fast enough to influence events outside the computer system. An air traffic control system is an example of a system operating in real-time mode. Most systems operating in real-time mode use a processor that is dedicated to that specific system.

For example, a computer-controlled chemical process uses sensors to input the temperature of the substances into the computer. The computer processes this information, controlling outputs that turn heaters on or off, and opening or closing valves when needed. The computer is operating all the time, receiving data, processing it and outputting information in time to influence events. There are many other examples of control situations when real-time processing is used. These range from very large systems such as the system that controls the operation of a nuclear reactor to small embedded microprocessor systems that control the functioning of devices such as washing machines, a service station petrol pump or a burglar alarm system.

The Tropical House at Kew Gardens provides an environment that enables plants from the tropics that would not survive in our climate to flourish. To maintain the correct environment, sensors measure such attributes as temperature and humidity and the computer system enables actuators to switch heaters on or off, open or close windows, or turn water sprayers on or off as appropriate.

The concept of feedback is essential to real-time processing. A computer has to process the data input from the temperature sensor in time to turn on the fan or the heater so that the system is maintained within allowable temperatures.

Batch processing

Batch mode is a method of computer processing used when there are large numbers of similar transactions that can be processed together. All the data to be input is collected together before being processed in a single operation. For example, when a survey has been carried out with the responses recorded on forms, the data from all the forms can be input into the system (perhaps using an OCR or OMR device) and, when it has all been entered to create a transaction file, the necessary processing can take place.

Early computer systems, using large mainframe computers, all operated in batch mode as the hardware did not make another mode of operation possible.

There are a number of tasks that are best carried out in batch mode. Batch processing is the most appropriate and efficient mode to use when a large number of records in a master file need to be updated.

In a typical batch processing system:

1. All the transactions are batched together offline then a transaction file is created.
2. This transaction file is sorted into the same order as the records in the master file.
3. Each record from the transaction file is read with the corresponding record of the master file.
4. An updated record is created and stored in a new master file.
5. This is repeated for every record in the transaction file.

The old master file is called the **father** file and the new version the **son**. When the **son** is in turn used to create a new version it becomes the **father** and the old father becomes the **grandfather**. A number of generations can be kept for backup purposes. As long as the relevant transaction files are also kept the current master file can be recreated.

Example of batch processing – a billing system

An example of a typical batch processing operation is an electricity billing system. The computer already has much of the data required to calculate the bill stored on disk in the master file. The data fields stored will include:

- customer number – the unique code used to identify the customer
- name of customer
- address
- last meter reading – to calculate the number of units used and the charge

- amount of electricity used in last four quarters – for checking that this quarter's usage is sensible
- special instructions for meter reader – for example, 'the meter round back of the house'

● The meter reader enters the meter reading into a palmtop computer. At the end of the day the reader takes the palmtop to the office.

● The data from the palmtop is used to create a transaction file. Each transaction record will need two items of data: the customer number, so that the correct record in the master file can be identified, and the current meter reading.

● The transaction records in this file are not in any order; they have to be sorted into the same order as the master file.

● The two files are read through together, record by record, the customer number being used to match transactions with the master file records.

● Each time a match is found, the details of the bill can be calculated. A record is created for a new version of the master file which will contain data updated from the transaction record. This new version of the master file will be used in three months' time when the next reading of the meter is made.

● When the new version of the master file is created, the old version is still kept as it provides a backup. If the new version were lost or corrupted, it could be recreated by running the update program again using the old master file and the transaction file.

Using batch processing for this billing system means that details of only one customer are processed at one time – the whole file does not have to be loaded in – so that the computer does not need a large amount of memory. Very large volumes of data can be processed efficiently in one run by using batch processing. Each input file is read through just once from start to finish.

Once the program is running there is no human intervention.

All the data has to be collected and entered at the start and no more can be entered once the system is running. This means that information can be out of date and new data can only be entered with the next batch.

You cannot perform an immediate search for information as response time for a specific query is slow.

Batch processing is suitable for payroll or billing systems, which are run once a week, once a month or once a quarter. It is not suitable for a system that needs an immediate response, such as an enquiry or booking system.

Activity 1

Outline the stages involved in a batch processing payroll system for a large organisation that inputs the number of hours worked by employees and produces pay slips.

Transaction (pseudo real-time) processing

Transaction processing is a mode of operation where data for each transaction is entered at source and processed immediately.

In a building society customers can be issued with passbooks. When wishing to make a deposit, that is put money into their account, a customer can take their passbook, together with a completed deposit transaction form, to a till at any branch office. The building society clerk will enter the details of the transaction (account number and amount of deposit) using the keyboard of a networked computer. The account details record in the master file is updated to reflect the transaction, the old values are overwritten. The passbook is placed into a special printer device and the details of the transaction and the new balance are printed.

In a booking system, for holidays or cinema tickets for example, the system deals with each booking as it is submitted. Each transaction is completed before the next can begin. The same seat cannot be booked twice.

Unlike batch processing the master file is updated with the data from the transaction immediately. Only one record of the master file is accessed, so the file must be organised in a way that allows each record to be located directly and independently. The great advantage of transaction processing is that the master file is always kept up to date. However, master file backup becomes more of a problem as there is no automatic production of backup files as there is when batch processing mode is used.

Many systems use a combination of processing in batch and transaction modes. The building society needs to produce annual account statements for members who may need the details for tax purposes. A printed summary is needed for each account. This is most efficiently produced automatically, in batch mode. It would be a long task if transaction processing were used, as a clerk would need to enter each account number in turn to initiate each transaction.

Interactive processing

Interactive processing involves the user 'having a conversation' with the computer. The user may use a number of input devices such as mouse, graphics tablet, joystick as well as a keyboard. The response time for interactive processing must be sufficiently fast to avoid frustration for the user. Ideally the user should think that the response is immediate.

Purchasing tickets via a touch screen at a railway station or using an automatic teller machine (ATM) to access bank account information are both examples of interactive processing.

Much home computer use involves interactive processing. Most computer games require interactive processing as do design and drawing packages.

Most transaction processing systems described previously will also involve interactive processing. For example, consider a mail order company that processes telephone orders on a computerised system as each order arises. This is interactive processing as the operator enters the data directly into the computer and responds to prompts for more data. The order is dealt with whilst the customer is on the telephone; the operator checks availability of each item for the user and confirms the price. The transaction is completed before the operator deals with another customer. Thus the system is based on transaction processing.

Activity 2

For each of the systems below, identify and *justify* the appropriate mode (or modes) of operation.

1. **Airline reservation system**

   A user sitting at a terminal will type in details of the customer's request, and details of suitable flights will be displayed. A booking can then be made and will be processed immediately.

2. **A nuclear reactor**

   A computer is used to monitor the temperature stability of the nuclear reactor. If this temperature becomes critical then an alarm system is activated.

3. **Play-a-Toy plc**

   Play-a-Toy is a large manufacturing company with around 6,000 employees. On the last working day of every month the computer system automatically transfers wages to the employees' bank accounts and produces individualised pay slips.

4. **British Telecom**

   Every three months British Telecom calculates a bill for each of its thousands of customers and prints the details on to preprinted paper for posting.

5. **The home user**

   Mary has a computer at home with a modem connection and access to the Internet. On occasions she uses a browser to surf the Internet and download interesting articles.

6. **Retailer**

   A local retail store has recently upgraded its premises. As part of the renovations a new set of automatic doors and an advanced air conditioning system have been installed. The doors allow customers to move in and out of the shop freely and the air conditioning system maintains a constant room temperature (the temperature is adjustable).

▶

7. Examination marking

When students enter multiple-choice examinations they fill in an OMR sheet with their choices marked in pencil. The sheets from every school are sent to the examining board, who read the data into a computer system that calculates the results. Individual student marks are summarised on a list for each school.

8. HSBC Bank mortgages

When a customer requests a mortgage, an advisor sits down with them in front of a computer. A program guides the advisor through a series of questions for the customer and the answers are entered. At the end the program produces details of any possible mortgage offer.

9. American Express

Each month a bill is produced for each customer that lists the details of all transactions made in the last four weeks, together with details of any payments made.

10. Zap 'Em

Zap 'Em is an arcade game in which buttons and joysticks are used to position a Zapper Gun to shoot down deadly aliens. These aliens are moving around the screen demolishing innocent Lemmings. As soon as a user hits a target, an alien is removed.

case study 1
▶ Howse, Hulme and Byer, Estate Agents

Howse, Hulme and Byer is a chain of estate agents with 50 branches around the country. The current data processing system, which has been in place for a number of years is based on batch processing.

The main categories of transactions that take place at the branch offices are:

- details of new potential purchasers
- details of a new house for sale
- details of a sale.

The current system

A branch employee writes details of a transaction on to a preprinted form. These forms are collected and, three times a week, are sent to the head office where they are put together with forms from all the other branches. A data entry clerk keys in the transaction data offline using a key-to-disk system. The data is entered again by a second clerk so that any mistakes made by the first clerk are highlighted.

As data from all the forms is keyed in it is stored on disk in a transaction file. This file is then inputted into a validation program that produces a valid transactions file as well as an error report that contains details of mistakes in the transactions.

The reports are sent back to the branch offices so that the transactions can be corrected and resubmitted.

The file of valid transactions is then sorted into the same order as the master file and used to update the old master file by creating a new version that includes the changes resulting from the transactions.

An updated list of houses available, ordered by area and price, is sent to each branch. Lists of any newly available houses that meet their requirements are sent to prospective buyers.

Howse, Hulme and Byer are considering changing from a batch system to an interactive system. To do this, computers will need to be installed in each branch office. These will be linked to a central computer. Transactions will be processed as they occur, the details being keyed in at the branch office.

The new system would bring a number of advantages. As the transactions are entered into the system as they occur, the information available is more up to date; details of new houses are available in the branches as soon as they are received. The details of all houses for sale are available in all branches as soon as the transaction is complete. The confirmation of a sale is immediately recorded, thus preventing potential purchasers being shown the details of a house that is no longer available. Any data entry errors that are made can be corrected immediately and do not have to wait until the next batch is run.

However, there are some issues that need to be considered before the system is updated. Obviously, there will be hardware and software cost implications. Currently processing takes place when there is little other use being made of the computer system. At present, all data entry is performed by trained staff in the head office; the new system will demand extra skills of branch employees; training will be needed in the use of the new system. There will be a greater security risk as computer records, at present only available at the head office, will be available at all the branches. Backup files, which are produced automatically in a batch processing system, will require more complex organisation.

■ Draw up a table of the benefits and drawbacks of moving to a new system based on transaction processing. Refer to the text and add some ideas of your own.

Worked exam question

A college uses a computer-based batch processing system for keeping the students' records. The students provide their details, or changes to their existing records, on preprinted forms. The completed forms are collected into batches ready to update the master files. These occur every night at certain times of the year, and once a week at other times.

a) Explain what the term batch processing means. (3)

b) i) Give **one** advantage of batch processing to the college. (1)

ii) Give **two** disadvantages of batch processing to the college. (2)

The college decides to install a transaction processing system with which student records are keyed in online by a clerk.

c) Explain what the term *transaction processing* means. (3)

January 2001 ICT 2

▶ **EXAMINER'S GUIDANCE**

Although this question is based around a scenario that you may not have studied, it is easy to adapt what you have learned from a similar scenario, for example, the estate agent Case Study.

Part (a) of the question requires you to write a definition of batch processing which can be taken from the text on page 188. There are 3 marks available for your answer which means that you have to make 3 distinct points. The following answer actually has 4 points, so if you left one out you would still gain full marks.

▶ **SAMPLE ANSWER**

All the changes to the student records are collected together to form one batch (1) over a day when the system is busy, and weekly otherwise, (1) to be processed in one computer run (1) without any human intervention. (1)

▶ **EXAMINER'S GUIDANCE**

Part (b)(i) is only looking for one advantage to the college. The advantages will be similar to those of the estate agency in the Case Study: processing can be done at night when the computer system is quiet, as the college is closed; it also requires few staff to run and has few hardware requirements – just one computer.

Part (b)(ii) can again be worked out by looking at the question and comparing it with the Case Study. A suitable answer would be: details may be out of date for up to a week and error corrections may take a further week.

(c) Again this is a formal definition (see page 190): transaction processing deals with each set of data as it is submitted (1) each transaction is completed (1) before the next is begun (1)

Characteristics of processing data ◀

▶ All data that is stored and processed by a computer is in binary form. A modern computer must store data of many types. The data may be in the form of text, pictures, sound or numbers. Whatever form it takes, the data must be represented by a binary code.

Different binary codes are used to represent different types of data. The smallest unit of storage is called a **bit**; a bit can be in one of two states: one state is represented by a 0, the other state by a 1. By building up combinations of bits, different codes can be stored. Two bits can store any one of four different codes: 00, 01, 10 or 11. Three bits can store one of eight codes:

000   100   001   101   010   110   011   111

4 bits can store 16 codes, 5 bits 32 codes, 6 bits 64 codes and so on.

As well as data, program instructions are also stored in binary code of 0s and 1s. The same bit pattern of, say, 16 bits could represent two text characters, an integer (whole number), part of a graphical image or a program instruction. The program that is running interprets the bit pattern appropriately.

Text

Data is commonly stored in text or character form. The word processor is the most common software package that processes text data.

Information Communication Technology

is an example of text and is made up of 36 characters – 34 letters and 2 spaces.

Each character (including a space) that can be used is assigned a unique binary code. Standard codes have been agreed so that data can be transferred and correctly interpreted between two systems.

The most widely used character coding system is **ASCII** (American Standard Code for Information Interchange). A character coded in ASCII is made up of 8 bits. The 8th bit acts as a **parity** bit to help ensure that any corruption of data is detected (see Chapter 12). The other seven bits can produce 128 unique codes, each a different combination of 0s and 1s. Thus 128 different characters can be represented.

Activity 3

Do you speak a language other than English? Does it use different symbols? Can you find the binary code for appropriate symbols in Unicode? Try
http://www.unicode.org
How many different codes can be stored in Unicode?

Pictures

Increasingly, computers are used to manipulate, store and display non-textual images. For example, a photograph can be scanned in and stored and used on a web page. Computer games can contain complex graphical images. Indeed, the most commonly used interfaces on a personal computer are made up of graphical images in the form of icons. These pictures, or graphics, also have to be stored in binary coded form.

There are two main ways in which images are stored: either as bitmapped or vector graphics.

Bitmapped graphics

A bitmap is the binary stored data representing an image. A picture is broken up into thousands of tiny squares called **pixels**. The number of pixels stored for a given area determines the **resolution** of the image. The more pixels that are used per square unit, the greater the resolution of the image. The greater the resolution of an image the better the image looks. The greater the resolution of the image, the more memory is required to store its bitmap.

Each pixel is allocated a number of bits in the bitmap to represent its colour. The more bits allocated to each pixel the greater the choice of possible colours, but the amount of memory required to store an image will also be increased.

If only two colours, black and white, are used then just one bit is needed to represent each pixel. A 0 can be used to represent white and a 1 to represent black. If four colours are to be represented then two bits will be needed for each pixel and the coding could be:

00 – white,   01 – red,   10 – green,   11 – black

Figure 16.1 shows a simple black and white image built up in pixels and the bitmap that would be used to represent it.

As processors have become faster both the main memory (RAM) and the backing storage capacity have increased hugely. Modern computers are able to store and process complex images of high resolution that are made up of many colours.

Bitmapped graphics can be created by using a drawing package where individual pixels can be set or lines 'drawn.' This is achieved using some kind of pointing device to modify an image displayed on a screen. Alternatively, an image can be input using a scanner or a digital camera. A software package can then be used to modify the image. For detailed changes the setting of individual pixels can be modified.

There are a number of standard formats that are used for storing graphical data. These are necessary, in the same way that ASCII is necessary for text storage, to allow graphical data to be transferred between different packages. An image developed in a painting package may then be used in a DTP package. One common format is Tagged Image File Format (TIFF).

A close up view of the lion's eye shows how the picture is made up of pixels

Figure 16.1 Greyscale image showing how it is made up of pixels

Activity 4

Draw out the image that is represented by the following binary codes. The image is in 4 colours and 2 bits are used to store the code for one pixel. The coding is:

00 – white,　　01 – red,　　10 – green,　　11 – black

The codes for the pixels are stored line by line and are printed in blocks of 8 bits for easier reading.

00000000 01000000 00000000 00010101 00000000 00000101 10010100
00000000 00010101 00000000 00000000 01000000 00001111 00000010
00001111 11111100 00100011 11110011 11110010 11111100 00001111
11101111 00000000 00001011 00000000

This starts: 00 (white) 00 (white) 00 (white) 00 (white) 01 (red) 00 (white) 00 (white) and so on…

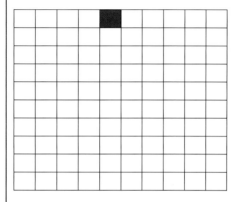

Compressed bitmap files

Data compression techniques are used to minimise the amount of storage space needed for graphical images. The Joint Photographic Expert Group (JPEG) has defined standards for graphical image compression. JPEG is now a commonly used format.

Problems associated with bitmapped graphics

■ Bitmapped graphics can be difficult to edit. For example, if a line needs to be redrawn, the pixels in the deleted line have all to be changed to the background colour and the pixels that make up the new line have to be changed too.

■ Image quality can be lost if enlargement takes place as the size of pixels are increased and the resolution of the image (the number of pixels per unit area) is reduced.

■ Distortion can occur if the image is transferred to a computer whose screen has a different resolution as pixels could be elongated in one direction.

■ Large storage space is required to store the attributes of every pixel.

Vector graphics

For applications such as CAD, where high precision is required, bitmapped graphics are not appropriate. With vector graphics the image is stored in terms of geometric data. For example, a circle is defined by its centre, its radius and its colour.

Vector graphics enable the user to manipulate objects as entire units. For example, to change the length of a line or enlarge a circle the user simply has to select the chosen object on the screen and then stretch or drag the image as required. The bitmapped graphic requires repainting individual dots in the line or circle. Using vector graphics, objects are described mathematically so they can be layered, rotated and magnified relatively easily.

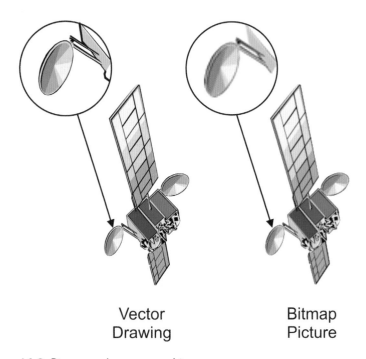

Vector
Drawing

Bitmap
Picture

Figure 16.2 Bitmap and vector graphic

case study 2
▶ **The Trinity House Lighthouse Service**

Trinity House provides nearly 600 aids to navigation sites such as storm-lashed lighthouses and buoys. Project teams consisting of specialist engineers are responsible for projects from initial design through to completion.

A CAD program is used to generate detail and assembly drawings that are used in the manufacture, construction and installation of navigational equipment. The CAD program uses vector graphics. This enables the engineer to represent the various components and services as objects that can be copied or adapted to serve different applications. Layering can be used to differentiate services such as water supplies, electrical cabling and control systems.

Input is normally via a digitiser and tablet with the primary output device usually being a pen plotter or A3 laser printer.

1. Explain why a bitmapped graphics package is not appropriate for use by the Trinity House Lighthouse Service. Give at least three reasons.
2. Explain why a digitiser and tablet is used for input rather than a mouse.

Moving pictures

Animations consist of a number of images or frames stored together and displayed one after the other. The more frames and the smaller the change between frames, the more realistic is the effect of the animation. An animation stored as GIF files can take up considerable storage space.

The MPEG file format uses a method of compression for video information in a similar way to that used in JPEG files for single images; the aim being to eliminate repetition between frames. MPEG files also allow a soundtrack. In spite of the size reduction resulting from compression, even a short piece lasting only a few minutes will have hundreds or thousands of frames and so the file size is likely to be large.

Numbers

Computers store numbers, as all other data, in binary coded form. There are three main ways of coding the numbers that we use.

Integers are whole numbers such a 7, 24567800, –56 or 0. When integers are stored in a computer, the number of bits assigned to the code determines the range of numbers that can be stored. One byte (8 bits) can store positive numbers in the range 0 to 255, while two bytes (16 bits) can store positive numbers in the range 0 to 65535.

The coding can be designed to store negative as well as positive integers. Integer arithmetic provides fast and accurate results; problems only occur if a calculation results in an integer that is too large to be stored in the number of bits assigned to the code.

A **real number** is a number that can have a fractional part. Unlike integers, real numbers can rarely be stored exactly in the bits assigned to store the number. Try dividing 100 by 3 (by hand) and you will find you can never write down all the digits after the decimal point. You could write down 33.3 or 33.33 or 33.333333333. Whatever you write will not be exact; the representation of real numbers in a computer always involves some loss of accuracy. The more bits allocated to store a real number, the greater the range of numbers that can be stored in the same way as integers, but the accuracy of the representation of the number is also increased. Performing calculations on real numbers is a more complex operation than doing so with integers and therefore is slower.

In systems where fractional values are needed but where accuracy is very important such as when data is representing money, then a third form of coding can be used. There are a number of applications where numbers that represent **currency** values are stored in a special format.

A **Boolean** value is one that can take one of only two values – one representing true (or yes) and the other false (or no).

Sound

Sound travels in waves and is therefore analogue in form. To be stored in a computer the analogue signal must be converted into digital form. The wave that is input through a microphone is **sampled** at regular intervals by an analogue to digital converter. This measures the height of the wave at the time of sampling and stores it as a binary code. The more frequent the sampling, the more accurate the representation of the sound. Obviously the amount of storage space required will increase as the sampling rate of the sound increases.

Typically, music stored on an audio CD has 44,100 samples per second, each sample using 16 bits with two channels (for stereo sound). This means that a CD stores about 10 megabytes of data per minute of music. A five-minute song therefore requires 50 megabytes of data.

Data compression techniques are used to reduce the amount of storage space required. MP3 is a standard coding system using compression techniques that stores the sound files in a smaller space. MP3 can compress a song by a factor of about 10 while keeping close to CD quality. The 50 megabyte sound file is reduced to about 5 megabytes when stored in MP3 format.

When the sound is output the digital representation is converted back to analogue form and the signal output through a loud speaker. How closely the sound resembles the original wave will depend upon the sampling frequency.

In the same way that there are a number of standard formats for storing text and graphics, so too are there standards for sound storage. WAV is the standard audio format for Windows and AIFF the Macintosh. Both platforms can also play and save sounds in the AU and SND audio formats as well as the MIDI format which is specifically for music. MP3 format, described above, is used to download and store music files from the Internet.

▶ **Four modes of operation can be identified and these are shown in the table below.**

▶ **These modes are not mutually exclusive. The appropriate choice of mode depends upon the nature of the application.**

Processing mode	Description	Examples of Use
Real time	Reacts fast enough to influence events outside the computer system	Control systems such as a computer-controlled greenhouse or a guided missile system
Batch	All the data to be input is collected together before being processed in a single operation	Invoicing systems – payroll systems
Transaction (pseudo real time)	Transactions are accepted from outside sources and transaction is processed before another one is accepted	Online order processing systems – booking systems
Interactive	In conversational mode	Designing; games; use of ATM

▶ **All data is stored in encoded binary form. Four categories of data are text, graphics, numbers and sound.**

▶ **Text data is stored in coded form where each code represents a single character. A commonly used code is ASCII, where each character is represented by eight binary digits.**

▶ **Picture (or graphical) data is stored in either bitmapped or vector form.**

▶ **A bitmapped image stores a code for each pixel, the tiny squares of which make up an image. This code represents the attributes such as colour of the pixel.**

▶ **Vector graphics store details of an image as a mathematical equation.**

▶ **Numbers can be stored in integer, real or currency format.**

▶ **Integers are whole numbers that can be processed fast with accuracy. The size of the number that can be stored is limited by the number of bits assigned to the code.**

▶ **Real number representation is used to store numbers where there is a fractional part. Very large and very small numbers can be stored but full accuracy cannot be achieved.**

▶ **Sound is stored in digitised form where the natural wave patterns are converted into binary codes using an analogue to digital converter. The quality of the sound stored depends upon the sampling rate.**

Chapter 16 Questions

1. a) Explain, using a suitable example, what the term batch processing means. (3)

b) Explain, using a suitable example, what the term transaction processing means. (3)

June 2005 ICT2

2. An airline uses two different types of processing in its computer systems. The airline booking system uses transaction processing for booking passengers' seats, and its aircraft use real-time processing for their on-board flight control systems.

a) Explain, using the booking system as an example, the term transaction processing. (3)

b) Explain, using the flight control system as an example, the term real-time processing. (3)

January 2004 ICT2

3. Graphical images can be stored in two different ways. One way is called **bit-mapped**.

a) Describe how data is stored for a bit-mapped graphic. (2)

b) Name the other method of storage. (1)

c) Describe how data is stored for the method named in **b)**. (2)

d) Name **two** advantages of the method named in **b)** over bit-mapped graphics. (2)

4. State **three** different forms that data can take, and illustrate your answer with an example of each. (6)

June 2004 ICT2

▷ Information itself is very important but the style in which it is presented is also important. Consider, for example, you might look at how two different newspapers report the same story.

The style and content of any computer output will depend on:

- the target audience (which person or group of people is the information aimed at?)
- the purpose of the output.

Within an organisation there are likely to be a number of different kinds of audience for whom information might be required.

- Company shareholders will want to be given information summarising the performance of the company over the last year.
- A group of salesmen and women may need to be briefed about the prices and specifications of new products.
- An operations manager needs to be informed of the performance and output of each factory.

Output format ◀

▷ A sales manager is writing a report on her company's sales. She can use different formats to present the same information depending on who will read the report.

- A director may want to see sales figures at a glance, probably including last year's figures for comparison. A **column graph** like the one shown could be suitable.

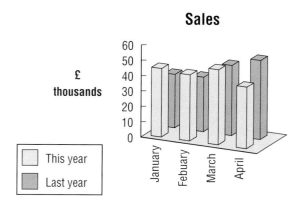

Figure 17.1 Column graph

Different types of graph could be used such as:
Pie charts (both 2-D and 3-D) are used to show the relative size of figures.

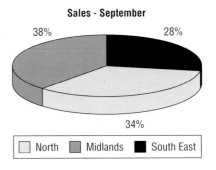

Figure 17.2 Pie chart

Line graphs are used to show trends in figures.

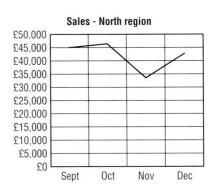

Figure 17.3 Line graph

- An accountant may want to see more information, possibly broken down area-by-area, month-by-month and compared with previous figures. The information can be presented in a *table* and studied in depth. It could be printed out on paper (hard copy) or presented on the screen (soft copy). Part of it might look like the table in figure 17.4.

	A	B	C	D	E	F
1	**2006**	Sept	Oct	Nov	Dec	Sept - Dec
2	North	£ 56,934	£ 53,192	£ 48,923	£ 59,204	£ 218,253
3	Midlands	£ 35,880	£ 32,901	£ 30,120	£ 41,245	£ 140,146
4	South East	£ 43,901	£ 38,103	£ 47,399	£ 58,104	£ 187,507
5	Total	£ 136,715	£ 124,196	£126,442	£ 158,553	£ 545,906
6						
7	**2005**	Sept	Oct	Nov	Dec	Sept - Dec
8	North	£ 56,191	£ 54,012	£ 49,231	£ 60,123	£ 219,557
9	Midlands	£ 26,712	£ 23,431	£ 29,012	£ 37,371	£ 116,526
10	South East	£ 41,021	£ 40,159	£ 46,912	£ 60,932	£ 189,024
11	Total	£ 123,924	£ 117,602	£125,155	£ 158,426	£ 525,107
12						
13	**Increase**	Sept	Oct	Nov	Dec	Sept - Dec
14	North	1%	-2%	-1%	-2%	-1%
15	Midlands	34%	40%	4%	10%	20%
16	South East	7%	-5%	1%	-5%	-1%
17	Total	**10%**	**6%**	**1%**	**0%**	**4%**

Figure 17.4

- The manager's immediate superior may want even more information. They may require an exception report including details of where the company has done exceptionally well or exceptionally badly. Reasons for good and bad performance may be included. A full text *report* may be necessary.

> Sales have risen year on year but an overall increase in sales of 4 per cent masks exceptionally good performance in the Midlands where sales rose by 20 per cent compared with last year, but in other areas sales actually fell. The good performance in the Midlands is the result of excellent work by our sales staff and an intensive advertising campaign in the region.

Figure 17.5

- A report to a group of directors could be presented on a screen using an LCD data projector and presentation software such as Microsoft PowerPoint. Such a presentation could include graphs, tables and text.
- PowerPoint gives the option of printing out the presentation in a variety of formats. A hard copy of all the slides with additional notes can be printed for the presenter. A hard copy of all the slides with additional space to make notes can be printed for the audience to take away with them for later reference.
- Spreadsheet software such as Microsoft Excel enables users to present information in a variety of chart formats. These charts can be copied and pasted into other software and then embedded into files in other programs such as Microsoft PowerPoint using OLE. This means that if the spreadsheet is updated, the graphs are updated both in the spreadsheet software and in the presentation.

Output media

All the output formats described above can be produced on paper for distribution to the appropriate people. However, there are times when the information needs to be presented to a group of people at a meeting.

Traditionally, acetate slides with information printed (or written) on to them have been used with an overhead projector (OHP). These slides are cheap to produce and only require a standard overhead projector and screen for display.

Nowadays many presentations are prepared using software such as Microsoft PowerPoint. Although individual slides can be printed out on to acetate and used as described above, the package allows for the information to be displayed as a slide show using a projector and a screen.

A data projector is connected to a computer and the image normally appearing on the computer screen is projected. Many rooms such as lecture rooms or classrooms have a ceiling mounted data projector. This projector is permanently fixed and can easily be connected to a computer e.g. a laptop.

A ceiling mounted projector is less likely to be stolen and the image is less likely to be interrupted by somebody or something getting in the way! Back projection where the data projector is behind the screen is also possible.

Data projectors can also be connected to video or DVD players where appropriate.

Features of presentation software

Using presentation software together with a data projector offers a range of extra features not available with an OHP.

1. Animation can be used so that the contents of a slide can be built up bit by bit to tie in with what the presenter is saying.
2. Animation can be set to occur automatically after a certain time delay.
3. Clip-art, sound and video clips can be added to the presentation.
4. You can get an on-screen pointer and use the mouse to pick out important points.
5. Links can be added so that it is possible to go through the presentation in a different order or to miss out slides, depending on the audience.
6. It is possible to make the screen go blank by pressing just one key. Pressing the same key again brings the slide back. In PowerPoint the key is B. This is useful if the

person making the presentation wants to grab the audience's attention.

7. The speaker can easily go back to the previous slide to review information.

8. The package will print out hard copies of the slides in a variety of formats so that members of the audience of a presentation can have a copy on which to add notes. Such presentations appear much more professional than ones based on standard acetates.

9. The speaker can use a remote control mouse to move the slides on and so can stand anywhere in the room.

10. Changes can be easily made, even at the last minute, which would be more difficult with acetate slides.

Problems with presentations

Using presentation software and a data projector will not make a boring presentation interesting. Cluttered screens, too small fonts, too much text, poor colour choice and overuse of animations are symptoms of poor presentations. This is usually because the presenter has focused more on the visuals than on the content. Some people call this 'Death by PowerPoint'.

Activity 1

On the Internet use a search engine to search for Death by PowerPoint.

Electronic whiteboards

The use of electronic whiteboards together with data projectors has opened up further possibilities for presenters. As well as carrying out a presentation as described above, the use of an electronic whiteboard allows the user to add notes to the image on the screen and store and print these annotations.

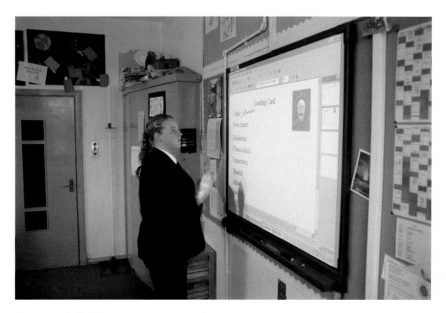

Figure 17.6 Electronic whiteboard

Electronic whiteboards may have a touch-screen feature, so that the presenter can navigate the Web using a finger to move the cursor and double-clicking with taps on the screen. An alternative is to use a special 'pen'.

An on-screen keyboard means that you can enter data at the whiteboard, rather than the computer.

Design principles for data projection

- Stick to one style of background, text and animation throughout.
- The font size of text should be chosen so that it is large enough to be seen when displayed on a screen. Check from the back of the room.
- The amount of text shown on one slide should be kept to a minimum; key points should be given rather than lengthy sentences. Some people recommend the 6 by 7 rule. No more than 6 points. Each point no more than 7 words.
- Care should be taken over the use of colour. Some colours show up better than others. Experiment with light text on a dark background and dark text on a light background to see which is clearer. Again this should be checked with the data projector in the room.
- The background chosen should not be too cluttered otherwise it will detract from the text.
- Too much animation will be a distraction.
- An organisation's logo could be incorporated into each slide.

Activity 2

Use a presentation package such as Microsoft PowerPoint to prepare a slide show to present a topic from the ICT AS specification to your class. Investigate as many features of the package as possible. Take care to ensure that your slide show keeps to the good design guidelines.

Getting the best of your printout

Design of printed output is just as important as you want to get your message to be read. There are many techniques available to make information more readable:

- Text can be formatted to different colours, sizes and fonts.
- Bullet points make lists stand out.
- Bold print and formatting borders can make tables easier to read.
- Borders around text attract attention.
- Words with a different colour background stand out.
- Start important sections on a new page to catch the reader's eye.
- Number pages for easy reference.

- In a formal report, sections and subsections can be numbered.
- Use the header for information that is the same for each page, e.g. section headings or titles.
- Use columns and text boxes.

Remember: You don't need to use them all.

Using the Internet for the distribution of information ◄

▶ The global nature of the Internet and its easy accessibility has meant that it is used for distributing information.

Many public bodies such as local councils use the Internet to publish agendas of meetings and their minutes. Just go to a search engine and type in *online minutes*.

This is much easier than printing several copies and posting them. It is also a way of giving the public easy access to information.

Reports can also be made available to subscribers such as the law reports at http://www.lloydslawreports.com.

The interactivity of the Internet means that it can be used for online surveys and questionnaires.

Activity 3

Check out your local council's website. Does it give access to minutes and agendas?

Design principles for web pages

With so many websites competing for our attention, many web pages (particularly those marketing a product) use different techniques to hold our interest, stop us moving to another site and persuade us to read the information.

These techniques include:

- text colour and background colour
- use of white space to make sure the page is not cluttered
- marquee – text scrolling across the screen
- bright images
- sound
- animated gifs – apparently moving pictures
- animations using JavaScript coding or special software such as Macromedia Flash
- video

Activity 4

Choose any website and make a list of the techniques used to hold the user's attention.

Web design disasters

Not all websites are well designed. Garish colours, poor contrast, unreadable fonts, too much animation and huge images that take a long time to load are some of the symptoms of bad web design.

http://www.webpagesthatsuck.com/ is a website that gives awards for poor web design. Every day it selects its daily sucker – another website that in their eyes is terrible.

Activity 5

Visit http://www.webpagesthatsuck.com/ and go to their daily sucker page. Do you agree with them that the site is not very good? Give reasons why you think the site is good or bad.

Style or substance?

If a web page is not attractively presented nobody will want to read it. When designing a web page don't forget that the purpose is to communicate information to the audience. It is crucial that the design, layout and text are suitable for the given audience.

Activity 6

Visit these two websites:
http://www.bbc.co.uk/radio1/
http://www.antique-furniture.co.uk/

They obviously have very different audiences.

Write down five differences between the designs of these two sites. Then write down five similarities.

For example, a similarity might be that they both have a search facility. A difference might be the position of the search facility.

Report generation ◀

▶ A report may be produced automatically using Report Generator software. (See page 177.)

This software can take data from one or more files and paste them into a report in a predetermined format. This format will include which fields to print and in which order.

Predetermined column headings will be used. It the data spills on to a second and subsequent pages, the column headings will be repeated at the top of each page.

Calculations can be performed on numeric fields such as comparing sales for this month with last month or the same month last year. Reports can include graphs of numeric data. Once the report has been set up with one set of figures, the next report can be prepared automatically with the same format.

Page formatting such as page numbering and orientation can also be carried out. Other information can be printed in the footer of each page.

SUMMARY

- ► **The way in which information is presented will depend on the target audience.**
- ► **Different formats are available such as text, graphs and tables.**
- ► **Different formats and techniques can be used to make a report more readable.**
- ► **Information can be disseminated to a larger audience in one place by creating a slide show using presentation software and presenting it with a data projector.**
- ► **Different techniques are used on the Internet to attract and hold our attention.**

Chapter 17 Questions

1. The head of a company's IT services department is to give the company's computer users a presentation about the facilities offered by operating systems.

  a) State **four** of the facilities offered by operating systems that should be included in the presentation. (See Chapter 14.) (4)

  b) He decides to develop a computer-based presentation to be displayed using an LCD (data) projector, rather than creating overhead projection transparencies.

   i) State **three** functions of the presentation software that are available for use with the LCD (data) projector (but which cannot be used with overhead projection transparencies). (3)

   ii) Give **four** factors that should be considered when designing an effective presentation. (4)

January 2005 ICT2

2. The head of a company's IT services department is to give a presentation on data security to all computer users within the company.

  a) Give **three** methods of ensuring data security that she should include in the content of her presentation. (3)

  b) She decides to develop a computer-based presentation to be displayed using a data projector rather than creating overhead projector transparencies.

   i) State **three** functions of the presentation software that are only available for use with the LCD data projector. (3)

   ii) Describe **two** design considerations that she needs to take into account in order to develop an effective presentation. (4)

June 2001 ICT2

3. A head teacher and the school's governing body want to consider the school's recent exam results at AS and A level at their next meeting. You have been asked for your advice on how the results could be presented. Produce a brief report on the options available. (5)

4. Presentation software and data projectors have almost entirely removed the need for overhead projectors (OHPs).

  a) State **four** advantages of using a data projector compared to an OHP. (4)

  b) State **two** disadvantages of using a data projector compared to an OHP. (2)

5. A manager of a stationery supplies company said, 'I haven't got time to read lots of figures. I want the facts in an easy-to-read format.'

  a) State which data format is likely to be the best for the manager. (1)

  b) As well as presenting data in this format, describe another software feature that is likely to be useful to the manager in this situation. (2)

▶ Computer systems work on the basis of input, process and output. The various parts of the computer (the hardware) can be defined as input devices, the processor, backing store and output devices.

Input devices are used to enter data. The processor is in the 'box' part of the computer and is made up of electronic printed circuits and microchips. The processor includes the computer's main memory. Backing store is where data is stored when the computer is turned off. Output devices are used to present the information to the user.

Processors ◀

▶ The **Central Processing Unit (CPU)** is where data is processed. When buying a computer you will see the **clock speed** of the CPU, measured in megahertz (MHz) or gigahertz (GHz) advertised. Usually the higher the clock speed, the faster the data is processed. This is important when using some software that has to perform many calculations very quickly, for example, a game with fast moving graphical images.

The computer's memory is associated with the CPU. There are two types of memory chip: **Read Only Memory (ROM)** and **Random Access Memory (RAM)**. Data in ROM cannot be changed and is permanently stored even when turned off. ROM is used to store the boot programs when the computer is switched on.

RAM is used to store any software and data while it is in use. The more sophisticated the software, the more memory it is likely to use. Multitasking – running several programs apparently at once – demands a large memory.

When the computer is switched off, data stored in RAM is lost.

The processor is housed in a box. Peripheral (input, output and storage) devices can be attached to the processor via ports – the sockets that can be seen on the side of the computer. Modern computers have a Universal Serial Bus (USB) port into which a variety of devices can be plugged. With USB, a new device can be added to a computer without an adapter card having to be added. The computer does not even have to be switched off.

Processors come in a variety of forms. The most common are the desktop personal computer and the laptop computer but PDAs are being increasingly used.

Desktop personal computer

The desktop computer, as its name implies, is designed to sit permanently on the user's desk and needs to be plugged in to a mains power supply. It usually has a range of peripherals permanently attached. These are likely to consist of:

- a large, clear screen which can be set up and positioned to minimise eye strain
- a sizeable keyboard that can be positioned in such a way as to minimise the risks of repetitive strain injury (RSI)
- a mouse or other pointing device
- a hard disk or disks. This will usually be located within the same box as the processor and is likely to consist of many gigabytes of storage
- other backing storage devices such as CD-ROM drive, floppy disk drive, or DVD-R drive. These can be built into the processor's box or plugged in externally
- a printer.

Depending upon the use made of the computer other devices may be attached.

It is likely that a desktop personal computer will have either a modem, built in or attached, or a network card to link it into a local area network.

A desktop personal computer is the appropriate choice for someone who regularly uses a computer in the same place. It is easier to set up the computer in a way that reduces the hazards of computer use (see Chapter 10).

Laptop computer

The main reason to have a laptop computer (or notebook, as many products are now called) is that it is portable. Laptop computers are relatively light, can fit into a carrying case and can be transported to wherever they are needed. As a laptop can run for a number of hours off a rechargeable battery it can be used when there is no access to mains electricity; it can be used on the move, for example on a train journey.

The weight of a laptop computer is of great importance as it has to be carried around; to help keep the weight down, the capacity of the hard disk is usually not as large as that of a desktop computer. Compactness is also a desirable feature, so most laptops have a rather cramped keyboard as the keys have to be contained in a smaller space. Most laptops will have a built-in touch pad which are designed to be easier to use in a confined space than a mouse.

Laptops are more vulnerable to loss or damage as they are more likely to be dropped or broken as they are moved around more than a desktop computer. Battery life is also an issue. Security is also a greater risk. Desktop computers can be locked away in an office, but laptops that are carried around can be stolen.

Many laptop users do not take sufficient care over the backing up of their data. Matt is a keen photographer who uses a digital camera. He stores his favourite images on his two-year-old laptop. Recently, Matt travelled to Australia on business. When he had finished his work he took a ten-day holiday with friends driving in a camper van from Perth to Darwin. It was a fantastic drive and he added many excellent photos to his collection. Unfortunately, whilst he and his friends were out eating one evening, thieves broke into the camper van and stole everything – including Matt's laptop. He had always meant to backup his photographs; now he had lost them all. His laptop and other possessions were insured, but there was no way to get back his lost data.

Personal Digital Assistant (PDA)

A PDA (or palmtop) is a small handheld computer that can fit into a jacket pocket. It can also function as a mobile phone and a digital camera. It combines microcomputer and wireless technology to enable the user to:

- access the Internet
- send and receive e-mails
- use application software such as a word processor and a spreadsheet
- keep a personal diary
- make phone calls
- take photos and movies.

Most PDAs use a stylus for input, either using handwriting recognition or an on-screen keyboard. Some PDAs can also react to voice input by using voice recognition technology.

Worked exam question

A company is replacing the personal computers used by its employees. The staff have been offered the choice of a desktop personal computer or a laptop computer. Describe one advantage, and one disadvantage, of these options to the staff. Your advantages and disadvantages must be different in each case.

a) A desktop personal computer (4)
b) A laptop computer (4)

January 2003 ICT2

▶ EXAMINER'S GUIDANCE

There are 4 marks available for each part of this question, 2 for an advantage and 2 for a disadvantage. This means that very brief answers will not gain full marks. Another possible pitfall is that an examiner will only give one mark for an idea. So it is no good saying that a disadvantage of a desktop computer is that it can only be used in one place, and an advantage of a laptop computer is that it is portable – you are just using the same idea twice and would only be awarded one mark.

To gain full marks you will need to give four full and different points.

Obviously the main advantage of using a laptop is that it is portable – but that is a big disadvantage of a desktop! Another advantage of a laptop is that it has a battery and so can be used when mains electricity is not available.

The advantages of a desktop and disadvantages of a laptop are easier to find; a desktop usually has a less cramped keyboard, a larger hard disk and has a range of peripherals permanently available. A laptop is easily stolen or broken.

So putting together a final answer, (remembering to expand each point for the second mark):

▶ SAMPLE ANSWER

An advantage of using a desktop personal computer is that its keyboard is less cramped and easier to use (1) so that problems of RSI are less likely to occur (1). A disadvantage is that the desktop computer is not mobile (1) and cannot be used in a different location (1).

An advantage of using a laptop computer is that it can be used with battery power and does not need to be plugged in to the mains supply (1) which means that it can be used when travelling on a train (1). A disadvantage is that a laptop can easily be dropped and broken (1) causing loss of data (1).

Input devices

◀

▶ (See Chapter 11 on Data Capture for more information.)

The keyboard and mouse are not the only input devices. OMR readers, OCR readers and MICR readers are used by commercial businesses. Games computers use a joystick. Hand-held computers use keypads. Computers controlling manufacturing processes may use sensors.

The **ergonomic keyboard** is an alternative keyboard that is reputed to reduce the risk of repetitive strain injury (RSI). A **concept keyboard** is a special keyboard designed for a particular purpose. Fast food chains use such keyboards where there is a grid of images, one for each menu item. The operator merely has to press the image that represents the dish that has been chosen.

Figure 18.1 A concept keyboard being used in a fast food restaurant

Touch screens allow users to make selections by actually touching the screen. In fact there is a grid of infrared beams in front of the screen. Pointing at the screen breaks the beams so giving the position of the finger. Touch screens are input and output devices combined. They are commonly used in railway stations for the purchase of tickets, in museums and galleries for interactive use and in towns and cities to help the visitors find out more about the area. Visitors can select from a number of icons representing such things as places of interest, special events and transport. On pressing an icon more information is displayed. A touch screen can provide a robust device that is very simple to use. (See figure 18.2.)

Figure 18.2 A touch screen

Typically PDAs use touch screen and character recognition technology to allow the user to 'write' on the screen and enter text into the computer.

Scanners can be used to input any image. The image could be a plan or a map, a chart or diagram, a photograph or even a signature. Pictures can be stored in a number of formats such as jpg or bmp. With the use of OCR software, text can be stored as a text file and imported into other applications.

Flatbed scanners are often sold with OCR software that enables text to be scanned in and stored so that it can be loaded into a word processing program (see Chapter 11). The accuracy of the text in the document produced by software depends on the image quality of the original document.

Digital cameras are widely used. The camera can connect to a computer via its USB port and images can be downloaded and stored. Image processing software can be used to modify an image, perhaps by cropping, altering the brightness or contrast or removing the 'red eye' caused by the use of flash. Photographs can then be printed out to a particular size, stored on to backing store (such as CD-R) or displayed as a slide show on the screen. Many digital cameras today can record moving images together with sound.

Graphics tablets have a stylus pen which is used to draw on a special flat surface. The drawing is automatically read by the computer. These allow very accurate images to be produced and are ideal for graphic designers, artists and technical illustrators.

Activity 1

(You will have to refer to Chapter 11 as well for this activity.)

Match the following input devices to the uses listed below and explain your choices:

OCR	OMR	MICR	Scanner	Bar code reader

1. Inputting a photograph
2. Reading the details from a bank cheque
3. Reading the turnaround document from the bottom of a gas bill
4. Identifying a tin of peas
5. Inputting the answers to a questionnaire

Graphics tablet	Concept keyboard	Keyboard pad	Joystick	Touch screen

Here's another set:
1. Playing a game
2. Finding out information about bus times at a bus station
3. Entering the design for a garden
4. Selecting a vegetable type when weighing at a supermarket
5. Cutting and pasting text using a word processor on a laptop

Output devices ◀

▶ Output devices include the screen, printers, plotters and loudspeakers.

Screens

The most commonly used output device is the **screen**. Screens can be black and white or colour and vary in size, resolution and type. The screen size is measured from one corner to the opposite diagonal corner. Common screen sizes for desktop computer screens are 12, 14, 17, 19, and 21 inches.

The screen's resolution determines the number of dots (known as pixels) that are displayed – the more pixels, the greater the resolution.

Traditional screens make use of cathode ray tube (CRT) technology and are bulky devices.

Flat screens were originally used in laptop computers because of their light weight and compact size. Now they have become very common with desktop computers. Their price has reduced considerably and their quality increased. They take up much less desk space than a CRT monitor, they use less electricity and generate less heat – this can be very important in a stuffy office.

Modern flat screens have bright displays and high resolutions. They are a type of liquid crystal display (LCD) screen usually using a technology known as thin-film transistor (TFT).

A problem with LCD displays is that due to the nature of the manufacturing process, occasional defects can occur. The screen is made up of a number of pixels. Each pixel is made from 3 sub-pixels; one red, one blue and one green. Pixel defects can occur at any stage in the LCD's life and cannot be fixed or repaired.

Printers

When choosing a printer thought needs to be given to the uses to which it will be put as this will determine the most appropriate printer. The volume of printing required will influence the choice as the speed of printers can vary

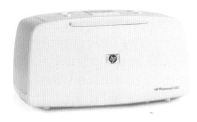

Figure 18.3 Printers

enormously. A home user who prints out the occasional letter and colour photograph has very different printer needs from a large organisation such as a bank that produces hundreds of thousands of statements in a day.

Some applications require the use of preprinted stationery such as headed notepaper or pay slips which are directly printed into envelopes so that the contents of the slip cannot be read casually by anyone. Sometimes multipart paper is used; invoices for car repairs at a garage are often printed on two-part paper with one copy for the customer and one for the garage.

Printers come in different sizes. The printer at your school or college may well be larger than a printer you would buy for home use as the volume of printing done at school is likely to be much larger and so a more powerful printer is needed. However, much smaller and much larger printers are in use. Very small printers can be built into equipment for specialist use – see Case Studies 1 and 2. Lightweight, portable printers can be used with laptop computers. At the other end of the scale, high-speed laser printers are floor standing and very hefty pieces of equipment. They will often be printing all the time.

The most common forms of printers all form their images out of dots – the smaller the dots, the better is the quality of the print.

Dot matrix printers are a type of impact or contact printer. They print by hammering pins against a ribbon on to the paper to print the dots. They are most commonly used in situations when only text, in black and white, is required. As it is an impact printer, a dot matrix printer can be used to print on multipart stationery; the pressure of the pins will cause the carbon paper to produce a print. The printers are easy and cheap to maintain as replacement ribbons are inexpensive.

Inkjet printers squirt ink on to the paper and form letters from tiny dots. They are quiet, quality is good and most versions support colour. Such printers are the most popular for home use as they are relatively cheap to purchase and produce a clear image. However, most inkjet printers are too slow to be used with high volumes of printing. On some inkjet printers, photo quality images can be printed on special high quality, glossy paper. Although the initial cost outlay is relatively low, the ongoing cost of cartridges can be very costly in relation to the initial cost of the printer.

Laser printers are very popular for business use. The way in which a laser printer functions is very similar to the way a photocopier works. In fact printers that can also function as photocopiers are available.

The cost of using a laser printer depends on a combination of costs: paper, toner replacement and drum replacement. Some laser printer models can accommodate a duplexing unit that allows printing on both sides of the paper in one run. This will reduce the paper costs and the space requirements for the physical filing of documents

The variety of types of laser printer available is huge. Printers that can produce colour are more expensive than those that can only produce black and white. Speeds can vary. The slowest can sit on a desk top and be used occasionally to produce letters and brief documents at a speed from 4 pages a minute. The fastest are large, high speed devices that can print thousands of pages in a minute and would, for example, be used by banks to print out statements.

The choice between inkjet and laser printer is not always clear cut. Many inkjet printers can produce excellent quality printouts; printer choice can be a compromise between print quality, speed and cost. Some of the more expensive inkjet printers produce better quality graphics than some laser printers.

A **thermal transfer printer** is a non-impact printer that uses heat to make an impression on paper. They operate quietly. Thermal transfer printers are particularly chosen for the printing of bar codes and price tags as well as labels. Thermal transfer printers are usually small and are cheap to maintain. A portable version of a thermal printer can be used for mobile POS, receipt or ticket printing. The printer is very small – only 58 mm wide – and runs off a battery. These printers can be found in restaurants, used by customers when they have made a payment using a credit or debit card. The printer is used to produce a receipt at the table.

Dye-sublimation printers (called dye-subs) are used to produce high quality graphical images, particularly colour photographs. These printers produce images with excellent colour reproduction, that look as if they came from a photographic laboratory. The purchase price of a dye-sublimation printer is high; this is a printer that would be used for printing artwork to a very high quality.

Activity 2 – Which printer?

When an exam question asks you to state an output device to be used in a specified application, the answer 'printer' is unlikely to be sufficient. You would need to state which type of printer would be required.

This activity requires you to choose from the printers listed, the most appropriate for each of the tasks listed below. For each justify your choice and discuss the specific requirements such as size, speed and preprinted paper needs.

Dot matrix	Black and white laser	Colour laser	Inkjet

►

- Producing a family newsletter which will include text and photographs.
- Producing the pay slips (enclosed in an envelope) for a small company.
- Producing household bills for an electricity supplier.
- Printing letters and legal documents such as wills at a solicitor's office.
- Printing out prescriptions at a doctor's surgery.
- Printing timed tickets for use in a car park.

Other output devices

Data projectors which project computer output onto a large screen are expensive but are now common in business demonstrations, projecting the output of a laptop computer. Prices continue to fall and quality is improving. They are now increasingly used in the classroom, often together with an electronic interactive whiteboard.

Loudspeakers are a common output device used to output music. However, sound is used in other ways as well. Many programs make beeping sounds to indicate errors; Microsoft Windows will make a distinctive sound when loading. The use of a **loudspeaker** that allows for speech synthesis is an expanding area of output, common in a range of applications including computer games. If you phone up directory enquiries or the speaking clock, you will be told the number you require or the time by the computer in synthesised speech.

Figure 18.4 Interactive whiteboard in use in a classroom

case study 1
▶ **Automatic teller machine (ATM)**

Figure 18.5 ATM

An automatic teller machine is so named because it replaces many jobs carried out by the human bank teller, a bank employee who used to work behind a counter and deal with customers' deposits, withdrawals and other transactions. Most transactions are now dealt with electronically – for some people via the Internet or the telephone but for most using an ATM. ATMs are located in a range of places including inside and outside the bank itself, in shopping centres, railway stations and airports.

An ATM has a number of built-in input and output devices. The user inserts his bank card into a magnetic stripe reader. The device will read the identity code of the customer. The ATM also has a keypad that the customer uses to enter his PIN number. A menu of options appears on a touch screen; the customer selects an option by placing a finger on the screen at the appropriate position, or on the keypad. Depending on their choice, a number of further questions will appear on the screen and these are answered in a similar way.

The ATM has a small, built-in impact or thermal printer that is used to print out receipts for cash withdrawals or statement of cash balance. A device that dispenses the cash completes the transaction.

1. Explain why a touch screen is used.
2. Explain why an impact or thermal printer is used.
3. Explain why the customer has to type in a PIN number.

case study 2
▶ **At the**
supermarket till

Figure 18.6 EPOS at a supermarket

The checkout at the supermarket has a large number of input and output devices. The most obvious input device is the flatbed bar code laser scanner. Products are passed over the scanner which interprets the product identification code that is encoded on to the bar codes. This code identifies the product and the price is found from a database. A specialised keypad allows numbers to be entered if several of the same items are purchased; this saves the operator from scanning every one. If, for some reason, the bar code cannot be read a beep sound is made (through a loud speaker) to alert the operator. The operator can then enter the product identity code, which is printed underneath the bar code, using the keypad. As products are scanned, a screen displays details of the latest purchase together with the current total cost for the customer to view.

Loose products such as fruits and vegetables will not be bar coded. These items must be weighed on special scales which use sensors to produce an electronic value equivalent to the weight. The operator must then choose the product type from a series of images displayed on a touch screen – if he is weighing red onions he touches the image of a red onion.

Customers can pay with cash or by using a credit or debit card. 'Chip and PIN' allows the customer's smart card to be read by a small device connected to the till. The customer enters his password using the device's keypad. The account is accessed via a wide area network and the transaction is authorised. A small, built-in printer is used to print out the bill which lists every item purchased together with its price.

Many supermarkets provide their customers with a loyalty card; they are allocated points according to the amount of money they have spent. The points can be redeemed for goods. A customer's loyalty card is read using a magnetic stripe reader to identify the customer's account which is then updated with the points earned during that sale.

■ Draw up a table of all the input and output devices used at the supermarket checkout under the following headings:

Device	Input or Output	Purpose

Backing storage devices

Backing store is a permanent storage medium on which data can be stored for retrieval later. When the computer is switched off, data stored in main memory is lost but data stored in backing store is not lost. Backing storage can be **fixed** or **removable**.

Fixed backing storage – hard disk

In most cases fixed backing storage takes the form of a **hard disk**. This is a magnetic storage device that is generally housed within the box containing the processor. The hard disk inside the computer can hold many gigabytes of data. It is used to store the operating system, generic software as well as data files. These files are vital and some form of backup is necessary in case of disk failure.

Removable backing storage

As well as storing data on a medium that is permanently attached to the computer, it is often necessary to use a device that stores data on a medium that is transportable.

The devices that enable electronically stored data to be removed from a computer have four main uses:

- Transferring software from the manufacturer to the user.
- Transferring data to another computer (this can be done without using a backing storage medium; a file can be sent via the Internet). A student who is working on their course work for ICT3 may do some work during the day in class, using a computer in the school's classroom, and then want to continue in the evening on his home computer. He will need to transfer the up-to-date version of his coursework from one computer to the other.
- Backing up data (see Chapter 19).
- Archiving data. This is removing data, that is not used frequently, from the main backing storage device of the computer (usually a hard disk) to a medium that can be stored away from the computer, but accessed if the data is needed. At a college, the details of students who left college three years ago would not be required on a day-to-day basis. However, they may need to be accessed occasionally, for example, if a request for a reference about a student was received. A home computer user who is a keen photographer could soon fill up her hard disk memory with digital images. To free up space without deleting the images, and losing them permanently, she should archive some of her images to a removable storage medium.

HARDWARE

Magnetic devices

It is now possible to have a removable, **external hard disk**; these are increasingly being used, especially by laptop owners, to provide better security. The removable hard disk is similar to the permanent hard disk that is found inside a typical PC. It houses the drive mechanism and the medium together in one sealed case. The drive connects to the PC via USB cable.

The removable 3½ inch **floppy disk** is a magnetic storage medium that normally stores only 1.44 Mb. For many years a floppy disk drive has been a standard part of all personal computer systems. It is mainly used for keeping backup copies of small files, such as text files of letters or small documents, or for transferring small files between two or more computers. Floppy disks are very cheap to buy. However, their usefulness has decreased as the size of files to be stored has grown and they are much slower than a hard disk.

Magnetic tape cartridges are used for backup of entire networks due to the high capacity, for example, of 120 Gb. Magnetic tape is a serial medium. This means that the data has to be read in the order in which it is stored on the tape. It is also sometimes used for archiving large volumes of data.

Optical storage devices

CD-ROMs (Compact Disk-Read Only Memory) are small plastic optical disks. Like floppy disks, CD-ROMs can be moved from computer to computer. However, they store larger quantities of data (650 Mb or 0.65 Gb) permanently. A CD-ROM drive of some sort is now standard in most PCs. The data stored on a CD-ROM is less prone to damage than that on a floppy disk as the data storage method uses laser rather than magnetic technology.

As the name suggests, data can be read from but not stored on a CD-ROM disk. Much commercial software is distributed on CD-ROM and many computing magazines are sold with a CD-ROM attached that holds free sample software.

CD-Rs (Compact Disk–Recordable) are writable compact disks. Using a special writable CD drive, up to 650 Mb of data can be recorded on a blank disk. This data cannot be altered but it can then be read by any other PC with a standard CD-ROM drive. This means that CD-R is suitable for archiving data that can be removed from the computer's hard drive, but still be available if it is needed.

CD-ROMs are used to store multimedia applications as the sound, graphics and animation files are likely to require large amounts of storage space. For example, a marketing manager might prepare a slide show presentation with information of new products and pricing policy which could be distributed to all sales staff.

CD-RWs (Compact Disk–ReWritable) are rewritable compact disks. Using the same writable CD drive, up to 650 Mb of data can be recorded, deleted and re-recorded on these disks. This means that a CD-RW can be used in the same way as a floppy disk without the limitation on size of file.

DVD (Digital Versatile Disk) is a high-capacity optical disk developed in the 1990s. A DVD is the same physical size as a CD. Current disks can store 4.7 to 17 Gb, the equivalent of over 25 CD-ROMs and are used for moving images in films as well as audio.

DVD drives can read both CD-ROMs and DVDs. 'Combi' drives that read DVDs but can write to CD-R and CD-RW are becoming increasingly common. Some DVD drives can both read and write to DVDs.

DVD-R (Recordable DVD) and DVD-RW (ReWritable DVD) are available but capacity is reduced.

Flash memory

Flash memory is a type of removable backing storage that was developed for small devices such as digital cameras and is now used extensively as a portable storage medium.

There are a number of proprietary formats which require special adaptors e.g. Compact Flash and Secure Digital. Flash memory is made up of a special storage microchip. Flash memory sizes range from 8 Mb to 4 Gb.

A USB **memory stick** or **pen drive** is a portable storage device that uses flash memory. It is 'plug and play'; the user simply plugs the stick into their computer's USB port and the computer's operating system recognises the stick as a removable drive. A memory stick is very small and light; it can be attached to a key ring or hung on a cord around the user's neck. Memory sticks do not require any battery or cables and are available in capacities ranging from 128 Mb to 4 Gb. However, memory sticks with greater capacities will soon be developed.

Memory sticks are used to record different types of data: graphical images, music and moving pictures as well as other computer data files. A 1 Gb Memory Stick can store between 250 and 1,000 minutes of video depending on the image resolution chosen.

Figure 18.7 Different types of flash memory

Activity 3 – Backing storage

Create a grid with the headings given below. For each of the devices or media listed, give a description of the device and list typical uses for the device.

Floppy disk, memory stick, magnetic hard drive, DAT (digital audio tape), CD-R, CD-RW, DVD-R.

Device/medium	Description	Applications

Activity 4 – Which medium?

For each of the following activities, state a suitable backing storage medium. Justify your choice in each case.

1. A software house distributing new software.
2. A businessman transferring a short text document from his laptop to his desktop computer.
3. Storing music downloaded (legally) via the Internet.
4. Storing frequently used software.
5. A charity archiving details of past transactions from its database.
6. An A-level student transferring an ICT project between home and school computers.
7. Backing up data from a laptop.
8. Backing up all the data stored on a network.
9. Storing holiday photographs.
10. Storing a multimedia presentation about your sixth form for distribution to local schools.

case study 3
▶ Garden design

Terry has built up a small business as a garden designer. He wishes to buy a computer to help him to run his business. He intends to produce letters, keep records on his customers and jobs, create garden designs as well as leaflets showing 'before' and 'after' shots of the gardens he produces. Some of these photographs will have been taken by Terry and some given to him by his clients. Terry wishes to store all the photographs and designs electronically.

1. What advice would you give to Terry about purchasing his computer? Make three distinct points.
2. List the input, output and backing storage devices that Terry should buy, explaining carefully why each is needed.

Communication devices ◀

▶ The hardware devices used in communication are discussed in Chapter 20.

SUMMARY ◀

Processors

▶ **The Central Processing Unit (CPU) is where data is processed. Its speed is measured in MHz or GHz**

▶ **There are two types of main memory: Read Only Memory (ROM) and Random Access Memory (RAM). Data in ROM cannot be changed. When the computer is switched off, data stored in RAM is lost.**

▶ The most common forms of computer are the desktop personal computer and the laptop computer.

▶ The desktop computer needs to be plugged in to a mains power supply. It has a range of peripherals permanently attached.

▶ A laptop computer is portable, light and can run off a rechargeable battery. A laptop is vulnerable to loss or damage.

Input devices include:

keyboard;

mouse;

OMR reader;

OCR reader;

MICR reader;

joystick;

keypad;

touch screen;

scanner;

digital camera;

graphics tablet.

Output devices include:

screen (**CRT** and **LCD**);

printers:

(dot matrix printer,

inkjet printer,

laser printer)

data projector;

loudspeakers.

Backing Storage devices can be **fixed** or **removable**:

▶ **Hard disk** provides very high capacity (10 to 120 Gb) fixed storage. It allows permanent online storage of software and data.

▶ Removable backing store is used for backup, archiving, transferring software and data between computers.

▶ The **floppy disk** has a low capacity of 1.44 Mb and is used to transfer small files between computers

▶ A **magnetic tape cartridge** has a very high capacity (e.g. 120 Gb). It can be used to backup an entire network or for archiving large volumes of data.

- ▶ A **CD-ROM** has a high capacity (650 Mb). It is read only and is used for distributing software and reference material.
- ▶ **CD-R** and **CD-RW** have a high capacity and can be used to archive, transfer and backup all types of data. Commonly used for storing multi-media presentations for distribution.
- ▶ A **DVD** is read only; it has a very high capacity (4.7 to 17 Gb). It is mainly used to distribute moving image and audio data.
- ▶ A **DVD-R** has a high capacity (4.7 Gb) and can be used to record moving image and audio data.
- ▶ **Flash media** have a medium capacity (128 Mb to 4 Gb) and are used for the transfer and backup of large files.

Chapter 18 Questions

1. A hotel is purchasing new computer hardware and software.

  a) State **two** types of printer that the company could purchase. (2)

  b) For each type of printer describe an appropriate use within the hotel. (4)

  c) Name **two** input devices that would be used. (2)

The hotel manager is considering purchasing himself a Personal Digital Assistant (PDA).

  d) Describe **three** uses he could make of a PDA that would assist him in his work. (6)

2. It is necessary to back up files that are stored on a computer system. For each of the following files state a medium that may be used for backing up. Explain why it is the most appropriate medium.

  a) A multimedia presentation (2)

  b) A word processed letter (2)

  c) A student's ICT coursework that consists of text and graphical images (2)

3. Floppy disk was once the usual medium for distributing software adopted by software houses and developers.

  a) Describe one occasion where it would still be sensible to use a floppy disk for software distribution. (2)

  b) State **two** different ways, other than by floppy disk, in which software can be distributed. Give, with reasons, an example of when each one might be used. (6)

4. Modern personal computer systems usually include a CD-Rewriter. State **two** legal uses for a CD-Rewriter. (2)

June 2002 ICT2

▶ Data stored on computer is vital to the success of any business. The loss of computer files is an extremely serious problem for any organisation, so it is vital that they take steps to protect the integrity and security of their data.

- Data integrity means the **correctness** of the data. Incorrect data may be caused accidentally or by malicious intent.
- Data privacy means keeping data **secret** so that it cannot be accessed by unauthorised users. The Data Protection Act (see Chapter 9) says that *personal* data must be protected but computer users will need to protect all confidential data.
- Data security means ensuring data integrity and data privacy as well as keeping data **safe** from physical loss. Loss could be due to accidental damage or deliberate destruction. Backup is an essential part of ensuring that data is not lost.

The importance of maintaining data security ◀

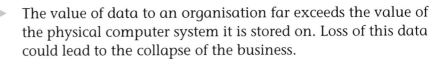

▶ The value of data to an organisation far exceeds the value of the physical computer system it is stored on. Loss of this data could lead to the collapse of the business.

A study by the University of Texas Centre for Research on Information Systems showed that businesses that lose their computer data for ten days or more never recover. The same study found that 90 per cent of data losses were due to accidents such as power failures, water leaks, loose cables, user mistakes, and other hardware, software and human errors.

Protecting data integrity

Data integrity is lost when data is altered in some way, making it incorrect. Such alteration may be caused by errors in data transmission (caused by background noise on the line), input errors (data typed in wrongly), operator errors (for example, an out-of-date version of the file has been loaded), program errors, hardware breakdown, viruses or other computer crime.

A number of measures to protect systems from illegal access, such as data encryption and virus checking, that were discussed in Chapter 7 are appropriate here. A number of further measures can be taken to help minimise the risks to data integrity.

Standard clerical procedures

Loss of data integrity often occurs not as a result of computer malfunction or illegal access, but as a result of user mistakes. For example, yesterday's transaction file could be used to update a master file instead of the correct one for today. This could result in yesterday's transactions being processed twice and today's not at all.

To ensure that such human errors do not occur, very careful operational procedures should be laid out and enforced. Files should be properly labelled and stored in a systematic, predetermined and clear manner. Detailed manual records of the location of files should be maintained.

Write-protect mechanisms

Data can mistakenly be overwritten if the wrong disk or tape is used. Floppy disks and memory sticks are both designed with special slider mechanisms. When the slider is moved to a particular position writing to the disk or the memory stick is prevented. Similarly, certain tapes require a plastic ring to be inserted before the tape can be written to. Care should be taken to write-protect any disk or tape containing data that needs to be preserved.

Password procedures

In a networked system only registered users are allowed access. Each authorised user is allocated an individual user identification code that they will enter to log on to the system. They are then asked to enter a password to confirm that they are indeed the identified user.

Passwords need to be kept private otherwise they have no value. They should be carefully guarded and never revealed to others. A user should take care over her choice of passwords. A password should not be easy to guess. For example, names should be avoided, as should words such as SECRET, SESAME, KEEPOUT. A password should not be too short otherwise it can easily be decoded. Ideally, it should not be a real word but simply a collection of characters, perhaps a mixture of numbers and letters. Some passwords are case sensitive; if so it is a good idea to mix up upper and lower case letters.

For increased security passwords should be changed regularly.

It is essential that a password is never written down. Far too often users write their passwords down in their diary, or on a piece of paper which is kept in an easily accessible desk drawer. Even worse is to write the password on a sticky label that is stuck on the screen of the computer.

Levels of permitted access (see Chapter 7)

Not all the users need to be able to access all the files on a networked system. Access rights should be set up that only allow certain users to have access to specific files or applications. Not all users need to access data in the same way as there are a number of different levels of access that can be permitted. These include:

- **Read only**: the user can view the data in a file but not alter or delete it.
- **Read/write access**: the user can modify data as well as view it.
- **Append access**: the user can add new records but not edit or delete records.
- **Delete access**: the user has the authority to remove a file or record.
- **No access**: a user cannot access the file in any way.

Backup and recovery ◄

What is backup?

Backup means the process of copying files. The purpose of backup is to ensure that if anything happens to the original file, the backup copy can be used to restore the file without loss of data and within a reasonable timescale. Backup is used to avoid permanent data loss and ensure the integrity of the data.

Procedures

Backing up files is not enough by itself to protect a computer system from data loss. An organisation needs to put procedures in place that will allow the lost or corrupted files to be restored by making use of backup copies.

These procedures need to be carefully planned and personnel made aware of them; the methods of recovery should be practised so that, when they are needed, they will run smoothly.

What is backed up?

While emphasis is placed on the need to backup data files, there are other electronically stored files that are crucial to the running of the system.

Without an operating system a computer will be virtually unusable. A modern operating system is complex and requires many stored files. Many of these are specific to the installation and include appropriate device drivers, fonts and control panel settings. Without suitable backup it would be difficult and very time consuming to restore the environment to its original state if the files were corrupted.

Applications, though usually installed from CD-ROMs, are usually customised once installed to meet the specific needs of the user. Without backup, all such customisation could be lost.

In batch processing (see Chapter 16), when a master file is updated the old version is still intact at the end of the process. This provides an automatic backup file. In all other processing modes data is overwritten as transactions occur, so backup copies of the file will need to be made.

case study I
▶ Bank recovers data lost on 9/11

Commerzbank is the world's sixteenth largest bank, handling US $30 billion in transactions every day. It has offices only 100 metres from the World Trade Center towers which were attacked by terrorists on 11 September 2001.

Although its building remained standing, hundreds of windows were shattered, equipment destroyed by smoke and dust and the offices evacuated.

Yet Commerzbank was able to resume business in hours. This was because the bank had a disaster recovery site, 30 miles away in Rye, New York State. The data held at the primary site, such as customer transactions, financial databases and e-mails, were backed up almost immediately to the remote site.

Backup media

Single user backup

An individual user, such as a home user working on a PC, should not ignore the need to backup. There are a number of measures that can be taken to make sure that, in the event of data loss, important files can be restored.

Automatic backup

Many software packages such as Microsoft Word offer automatic backup procedures. When it saves a file, the previous version of this file is saved as a backup. The old version is automatically renamed before the new one is saved. The old file is usually given the same name but a BAK extension. For example, a file named LETTER.DOC would be backed up as LETTER.BAK. The latest version will be saved as LETTER.DOC.

Of course, the second copy will take up disk space and the time to save is longer.

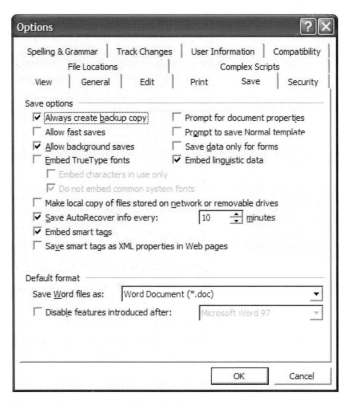

Figure 19.1 Microsoft Word offers an automatic backup copy option and AutoRecovery

Another software feature that maintains data security is the auto save feature. The software will save the work automatically every few minutes. This feature is available in Microsoft Word and Microsoft Excel on the **Tools**, **Options** menu. Click on the **Save** tab.

If correctly set and the system crashes, even if the user has forgotten to save their work, a recovery file has been stored.

Other media

Careful use of automatic backup facilities will not protect a user from hardware problems such as a disk failure.

One way of guarding against disk failure is to use fault tolerant systems such as RAID (Redundant Array of Inexpensive Disks). RAID is a set of two or more disk drives used instead of one disk to store data. By using two disks to store the same data, a fault in a disk is less likely to affect the system.

Another way of guarding against disk failure is to use another medium, such as floppy disks (for small files), memory sticks, external hard drives, CD-R or DVD-R. If you have fast Internet access, you can even backup to a website that offers free file storage.

Network backup

Larger networked systems usually store all the data on a central file server. This means that individual users do not have to backup as all the data can be backed up automatically. As there are likely to be a large number of files to backup they need to use a backup medium with a large capacity. Magnetic tape, although not used commonly for storing data files is very suitable for backup.

Commercial backup

Large businesses with a lot of essential data are likely to use high capacity storage media such as magnetic tape. They may also use an autoloader – a magnetic tape drive that can fetch tapes from a library automatically and load them. This makes unattended large-scale backups possible. They are frequently used when backing up data stored over a network. The volume of data that can be backed up without the need for human intervention has increased hugely and runs into thousands of gigabytes. It is limited only by the number of tapes that the library can hold.

The backup medium used will depend on its capacity, its speed, its cost and the importance of the data.

It is not always necessary to have a device that is dedicated to backup. Smaller businesses and home users may use storage devices for backup that were designed for archiving or transferring data. Examples of these are:

Floppy disk	Very low capacity; suitable for storing a few files.
Memory stick	Easy to use and highly portable. Can store up to 1 Gb.
CD-R and CD-RW (Compact Disk Recordable and Rewritable)	Normally can store up to 700 Mb on each disk
DVD-RAM (Writable Digital Versatile Disk)	Capacity up to 4.7 Gb
External hard drive	Capacity up to 120 Gb. They connect to a USB port and can be used to increase disk capacity or as a backup
Removable cartridge devices	External cartridges such as the *Iomega REV* can store up to 90 Gb. Also connects to a USB port.
Mirroring devices	Usually simply a second hard disk. All data is written to both disks in case one copy is lost.

When to back up

Frequency of backup

How often should a backup be performed? Obviously the more frequent the backup the less out of date will be the data when it is restored. However, when a backup is performed, processor time is tied up and files can be unavailable for use.

An appropriate balance needs to be found and factors such as the time to restore files in the case of failure as well as the importance and nature of the data. Sales data for a supermarket, which affects orders and deliveries, will be backed up hourly, if not more frequently. User data, such as user names and passwords need only be backed up every week.

Time of backup

When should a backup be performed? If a backup is performed daily, it is likely that the backup will take place overnight when computer system use is much less. However, with more and more organisations running 24-hour operations, this is not necessarily the case.

Recording of transactions in a log

Unless a file is backed up after each transaction, which is most unlikely to be feasible, a record will need to be kept of all the transactions that have taken place since the last backup occurred. In the case of file failure, the latest backup copy would be used to restore the file. It could then be brought up to date by rerunning all the transactions stored in the log, that have occurred since the backup was made.

Full or differential backup?

A backup takes time. If the contents of a hard disk are backed up every day, many of the files that are backed up, probably the majority, will not have been altered since the last backup was taken. To keep re-backing up the same data again day after day wastes both time and backup media space.

A backup where all files are copied is known as a **full** or **global backup**.

A **differential backup** only copies files that have been created or changed since the last full backup was made.

An **incremental backup** only copies files that have been created or changed since the last backup (full, differential or incremental). A common backup regime might involve an organisation making a full backup once a week with incremental backups made nightly.

Find out more about backup at http://www.backup4all.com

It is important that after files have been backed up, the backup is verified; in other words it must be checked against the original to ensure that it has been copied exactly. If this is not done, the backup files could prove to be useless and the original file could not be recreated.

Recovery procedures

If the original data files or software files are lost or corrupted, the data can be recovered by using programs that restore the data from the backup files.

It is necessary to restore the files in the correct order by following agreed recovery procedures. The file will first be recreated using the most recent full backup and then each subsequent incremental backup file should be accessed, in time order, to update the file. Any transaction log should then be used to restore the most recent transactions.

If the files are used in the wrong order, the restored file will not be correct. Care must be taken in the careful labelling and organisation of backup tapes and disks to ensure that no mistakes are made.

If the hardware has been damaged, for example, in a fire, it will be necessary to use alternative hardware on a different site either owned by the company as in Case Study 1 or rented from a supplier.

It is important that staff have been trained how to restore data and know exactly what they each have to do. It is likely that these recovery procedures have been practised. It is also necessary to test regularly that the backup has worked. It would be frustrating to go to a backup tape after data has been lost and find that the tape is blank.

Physical security of backup medium

As data can be lost due to disasters such as fire, it is essential that backup files are kept in a separate place from the original files. It is a good idea to take backup media off site. Otherwise a fireproof safe should be used.

case study 2
▶ **A remote backup service**

Backup Direct™ is a British company that offers businesses a daily, automated, off-site backup service. Data from the business's computer is automatically encrypted and backed up after business hours to one of Backup Direct's two state-of-the-art UK data centres.

Using Backup Direct's backups, businesses are guaranteed fast recovery of lost files. All client data held by Backup Direct is stored in compressed and encrypted form. Encryption is carried out using a military grade 112-bit algorithm. Backup Direct and its employees do not possess the ability to decrypt this data.

Backup Direct protect over two million computers worldwide and offer 24/7 telephone support for their clients.

Remote backup has many advantages. Many users forget to perform a backup even though they have a tape drive. Other users think they may be doing a backup correctly, but when they need to restore a file they find out that their tapes are useless. Few users take their tapes offsite so, if they have a fire or other disaster, they lose all their data.

Find out more at: http://www.backupdirect.net/

1. Why is the data compressed?
2. Why is the data encrypted?
3. Give three advantages to an organisation of using the services of Backup Direct.

Activity 2

All too often an ICT student who is approaching a project deadline reports that all his work has been lost due to hard disk failure. Suggest in detail the steps that a student (and you) should take to ensure that work is not lost in this way.

Worked exam question

An international airport is open 24 hours every day of the year. Its computer-based flight information system for arrivals and departures is essential to the smooth running of the airport. Describe **four** factors that the airport must consider when designing backup and recovery procedures for this system. (8)

January 2003 ICT2

▶ **EXAMINER'S GUIDANCE**   *This question is about an airport that it is open 24 hours a day. This must be reflected in the answer. You need to describe four factors. One mark will be for stating the factor the second for describing why it needs to be considered.*

▶ **SAMPLE ANSWER**   Possible answers include:

One factor is the testing of the recovery plan so that they know that it works properly and no data is lost.

Another factor is selecting the backup media to be used so that they never lose data from a large online system which is used 24 hours a day.

Another factor is the location of the backup media. In an airport there may be a danger to backup media. If the media is stored off site, where should it be stored?

Another factor is the training of staff. It is important that everyone knows how to carry out their role and what to do in an emergency.

SUMMARY

Data is a most valuable commodity to organisations.

Data can be lost because of:

- disk failure
- user mistakes
- data theft
- virus attacks
- natural disasters.

Backing up refers to the process of copying files.

Some software packages offer automatic backup facilities such as:

- backup on saving
- auto save

The following factors need to be considered when establishing a backup regime:

- the appropriate medium for backup storage
- the frequency of back up
- when to back up
- what files to back up
- the use of a log to record transactions
- the use of full (global) and/or incremental backups
- the number of generations of backup that should be kept
- whether to use a remote backup service
- where the backup medium is to be stored
- recovery procedures.

For recovery procedures to be successful:

- backup tapes must be kept securely
- files must be restored in the correct order
- backup tapes must be carefully labelled and organised
- alternative hardware must be available if required
- staff must be trained in what they have to do
- recovery procedures must be practised
- backup must be tested regularly.

Chapter 19 Questions

1. Passwords, entered at a keyboard, are often used as a method of protecting data against malicious access. Give **two** other methods of preventing access to data. (2)
January 2002 ICT2

2. A company has procedures to backup the data files held on its computer system on a regular basis so that data can be recovered if it is lost or corrupted. Give **three** other items that need to be considered for the recovery procedure that should also be in place. (3)
June 2005 ICT2

3. A student is working on an ICT project using the computers at her school and her own computer at home. Describe a suitable backup procedure that the student could use. (4)
June 2004 ICT2

4. A company has procedures to backup the data files held on its computer system on a regular basis.
Explain why recovery procedures should also be in place. (3)
January 2002 ICT2

5. An Internet sales company carries out its business with the assistance of a database system running on a network of PCs. The main tasks are the processing of customer orders and the logging of payments. You have been asked to advise the company on backup strategies and to explain their importance.
   a) Give **two** reasons why it is essential that this company has a backup strategy. (2)
   b) State **five** factors that should be considered in a backup strategy, illustrating each factor with an example. (10)
January 2001 ICT2

6. A doctor's surgery has recently converted its manual patient record system to a computer-based system.
   a) Describe **two** methods that the surgery could use to keep these computer-based records secure. (4)
   b) The surgery also needs to ensure the privacy of the records. Using an example from the above system, describe the difference between security and privacy. (3)
June 2003 ICT2

7. Give **two** functions that should be incorporated into a software package to prevent accidental deletion/alteration of data. (2)
June 2002 ICT2

8. All employees of a company have an eight-digit password to access the company's computer network. State **three** rules that the employees should follow to ensure the effective use of the password system. (3)
June 2002 ICT2

9. It is estimated that 25 per cent of companies do not have systematic backup procedures.
   a) Explain why it is necessary for companies to have systematic backup procedures. (2)
   b) In setting up these procedures, one item that has to be considered is which medium to use to store backups. State **three** other items that should be considered in adopting backup procedures. (6)

▶ A computer network consists of two or more computers and peripherals that are linked together.

Stand-alone computer ◀

▶ A computer that is not part of a network is called a **stand-alone** machine. Stand-alone computers can only access data files that are stored on a backing storage device that is linked directly to that computer. To be able to use any peripheral device, such as a printer or scanner, the device will need to be directly linked to the computer. Typically such a computer would have a number of backing storage devices such as hard disk, floppy disk drive and a CD-ROM or DVD drive attached directly to it. All modern computers have a USB port that allows devices such as printers, digital cameras and USB flash memory devices (memory sticks) to be attached. A user of a stand-alone computer has sole use of the data stored on the hard disk; no one else can access it. The computer and installed software can be customised to meet the user's needs exactly.

Most home computers are stand-alone. However, when they are linked to the Internet the stand-alone computer becomes a networked computer.

Networked computer ◀

▶ Data files stored on networked computers can be accessed by different network users. Networked computers can share hardware (such as printers) and software. Very often a networked computer will not have a dedicated printer directly attached. A network will have extra hardware installed to allow the computer to link in to the network; extra cabling may be necessary although the use of wireless networking is quite widespread. To provide the security necessary to prevent unauthorised access, it is usual to present the user with a login screen when the computer is turned on. When several users use the same stand-alone computer, each user must enter a unique code to identify himself to the network operating system together with a secret password to confirm his identity. This is often the case when several users use the same stand-alone computer.

A network user has access to a greater range of disk drives. Some of these are called logical drives as they are merely part of a shared central file server that is used by many users. A user can be allocated their own private space on such a disk (often referred to as the f: drive); other drives, each identified by a different letter, may be shared by a group of users.

It is necessary to plan a network with great care; the number of computers in the network will be an important factor in deciding how it should be set up. It will also be crucial to work out the potential usage at peak times and any likely future expansion of the network.

Advantages of networking computers

- **Hardware can be shared**. Resources such as printers, scanners and modems can be shared, so saving money. A common Internet gateway can be used which can make it easier to maintain security.
- **Data can be shared** rather than each user having their own copy of the data. This could be a centralised database containing details of stock prices and sales data. A standardised template for a word processing package could be stored centrally to allow all users to produce documents in the same format.
- **Improved communication between users**. This is particularly useful for e-mail and sending data accurately so that it does not have to be typed into the computer again (for example, examination board entries, newspaper stories and National Lottery tickets sales). Intranets can be used for publishing company information. Team members can work collaboratively on projects since everyone can access common files.
- **Software can be shared**. When buying a network of say 20 machines, you can buy a network licence to run a program such as Microsoft Office. This will be cheaper than buying 20 copies of Microsoft Office, which you would need to do if you had 20 stand-alone machines. You will only need to install the software once and it will be available to all network stations. With 20 stand-alone machines the software will need to be installed twenty times.
- **Improved security**. Access to the network is only accessible to registered users who have an individual user id which can only be used with a password. Different users can have different access privileges which can restrict the data they can access. There can be greater control over the software that is loaded and stored on to computers; this is especially true if the networked computers do not have individual floppy disk and CD-ROM drives.
- **Backup can be controlled centrally**. One person can be given the responsibility for backing up files rather than rely on individuals to carry out the process.

Advantages of a stand-alone system

- **Fewer hardware requirements**. A network requires extra hardware. Cables, unless wireless connections are used, are needed to link computers together. They may be difficult and expensive to install. Each computer on the network requires a network card; extra devices such as switches or bridges may be required.
- **Reliability of performance**. A stand-alone computer should always work at the same speed whereas a user working at a computer connected to a network may notice a slowing down in response time that may be due to high network traffic or the speed of connection. If the network server fails then every computer in the network will be unable to access the network resources.
- **Fewer security problems**. A virus introduced on one network computer may quickly spread to the rest of the network. A stand-alone computer is only susceptible to viruses through software or files loaded through media such as CD-ROM or floppy disk. The only way for someone else to access your data if it is stored on a stand-alone computer is to physically use that computer.
- **Less ICT knowledge needed**. Any problems occurring will be local to the computer. With a network problems are harder to trace.

case study 1

▶ A graphic design studio

Three graphic designers, Adrian, Mike and Sanjit, have decided to set up a new business together. They will be employing two assistants. They have to decide on the IT equipment they need to buy for the business. One of the decisions they need to make is whether to install a small network or to have stand-alone computers.

If each designer were to have his own computer they would each need specialist peripherals: a scanner and high quality printer. This would prove expensive. However, there would be no need for one of them to wait while a device was in use by someone else, as might occur with a network.

If they chose to install a network the designers and assistants would be able to share data; this would allow two or more of the team to work on the same project.

Software would only need to be installed on one central server so any upgrades could be made quickly, without the need to install it on every computer. On the other hand, the transfer of software and the very large files that would be needed to store the complex graphics of their designs would generate considerable network traffic. This could slow down the response time at the individual computers when all the designers were working.

A network would allow the team to communicate with each other through e-mail, share online diaries and access each other's documents for proofreading. ▶

The designers agreed that if they were to install a network, somebody would have to take responsibility for managing it.

1. Should the designers install a network or maintain stand-alone computers? What would be your recommendation to the designers? Give three reasons to justify your answer.
2. Describe three tasks that would be involved in managing this network.
3. A General Practice team of doctors, nurse, practice manager and receptionist currently uses a number of stand-alone computers to manage patient records, appointments, correspondence and all financial accounts. The practice manager is considering installing a network. Describe three advantages and two disadvantages of installing a network in this particular application.

Activity 1

Carry out the following tasks on a stand-alone computer and a networked computer. Note down *every* difference (however small) that you find in the process. (For example, you may in one case print to a device attached to the computer and in the other case then print to a device on the other side of the room.) How many differences can you find?

1. Switch on and start up the computer.
2. Load a word processing package.
3. Enter some text.
4. Save to a file.
5. Print the document.
6. Close the application.
7. Shut down the computer.

LANs and WANs ◀

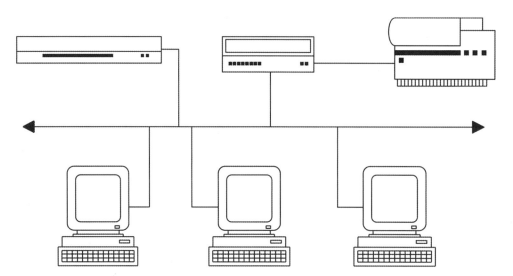

Figure 20.1 A LAN

A network may be restricted to one room or one building or cover a small geographical area. Such a network is called a Local Area Network or **LAN**. It will usually be connected via direct lines – physical links using its own dedicated cables. These can be twisted wire, coaxial or fibre optic cable. The development of wireless networks means that some networks now operate without physical cables. (See page 250.)

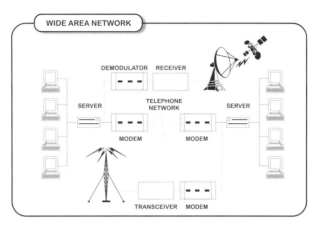

Figure 20.2 A WAN

Alternatively a network may be spread over a wide geographical area, possibly covering different countries. Such a network is called a Wide Area Network or **WAN**. It can be linked by public telecommunications systems such as telephone lines, satellite links and microwave signals.

There has been a great increase in the use of WANs over the past ten years due to the increased importance of the Internet for information and e-commerce, the increased importance of e-mail and the increased speed of transmission and access.

Examples of the use of WANs include: airline, theatre and hotel booking systems; home banking; bank ATMs; the National Lottery; e-mail; videoconferencing; stock control. The Internet is a huge WAN, but there are many other WANs as well.

case study 2
▶ Networking in an FE college

Faxton College is based on two sites, a mile and a half apart. All the students on the main site are full time students aged 16–19; the second site is used for part-time adult courses. All financial, examination support and personnel functions are carried out at the main site. Each site has had its own LAN for several years and both have been managed by the shared IT team. Software had to be installed and maintained on two servers, one for each site. Computers were connected by cable.

A few years ago, the IT Manager decided to link the two LANs with a WAN. The link between the two LANs was established using a dedicated telephone line. Central file servers in one site hold the database files management information software for the whole college and staff on both sites share the software and access common information. One further outcome of installing a WAN means that files can be backed up in a different location.

Examination question

Three colleges in a large city are to merge and become a single college spread across the three sites. Each college has a LAN and these networks are to be joined together to form a WAN.

a) Explain two differences between a LAN and a WAN   (4)

b) Give two advantages to the merged college of using the new WAN.   (2)

c) State two problems that could occur when using the new WAN.   (2)

January 2004 ICT 2

Server-based networks and peer-to-peer networks ◄

▶ There are two different types of local area networks.

Server-based networks

Server-based LANs have a central computer called a server. Other computers in the network are called clients. Devices are treated as either servers or clients; they cannot be both.

Servers provide central services such as backup and software installation as well as providing centralised storage of data files. This central storage provides a pool of data that is accessible to all workstations on the network. Clients send requests for services, such as the retrieval of data or printing, to the appropriate server which carries out the required processing. Some processing tasks are carried out by the server and others on the client computer.

As software is installed centrally, it only has to be installed once. Backup is easy to perform and there is no need to rely on users backing up their own files.

Individual users can be set up centrally with appropriate access rights. Each user is allocated a user name, a password and disk space on the server. Security is therefore very high.

Large LANs may have more than one server. The performance of this sort of network is heavily dependent on the servers. They need to have fast processing speeds, large main and backing storage. They are therefore relatively expensive and server-based networks can be complicated to install. If a server fails then the clients on the network cannot access the resources provided by the server.

Peer-to-peer LANs

A peer-to-peer LAN is a very simple network that provides shared resources to the computers that make it up. All the computers in the network have the same status and there is no central server.

Computers on a peer-to-peer network can access files and devices on another linked computer providing the appropriate access privileges have been set. Any computer can communicate and exchange data with any other on the network. Such a network cannot have complete security.

Installing software takes more time, as it has to be installed on each station. Backing up must also be done separately for each individual station.

As a server is expensive to buy, a small peer-to-peer network would probably be much cheaper than a small server-based network. A peer-to-peer network would be ideal in a small office where four PCs need to be networked to share data.

Both types of LAN can share printers and other peripherals such as scanners. Both types of network can be used to send and receive e-mails from other network users.

Worked exam question

The manager of a small hotel uses a stand-alone computer to administer the booking and billing systems. He is considering setting up a small local area network to replace the stand-alone computer, with workstations in reception, in his office and in the dining room.

a) State **two** different types of network that would be suitable. (2)

b) i) Give **two** advantages of this change for the **manager**. (2)

ii) Give **two** advantages of this change for his **customers**. (2)

▶ EXAMINER'S GUIDANCE

a) This part of the question is straightforward bookwork; you should have no difficulty gaining 2 marks with the answer: server-based or peer-to-peer. You could also have chosen two topologies from bus, ring or star. However, don't mix the two – an answer of peer-to-peer and ring, for example, or peer-to-peer and star.

For parts (b) and (c) you have to first think a bit about how the network would be used in the hotel and what effect it might have before trying to answer the question. The computer in reception would probably be used for making reservations and producing bills for guests when they have completed their stay. The restaurant computer would be used to record all details of meals consumed by guests to be included in their bill. The manager would use his computer to check on current level of bookings and for planning purposes. He would have access to all the information that would be available at the reception desk. He could e-mail his restaurant and reception staff.

You are asked about advantages of the networked system – but generalised advantages will not do.

Part (b) asks you to look at the system from the manager's perspective and give two advantages of linking the three computers into a network.

▶ SAMPLE ANSWER

He will be able to communicate with his staff at all times (1); because all three computers are able to access the same records he will always have access to up-to-date information (1) which he can use for realistic planning (1). He can access the information from any of the three computers (1)

▶ EXAMINER'S GUIDANCE

For part (c) you need to change focus and consider the networked system from the customer's point of view. This is a bit trickier as the customer will not be using a computer himself. What do customers do? They make bookings, they consume meals and they pay their bill and check out.

Elements of a network environment ◀

Figure 20.3 A network interface card

Hardware

Extra hardware is required when linking computers together to form a network.

Network interface card

To connect a computer to a local area network a network interface card is needed. The card is an electronic printed circuit that fits inside the computer into an empty slot on the computer's motherboard (main printed circuit). It allows the computer to be recognised by the network and allocates it a unique identifying number. The network interface card determines the maximum speed of data transmission that will be available around the network.

Cabling

Cables are the most common form of transmission media used to connect network stations to the rest of the network. The network cabling connects to the network card. They are usually made of copper wire. Common examples are Ethernet cabling (coaxial like a television aerial) and UTP (Unshielded Twisted Pair) cabling. Fibre optic cables are becoming more common; they are faster than copper cabling but more expensive. Different types of cable have different physical capacities; this affects the speed that data can be transmitted around the network.

Bridge

A bridge is a device which allows two local area networks to be linked, thus extending the network. This may be necessary if a network has reached a maximum size, either in the number of terminals covered or in the distance covered. An intelligent bridge can enhance security by only allowing messages from designated workstations to cross the bridge.

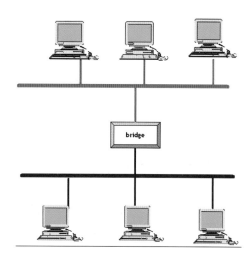

Figure 20.4 Diagram of a bridge

Repeater

Transmitted signals deteriorate as they travel longer distances until they reach a stage when they are unrecognisable. To prevent this happening, a repeater is installed between segments in the network. A repeater is an electronic device that receives a signal and outputs it in boosted form.

Modem

A modem is a device that can be plugged into a computer or, more usually, housed inside a computer. It is connected to a telephone line and provides access to a wide area network. The modem (standing for modulator/demodulator) converts the digital signal that is used within the computer into analogue form that is required for transmission over a telephone wire.

case study 3
▶ The National Lottery

The National Lottery, run by Camelot, sells tickets in around 35,000 retail outlets. Tills in all the retailers are connected to Camelot's wide area network either by cable or by satellite. As lottery tickets are sold, details of the numbers chosen are entered by optical mark reading (OMR).

The data is transmitted to Camelot's computer centre in Rickmansworth, Hertfordshire. The network needs to be very sophisticated to cope with the large volumes of sales (particularly early in the evening before the draw is made) which have reached over 50,000 transactions a minute. Camelot say that the network has been designed to cope with considerably more traffic than this.

1. What data needs to be transmitted from a lottery network station to the central computer?
2. Give five reasons why Camelot use a WAN for collecting data from shops.
3. Describe the hardware that would be needed to enable lottery sales in a new store.

Wireless networks

Cables are no longer necessary to connect network stations. A wireless network does not need cables. At present wireless networks are not as fast as conventional networks but are very useful when connecting portable laptop computers to a network, operating in temporary buildings or operating where conventional cabling is impossible to install.

Wireless networks require a transmitter, which transmits via an antenna to a wireless network card fitted into the computer. Antennae have a limited range and a line of sight may be required.

Software

A special **network operating system** is required to enable the running and management of a network. It sets up the correct protocols to be used across the network. A **protocol** is a standard set of rules that defines how communications take place between computers.

The use of protocols means that a network does not have to be restricted to one manufacturer's equipment; it allows for the existence of what are known as open systems. This means that several disparate pieces of equipment can be connected together and can be expected to communicate effectively. A network could have some Dell computers and a number of Sony ones that could all intercommunicate.

It is important that a network offers different users different levels of access.

The network manager will have unlimited access to all areas and drives. The manager will need greater privileges than ordinary users, in order to install new software, add and delete users, set up menus and so on. The manager's programs obviously must be protected by passwords.

Users, however, need read/write access to a dedicated area of the disk where their files are saved, read-only access to some areas (for example, where software is loaded from) and no access at all to other areas (for example, other user areas).

Communications ◀

Connecting to the Internet

The speed at which a networked computer can receive data depends on the **bandwidth**. A home computer connected to the Internet through a modem can only operate at the speed of the modem typically 56 Kbps (kilobits per second). In fact, error checking procedures mean that even these relatively slow speeds are not achieved. ISDN digital telephone lines offer faster speeds of 128 Kbps.

In practice these are still too slow and demand has grown for greater bandwidth and faster Internet access. Many companies now offer broadband technology using fibre optic cables offering speeds of at least 2 Mbps (megabits per second). However, these speeds are still slow compared with LANs that have speeds of 100 Mbps.

Asymmetrical Digital Subscriber Line (ADSL) technology has been developed to give broadband performance using a standard copper telephone cable. Special hardware and efficient compression techniques mean that ADSL can operate at speeds of around 2 Mbps. It is called asymmetrical because it can download (or receive data) at speeds of 2 Mbps but upload (or send) data at speeds of 256 Kbps.

As most Internet users receive a lot of data and only send e-mails, ADSL is an attractive option and cheaper than dedicated fibre optic cables. It is not suitable when a user needs to send data at high speeds, e.g. net hosting.

Topology

A topology is like a schematic map. An underground map of London shows you how the stations link together, rather than the exact path taken by the tracks with all the twists and turns. In the same way a network topology shows how the computers link together, rather than the detailed path of every cable.

There are several possible topologies, but the most common are the star, the ring and the bus.

Star topology

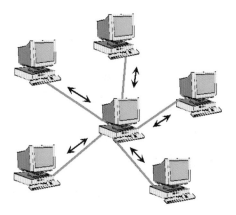

Figure 20.5 Star topology

In a star topology, each computer is connected to a central host server by a dedicated cable. The central server is a high specification computer with a fast processing speed and large main storage (RAM). This central computer controls the network and stores the network operating system. All data from one computer to another passes only through the central computer and none of the other computers in the network.

Advantages of a star topology

There are several advantages that arise from the fact that in a star network each computer is connected through a dedicated cable to the central computer. If a cable linking one user computer to the central computer fails, the other user computers are not affected. It is easy for technicians to find the cause of a fault and it is easy to add extra user computers without disturbing the network. There are fewer problems of lack of security as only the two computers involved in a data transfer have access to the data. The star network provides a consistent level of performance, even when it is being heavily used, as each computer has a dedicated cable.

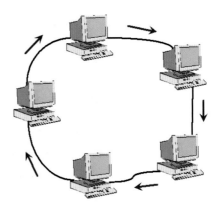

Figure 20.6 Ring topology

Ring Topology

In a ring network all the computers are connected, one to another, to form a closed loop. There is not necessarily a main computer acting as server; if there is a server, it is just one computer in the ring. Communication is achieved by passing data around the ring in one direction; all the data passes through all the computers. This makes the data less secure than in a star network. As the cabling is organised in a loop, adding a new computer can only be achieved by closing down the whole network whilst the installation occurs.

Advantages of a ring topology

The ring network allows for very fast transmission rates. It is not dependent on a single, central computer. It is cheap to install as a file server is not strictly necessary and there is a minimum of cabling required.

Bus Topology

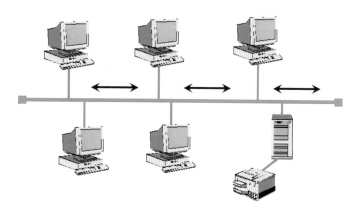

Figure 20.7 Bus topology

In a bus network there is one main cable, terminated at either end, to which all computers are joined. A computer transferring data transmits in both directions along the bus and the receiving computer picks up the response. The message is accessible to all computers linked in to the network which can cause security problems. If the main cable fails, all the computers are affected.

Advantages of a bus topology

A bus network is cheap to install as only one main cable is required. It is straightforward and the easiest topology to install; extra computers can be added easily too.

SUMMARY

▶ A **computer network** consists of two or more computers and peripherals that are linked together.

▶ A **stand-alone computer** is a computer that has no connection to any other computer.

Advantages of networking computers	Advantages of a stand-alone system
▶ Hardware can be shared	▶ Fewer hardware requirements
▶ Data can be shared	▶ Reliability of performance
▶ Improved communication between users	▶ Fewer security problems
▶ Software can be shared	▶ Less ICT knowledge needed
▶ Improved security	
▶ Back up can be controlled centrally	

▶ A Local Area Network (**LAN**) is a number of computers that are linked together. Direct physical connection using cables is possible. It may be restricted to one room or one building or cover a small geographical area.

▶ A Wide Area Network (**WAN**) is a number of computers and/or LANs that are linked together and spread over a wide geographical area, possibly covering different countries using a range of telecommunications links.

▶ A server-based **LAN** is a local area network that has a central computer called a server. Other computers in the network are called clients. Devices are treated as either servers or clients, they cannot be both. Servers provide central services for the clients which are operated by the users.

▶ A peer-to-peer **LAN** is a very simple network that provides shared resources to the computers that make it up. All the computers in the network have the same status and there is no central server.

Elements of a network environment

Hardware

Extra hardware is required when linking computers together to form a network including:

▶ network interface card

▶ cabling

▶ bridge

▶ repeater

▶ modem.

Software

A special **network operating system** is required to enable the running and management of a network.

A **protocol** is a standard set of rules that defines how communications take place between computers.

▶ Topologies

The **topology** of a network is the description of the network in terms of its layout.

Star topology: each computer is connected to a central host server by a dedicated cable.

Ring topology: all the computers are connected one to another to form a closed loop.

Bus topology: consists of one main cable, terminated at either end, to which all computers are joined.

Chapter 20 Questions

1. A school has a local area network (LAN).

   a) Describe **two** advantages to the students of using a LAN rather than stand-alone computers. (4)

   b) State **two** disadvantages to the students of using a LAN rather than stand-alone computers. (2)

   June 2005 ICT2

2. The term used to describe the arrangement of computers in a network is topology. One type of LAN topology is a star.

   a) Draw a diagram to illustrate a star topology showing the direction of flow of data. (1)

   b) Name **two** other LAN topologies. For each draw a diagram to illustrate the topology showing the direction of flow of data. (4)

   c) State **one** different advantage for each topology that you have chosen. (2)

3. A personal computer (PC) can be connected to a Local Area Network (LAN).

   a) Describe the extra hardware required for a PC to be linked to a LAN. (2)

   b) Describe the extra software required for a PC to be linked to a LAN. (2)

   c) Describe the extra hardware required for a PC to be linked to a WAN. (2)

4. A local area network can be a peer-to-peer network or a client server network.

   a) Explain the term peer-to-peer network. (2)

   b) Describe when it would be appropriate to install a peer-to-peer network. (2)

   c) Explain the term client-server network. (2)

   d) Describe **two** advantages of a client-server network. (4)

5. A small company that develops games software employs several program developers as well as administrative staff. The company has installed a local area network. The developers sometimes use their computers in 'stand-alone' mode rather than as part of the network.

   a) Explain **one** advantage to the developers of using their computers in 'stand-alone' mode. (2)

   b) Describe **two** advantages to the company of installing the network. (4)

   c) State **two** items of hardware that are required when joining a computer to a local area network. (2)

   d) Name and explain the purpose of the item of software that will be required when the local area network is installed. (3)

▶ The **Human/Computer Interface** (HCI) is the point of interaction between people and computer systems. The HCI aims to make it easier for humans to communicate with the computer. In particular, the HCI looks at

- the choice of hardware devices (both input and output devices)
- the look and feel of the software including screen layout design

Designing the HCI ◀

▶ The design of how humans and computer systems interact is crucial to the successful use of a computer system. The choice of HCI will depend on the application and the needs of the user.

- If an application requires large amounts of text to be entered then the most appropriate form of interface will probably involve a keyboard. However, human/computer communication is not just entering data at the keyboard and reading text on the screen. A voice recognition system may be more appropriate.
- Software for use in a primary school will need screen designs to be very simple with visual clues as the children may not be able to read very well. A concept keyboard with pictures overlaid on to a pressure sensitive pad may be more suitable than the standard keyboard.
- A computer system that controls machinery in a factory would require a very different interface. The operator might be working on machinery that requires the use of his hands and the environment might be dirty. The use of voice data entry, based on a simple set of commands, might be most appropriate in such a situation.
- Adventure games have video-quality graphics and CD quality sound. A keyboard or mouse would not be quick enough as an input device – a joystick – is needed.

The earliest computers had interfaces that were not user-friendly and could only be used by people with extensive technical knowledge. As the capabilities of computers have increased, HCIs have improved.

The use of graphics is now used extensively in HCIs. As the memory capacity and the processing speeds of computers have increased, the use of graphics has become more widespread.

Icons – tiny pictures designed to convey an easily understood meaning – are fast and easy to interpret and are not language specific.

Sound can be a feature of a HCI. Audible error messages can alert a user, for example, if you press the CAPS LOCK key. Printer drivers can include sounds so that users get audible messages such as 'Please load paper in the cut sheet feeder' or 'There is a paper jam in the printer'.

An HCI should be easy to use, appropriate for the users, safe and robust.

Types of interface ◀

Command line interface

A command line interface is an interface where the user types in commands for the computer to interpret and carry out. For example, to run a word processing program the user may have to type in WORD.

As the command is typed in, it appears on the screen. The user has to know the commands and there are no clues to help guess them.

The screen is usually monochrome and **C:>** (called the C prompt) appears on the left of the screen. This means that the computer is looking at drive C – its internal hard drive. Any file references typed in refer to that drive.

The MS-DOS operating system uses a command line interface. Some operating systems, such as Unix and Linux, use both command line interfaces and graphical user interfaces.

Figure 21.1 shows a typical command line in the Unix operating system. The **ls** command lists the files in the current, or specified, directory. It has many options; **-l** produces a long (detailed) listing.

Figure 21.1 Unix command line interface

Many commands are complex. There may be additional parameters, usually extra letters at the end of the command that modify its meaning.

For example, in MS-DOS to get a directory the user has to type in **DIR** and press Enter.

DIR/P gives the same list but pauses at the bottom of the screen and waits for a key to be pressed before continuing.

DIR/W gives the same list but displays the files in columns on the screen. W stands for wide.

DIR A: gives a list of files on floppy drive A.

The user has to learn all these commands. As a result command line interfaces are normally only used by experienced and expert users. For someone with little experience they can be very frustrating and frequent reference to manuals may be needed.

Little computer memory is required for command line interfaces. Complex commands can be entered quickly in one line. Precise sequences of instructions can be entered allowing complex tasks to be performed. The first computers, with tiny memory and limited processing power used a command line interface.

Figure 21.2 The C prompt

Menu-based interface

A menu-based user interface is a form of interface that displays a set of choices on the screen so that the user can make a selection from the range of choices offered. They can operate in a number of ways:

- The selections may be numbered and the option selected by pressing a number key.
- The user may scroll through the selections using the cursor keys or a mouse until the required option is highlighted and then press enter.
- If a touch screen is used, the user touches the screen at the place where the chosen option appears.

Choosing one option may lead to a submenu. A balance needs to be made between the number of options on a screen at one time and the number of levels of submenu required. The more levels needed the longer the system takes to operate and the user is more likely to get irritated.

Figure 21.3 An iPod uses a full screen menu interface

A menu-based interface can only deal with situations where the user's requirements are known in advance as the user is limited to the predetermined choices that are built into the menus. A menu-based interface is easy to use and appropriate for relatively inexperienced and occasional users of a system.

A well designed menu-based interface should have a consistent layout. It should use the same prompt for the same operation in all menus and the prompt should be in the same position on the screen.

You have probably seen menu-based user interfaces in the following applications:

■ Mobile phone
■ An MP3 player such as an iPod
■ Digital camera
■ A bank cash machine

case study 1
▶ Mobile phones and HCI

Mobile phones use menu-based user interfaces. There are a variety of different interface techniques to make phones easy to use. These include:
■ A hierarchy of menus and submenus.
■ One submenu is an address book so that you can select commonly used numbers from a list.
■ The names in the address book appear in an alphabetical list for easy selection.
■ Pressing a letter takes you to all the names beginning with that letter.
■ Some phones use voice recognition to select a name from the list.
■ Predicted text makes it quicker to enter text messages.
■ Silent mode means that a call can be received in sensitive areas

1. What are the submenus on your mobile phone?

Graphical user interface

A Graphical User Interface (GUI) is a form of interface that uses high-resolution graphics, icons and pointers to make the computer as user-friendly as possible. Options can be chosen easily with a pointing device – usually a mouse.

A GUI is sometimes called a WIMP environment as it uses:

■ Windows
■ Icons
■ Menus and
■ Pointers.

GUIs were first developed for the Apple Macintosh but soon afterwards Microsoft Windows was developed as a GUI for the PC. GUIs tend to be resource hungry; they need a lot of memory and disk space and take time to load. However, today's computers are more than powerful enough to cope with a GUI.

case study 2
▶ Railway ticket machines

Automatic ticket machines are common at many railway and underground stations. These machines use a GUI to allow customers to purchase a ticket quickly and easily without having to queue in a ticket office. Customers use a touch screen to choose their destination from a list and the type of ticket, such as single or return. Payment is by credit card; the ticket machine can automatically read the card details from the magnetic strip on the back.

A touch screen is used because:

- ■ it is more durable than other pointing devices such as a mouse
- ■ it is easy to operate, even for the inexperienced user.

The instructions for use are printed on the screen and are very simple to use. The user has few decisions to make. The HCI is robust and very easy to use.

Figure 21.4 An Underground ticket machine uses a GUI

Features of GUIs ◀

Windows

A window is a rectangular division of the screen that holds the activity of a program. There can be several windows on the screen at the same time. The user can switch between windows and change the size and shape of the windows. The active window – the one in which the user is currently working on – appears in front.

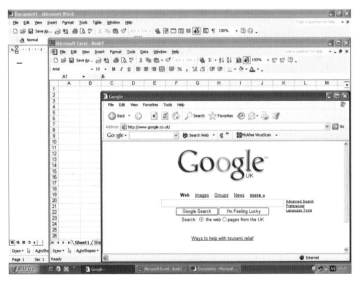

Figure 21.5 Three windows on one screen

A dialogue box (dialog box in the USA) is a window that appears on the screen when information is wanted from the user.

For example, a wizard can be used in Microsoft Access to create a report. Several dialogue boxes appear on the screen, one after the other, asking the user to choose settings so that the report appears as the user wants.

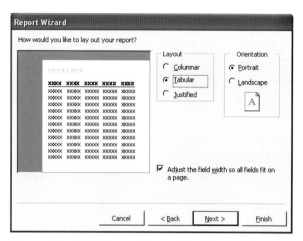

Figure 21.6 A dialogue box in the Microsoft Access report wizard

Icons

An icon is a small picture on the screen. Clicking on the icon performs an action such as saving a file. The same action can be performed using the menu system but the icon is used as a short cut. The action performed when you click on an icon should be easily recognisable from the image.

Today icons are used in nearly all software. Icons used in different programs are often very similar, as most software will use icons to open files, save files, etc.

Icons can be grouped together in toolbars on the screen. In many applications packages, icons and toolbars can be customised to suit the user. Icons can be added or removed. The image on an icon can be edited.

Software like Microsoft Word offers large icons which are useful for people with a visual impairment or who find it difficult clicking on a small icon.

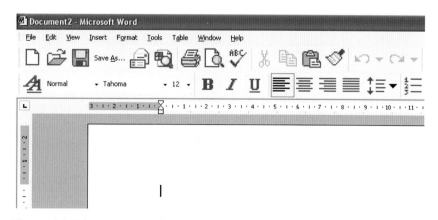

Figure 21.7 Large icons in Microsoft Word

Figure 21.8 A pull-down menu

Menus

A pull-down menu is a menu that expands downward when selected with a mouse or other pointer. The user then scrolls through the options and clicks a second time to make the selection. Windows software typically has a menu bar of pull-down menus across the top of the screen.

A pop-up menu is a similar menu that expands upward when clicked on with the pointing device. In Microsoft Excel and Microsoft Word, the Drawing toolbar typically appears at the bottom of the screen. When you click on an item on this toolbar, a pop-up menu appears.

In most Windows software if you click the right mouse button a shortcut menu appears. If you right click near the top of the screen, a pull-down menu appears. If you click near the bottom of the screen a pop-up menu is displayed.

In many applications packages, menus can be customised to suit the user. Options can be removed, new options added, whole menus removed or new menus added.

Pointers

A mouse is a very common pointing device and can easily be used for selecting a choice from a menu or pointing to any place on the screen. However, there are other pointing devices associated with GUIs. A laptop computer usually has a built-in touch pad. If a computer is to be used by members of the public, a mouse may not be robust enough. In this case a touch screen is often used. A tracker ball may be used in a similar way.

WYSIWYG software

A very useful feature of modern word processing and DTP packages is that they provide a screen display that is identical to the version that will be printed. The display exactly reflects layout, font, highlighting (such as bold and italic) as well as other features. This is known as WYSIWYG. (What You See Is What You Get — pronounced wizzy-wig)

Early word processing packages did not support WYSIWYG. The user had to insert codes that denoted formatting such as bold or italics. Special symbols on the screen were used to represent formatting. For example to put a heading in bold, it might look like this on the screen.

<b>What You See Is What You Get<b>

Often the only way to see exactly what a document was going to look like was to print it out, which led to many draft copies being produced before a final version was arrived at. Considerable amounts of paper could be wasted.

The high-quality monitors, fast processing speeds and large memory of today's computers mean that WYSIWYG software is standard. With WYSIWYG it is possible to see and manipulate the eventual layout of the document on the screen with much greater ease.

On-screen forms

On-screen forms are widely used to enter into a computer system. Forms are used to capture a standard set of data items, for example, when ordering goods or filling in a questionnaire.

On-screen forms reduce the chances of an error because the user is prompted to fill in each field in turn. Forms can be designed so that if an essential field has been left blank, the form will not be accepted until this field has been filled in.

It is a good idea for on-screen forms to mimic the style of paper forms, so that it is intuitive for an inexperienced user. On-screen forms should be filled in from left to right and from top to bottom like paper forms. On-screen forms should also enable the user to go back to make changes.

On-screen forms can include check boxes for yes/no fields and can allow the user to choose from a menu or list, where appropriate. This has several advantages; it restricts the user to allowable options, reduces the possibility of error and is usually faster. Choices can be made from a menu using a drop-down (or combo) box or by using option buttons.

Another way of speeding up data entry is to use default settings – the most likely entry is provided and it can be accepted or rejected by pressing a key to move the cursor to the next field on the form.

If there are a lot of questions, more than one screen per form is needed and the form should be split up into logical divisions. For example, a paper booking form for a holiday might require information on customer, holiday destination, mode of travel and car hire all on the same page. This would not fit onto one screen. The form could be split up to have one screen for each of the sections mentioned.

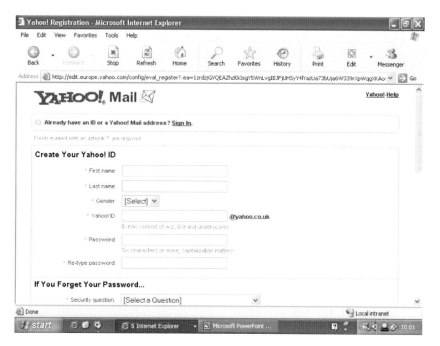

Figure 21.9 An on-screen form at Yahoo Mail

Advantages and disadvantages of various types of interface

◀

	Advantages	Disadvantages
Command Line Interface	✓ Little computer memory is required ✓ Wide variety of commands ✓ Commands entered quickly on one line	✗ Commands are complex ✗ The user has to learn all the commands
Menu-based interface	✓ Easy to use ✓ Uses little computer memory ✓ Can include short cuts ✓ Suitable for devices with small screens such as a mobile phone	✗ Only suitable where there is a choice of actions ✗ There may be several submenus
Graphical User Interface	✓ Easy to use and intuitive ✓ Flexible – many uses ✓ Uses graphics to show meaning ✓ Can use a variety of pointing devices ✓ Can be customised to suit the user ✓ Can include online help	✗ Needs a lot of memory ✗ Needs more disk space than menu driven or command line ✗ Takes time to load
Form-based interface	✓ Similar in style to paper forms ✓ Easy and intuitive to use ✓ Can use a variety of data entry techniques such as drop-down boxes ✓ Can be automatically validated	It is a version of a GUI so it also: ✗ needs a lot of memory ✗ needs more disk space than menu driven or command line ✗ takes time to load

case study 3
▶ **Travel agency**

A travel agent uses an information system to help customers choose their holidays. Different types of user use the system in different ways.

Customers can interrogate a local offline system to find details of all the holidays on offer. Many customers will not have good IT skills. The use of a touch screen might be appropriate so that the user can simply select from a number of choices on the screen to obtain the information they require. The user will not be required to enter any data other than choices. The layout of the screen should be simple and uncluttered to attract the user. The text should be large and good use should be made of colour. There could be a built-in printing device so

▶

that the customer can print out the details of any holiday that meets their requirements.

Travel agents based in the branches use the system to make bookings on behalf of clients. The system that they use could be built around a menu and forms dialogue. Although the agents will be regular users, using the system will only be part of their job, so it will need to be straightforward. Most of the data will be entered using a keyboard, although a mouse or similar pointing device would be used to make menu selections.

ICT specialist staff at the head office set up the system and maintain the accuracy of the database. These users are expert and would spend the majority of their working time using the system. They are likely to be using the system in a variety of ways and will be very knowledgeable about its workings. For these specialists, a command line interface might be the most appropriate as they could carry out complex tasks in the minimum of time.

case study 4
▶ HCIs and disabilities

ICT offers many opportunities for people with disabilities, particularly those who have difficulty communicating. There are various computer adaptations available for people who cannot use a mouse or keyboard or who cannot see a normal monitor too well.

Someone who can operate a pointing device like a mouse but not a standard keyboard can use an on-screen keyboard. This provides point-and-click access to standard keyboard letters, whole words and communication phrases.

Someone unable to operate a keyboard or a mouse may use a computer system with speech recognition.

Output can be to large screens, spoken – i.e. created by speech synthesis – or in the form of Braille to help users with poor eyesight.

Common user interfaces shared between generic packages

▶ Many Microsoft generic packages like Microsoft Excel and Microsoft Word have a similar look and feel as they share common interface features. Examples of these features include:

- identical icons such as cut, copy and paste
- similar toolbars
- similar pull-down menus – File, Edit, View, etc – with similar contents

- help facilities can be accessed by pressing F1
- common error messages.

There are many similarities between the layouts of Microsoft Excel and Microsoft Word as can be seen from these screenshots

Figure 21.10 Common interfaces of Microsoft Excel and Microsoft Word

These similarities make it easy for a user to learn to use a new package, as many of the commands and methods of operation will already be familiar and they will already be able to carry out basic procedures. With this knowledge, they are more likely to have the confidence to investigate the working of other, new features for themselves. The training costs for an organisation will thus be reduced and the productivity of staff will be increased.

The advantages of producing a screen layout with which users are immediately comfortable has resulted in standards for screen design. Most Windows software uses pull-down menus. The first menu is always the File menu. It nearly always contains commands such as New, Open, Close, Save, Print, and Exit.

Interface features that are commonly shared

Some of the features that have become standard in many packages include:

- the layout of the screen – common toolbars have icons in the same place
- the names given to commands (e.g. open a file rather than load)
- the shape, colour and design of icons are similar
- the order that the menus appear on the menu bar and the way in which options are allocated to menus (e.g. the 'File' menu is the first one on the menu bar and the first option in 'File' is usually 'New')
- the cut, copy and paste commands
- print and print preview commands
- the layout and contents of dialogue boxes.

Activity 1

For this activity you need to have access to a software package with which you are unfamiliar. Ideally it should be produced by the same manufacturer as a package which you have used and of which you have a good understanding. For example, you may be a confident user of Microsoft Word who has made use of Microsoft Excel but have never used Microsoft FrontPage or Windows Movie Maker.

Load up the unknown package and explore it. Note down all the features with which you are already familiar — you can include anything here from familiar icons to printing methods. Use the Help facility to find out how to use unknown features in the package.

Activity 2

Design an interface for each of the following systems. For each system specify hardware devices, type of interface (such as command line, menu-based, GUI) as well as designing any necessary screens.

- A simple painting program for young children
- An information system for use by tourists that gives information about a town's highlights
- A theatre booking system

Ten rules for good interface design ◀

1. All system interfaces should be consistent and should look, act and feel the same throughout. Keep the layout clear. Too much on one screen will make it cluttered and confusing.
2. Put features such as headings, error messages and requests for user responses in a consistent location.
3. Make good use of colour and contrast. Do not, for example, use red on a green background.
4. Make sure your text is not too big or too small. Stick to one clear font.
5. Start at the top left of the page and work down.
6. Don't use jargon, particularly with inexperienced users.
7. Whenever you are deleting work or closing a program, confirm all requests for action from the user; for example, 'Are you sure? Y/N'.
8. Make sure that the choices in a menu are easily distinguished from each other. Leave plenty of blank space between them.
9. Keep the level of complexity appropriate to the experience of the expected user. If the level is too high, the user will become confused. If it is too low, the user will be bored and make errors due to lack of attention.
10. Use the same name throughout for the same thing. For example, stick to the word 'save' and don't use 'keep', 'store' or 'write.'

Natural language interface

◄

► In the real world humans communicate in natural language such as English. A natural language computer interface, where humans and computers could communicate in normal English would be enormously advantageous.

Natural language is extremely flexible and powerful. However, to interpret natural language, a computer needs it to be precise with a limited number of commands and strict syntax rules.

English is not like this. It is not precise and has a huge vocabulary. New words appear and the meanings of other words change over time. Sentences can be ambiguous. It is only when the context and tone are taken into account that the meaning is clear.

It is not yet possible to develop systems that accept a natural language but some systems have been developed using a limited subset of a natural language by restricting instructions to a limited number of commands.

Commands are usually typed in at a keyboard, but if such a system is combined with speech recognition, there is potential for humans and computers to have a limited dialogue.

Pure natural language interfaces may still be the stuff of science fiction but there are many research projects exploring the possibilities of talking to computers. The Spoken Language Systems (SLS) Group at MIT's (Massachusetts Institute of Technology) Laboratory of Computer Science has been trying to get computers to communicate the same way as humans since 1989. Progress has been made as can be seen from the following excerpt from a conversation between a user and JUPITER, an SLS-based weather forecasting system.

User: Yes I would like the weather forecast for London, England, please.
JUPITER: In London in England Wednesday partly cloudy skies with periods of sunshine. High 82 and low 63. Is there something else?
User: What is that in degrees Celsius, please?
JUPITER: In London in England Wednesday partly cloudy skies with periods of sunshine. High 28 and low 17. What else?

Check out their progress at their website:

http://www.sls.lcs.mit.edu/sls/whatwedo

The search engine Ask Jeeves (http://ask.com/) uses a system called Natural Language Processing (NLP) that allows the user to ask questions in natural language. It builds up a bank of questions and uses these to help interpret new ones.

With NLP, Jeeves appears able to understand the context of the question and so can offer answers and suggestions in the same human terms in which we all communicate.

In Microsoft Office software, such as Microsoft Word, if you press F1 a help dialogue box appears. You can type in a natural language question to get help.

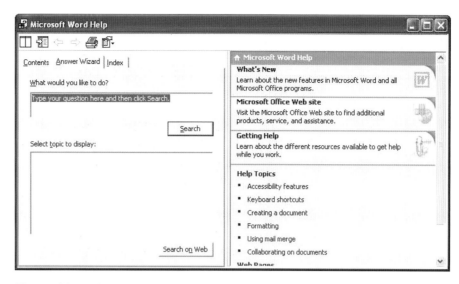

Figure 21.11 Microsoft Word help

Ambiguities in language

One of the problems in creating a natural language interface is the fact that natural languages like English can be ambiguous. For example, the word '*lead*' has several meanings. It can mean the leash for a dog. It can mean the person in front in a race. Pronounced differently it can mean the writing part of a pencil. The written sentence: '*I want the lead*' could mean:

a) *I want the leash for my dog*
b) *I want the lead to put in my pencil*
c) *I want to be in front*

The word 'by' is interpreted in different ways in different contexts:

'The lost children were found by the searchers' … (who)
'The lost children were found by the mountain' … (where)
'The lost children were found by nightfall' … (when)

The structure of a sentence can also be ambiguous. If you were to say: 'My car needs oiling badly' would you really want someone to make a bad job of oiling your car? What do you make of the sentence: 'Fruit flies like a banana'?

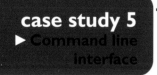

case study 5
▶ Command line interface

Ping

When network developers are installing a new network, they use a utility program called **ping** to test that one computer on the network is connected to another.

Ping sends a small packet of information to a specified computer, which then sends a reply packet in return. From this reply the ping program can check whether you can reach the other computer and how long it takes to get the reply.

Ping uses a **command line interface** as users can do a variety of different tests by typing in different commands.

Activity 3 – Experimenting with ping

You can use the MS-DOS prompt on a PC to experiment with ping.

1. Click on **Start**, **Run**

   Note: This may be disabled on your college/school computers but should work on a home computer.

2. Type in **command** (Windows 98) or **cmd** (Windows XP)

   The MS-DOS prompt screen opens

```
C:\WINDOWS\System32\cmd.exe                                    _ □ ×
Microsoft Windows XP [Version 5.1.2600]
(C) Copyright 1985-2001 Microsoft Corp.

C:\
```

3. To test a connection to another station on a local area network type in **ping** followed by the IP address of the other station e.g. **ping 192.168.0.2**

```
C:\WINDOWS\System32\cmd.exe                                    _ □ ×
C:\>ping 192.168.0.2

Pinging 192.168.0.2 with 32 bytes of data:

Reply from 192.168.0.2: bytes=32 time<1ms TTL=128
Reply from 192.168.0.2: bytes=32 time<1ms TTL=128
Reply from 192.168.0.2: bytes=32 time<1ms TTL=128
Reply from 192.168.0.2: bytes=32 time<1ms TTL=128

Ping statistics for 192.168.0.2:
    Packets: Sent = 4, Received = 4, Lost = 0 (0% loss),
Approximate round trip times in milli-seconds:
    Minimum = 0ms, Maximum = 0ms, Average = 0ms

C:\>
```

   The above screen shows that a connection has been found.

4. If you are not connected to a local area network but are connected to the Internet, try **ping** followed by a known Internet URL e.g. **ping www.google.co.uk**

```
C:\WINDOWS\System32\cmd.exe                                    _ □ ×
C:\>ping www.google.co.uk

Pinging www.google.akadns.net [66.102.11.99] with 32 bytes of data:

Reply from 66.102.11.99: bytes=32 time=78ms TTL=246
Reply from 66.102.11.99: bytes=32 time=76ms TTL=246
Reply from 66.102.11.99: bytes=32 time=70ms TTL=246
Reply from 66.102.11.99: bytes=32 time=77ms TTL=246

Ping statistics for 66.102.11.99:
    Packets: Sent = 4, Received = 4, Lost = 0 (0% loss),
Approximate round trip times in milli-seconds:
    Minimum = 70ms, Maximum = 78ms, Average = 75ms

C:\>
```

The Human/Computer Interface (HCI) considers how people communicate with computer systems. The choice of HCI will depend on the application and the needs of the user.

Common interfaces are:

▶ Command Line Interface (CLI)

▶ Menu-based interface

▶ Graphical User Interface (GUI)

▶ Form-based interface

▶ Natural language interface

The HCI must be designed specifically for a given environment – different situations and users at different levels need very different interfaces.

A GUI is much easier to use but demands fast processing speeds and a large computer memory. GUIs are associated with these features:

▶ Windows

▶ Icons

▶ Menus

▶ Pointers

It is very difficult to enter instructions into a computer system in a 'natural language' like English. This is because computer instructions need to be very precise and English has a large vocabulary which can be ambiguous.

Advantages of a natural language Interface

▶ It is the natural language of humans, who can express themselves freely without constraint

▶ No need for special training

▶ Extremely flexible

Limitations of a natural language interface

▶ Natural language is ambiguous and imprecise

▶ Natural language is always changing

▶ The same word can have different meanings

Chapter 21 Questions

1. An Internet search engine is said to have a *natural language interface*. (8)

   a) Explain, using examples, **two** advantages to the user of the natural language interface (4)

   b) Explain, using examples, **two** limitations of a natural language interface. (4)

January 2002 ICT2

2. After logging in to the network, the desktop screen appears as shown (figure 21.14). Describe **three** ways in which this screen provides an effective human/computer interface. (6)

June 2004 ICT2

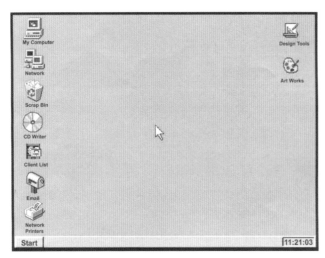

Figure 21.14

3. WIMP (windows, icons, menus and pointers) interfaces are provided by software on most personal computers. However, there are also other types of human/computer interface. Describe what is meant by each of the following, and for each one give an example of an appropriate use:

   a) menu-driven interfaces (3)

   b) command line interfaces. (3)

(The use of brand names will **not** gain credit.)

June 2003 ICT2

4. A mail order company receives orders from its customers, handwritten on preprinted forms. These are then used by clerks to enter the data into a computerised system. A sample blank customer order form (figure 1) and input screen (figure 2) are shown below.

   a) With reference to figure 1 and figure 2, describe **three** features of the input screen that provide an effective human/computer interface. (6)

   b) Identify **three** data items that the software will enter automatically and, for each item, state the event that triggers the automatic entry. (6)

Customer Order Form

Date: _____

Customer Number: _____   Title: Mr/Ms/Mrs/Dr/Other _____

Forename: _____   Surname: _____

Address: _____

_____

_____

_____ Postcode: _____

Item Code	Description	Unit Cost	Quantity	Cost
				Total

Figure 1

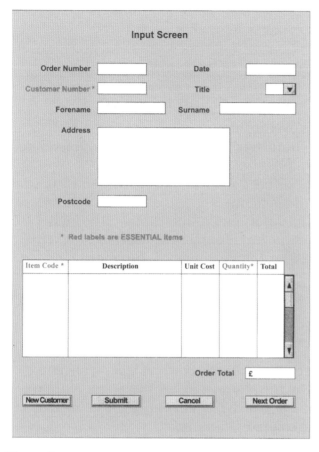

Figure 2

June 2002 ICT2

5. Most modern PCs make use of a GUI (graphical user interface) and have a WYSIWYG (what you see is what you get) word processing package.
  a) State **four** characteristics of a GUI. (4)
  b) Describe **three** advantages to the user of a WYSIWYG word processing package. (6)

June 2001 ICT2

6. All the staff in a small office use the same word processing, spreadsheet and database packages. These packages all have a common user interface.
  a) Give **four** advantages of having a common user interface. (4)
  b) State **four** specific features of a user interface which would benefit from being common between the packages. (4)

January 2001 ICT2

ADSL	Asymmetric Digital Subscriber Line. A method of providing broadband Internet access over regular phone lines.
Alphanumeric characters	Letters, numbers or other characters, for example punctuation marks
Application	A computer program that has been written for a specific task e.g. word processing or database management
ASCII	American Standard Code for Information Interchange. The binary code used in computers to store alphanumeric characters.
ATM	Automatic Teller Machine. The official name for cash machines outside banks.
Back-up	To make an extra copy of stored data in case the original is lost or corrupted.
Bandwidth	Physical limitations of a system's speed of transmission (usually in bits/sec).
Batch processing	A form of processing where all the data is batched together before being processed.
Bit	Binary digit. A binary number which can only have the value 0 or 1.
Bitmap	An image which stores the colour of every pixel.
Blog	A blog, or weblog, is a web page that contains periodic posts. They are often simply individuals' diaries or journals.
Bluetooth	A protocol for the wireless connection of different types of devices; such as a mobile phone with a desktop computer. Bluetooth devices have a short range and do not need a line-of-sight connection.
Boot	To start up a computer.
Broadband	A data transmission method that involves several channels of data and so is faster than older methods
Browser	A program that allows the user to access a database (typically the Internet).
Buffer	Memory where data is stored while waiting to be processed, typically in a printer.
Bugs	Errors in computer programs.
Byte	A group of eight bits, normally storing one alphanumeric character.
Cache	A very fast but more expensive computer memory.
Caching	Storing Internet files locally – usually on the computer's hard drive – to enable the files to load quickly if revisited.
CAD	Computer-Aided Design
CD-ROM	Compact Disc-Read Only Memory. A small plastic disk with an optically readable coating used to store data.
Clipboard	Part of the computer's memory (RAM) where data can be temporarily stored and then pasted into an application.
Clock speed	The instruction processing speed of a computer measured in megahertz (millions of cycles per second). The higher the number, the faster the computer operates.

Compression	A method of reducing the size of a file (zipping), typically to use less disk space or to send it faster over the Internet.
Configure	To set up a computer system for the appropriate hardware and software. A system will need to be configured for the printers, sound cards and so on.
Cookie	Data sent by a website server to a browser when the user visits the site. The data is sent back every time the website is accessed. This can be used, for example, to authenticate a registered user of a website.
Crop	To trim part of a picture.
CSS	Cascading Style Sheet. A way of specifying the appearance of pages on a website. The background, font, colour and font size of several pages can be altered simply by altering the CSS.
Cursor	The screen pointer, usually an arrow, which is controlled by the mouse.
Cyber-	A prefix alluding to computer communication often with reference to the Internet as in cybershopping, shopping by computer, cyberspace, everything accessible by computer communications.
DAT	Digital Audio Tape
Database	A structured set of data stored on a computer.
Data integrity	The reliability of data, that is ensuring it is accurate.
Data security	Keeping data safe from loss.
DBMS	Database Management System. A set of programs allowing the user to access data in a database.
DDE	Dynamic Data Exchange. Shared data in two applications is linked so that when it is updated in one program, it is automatically updated in the other program.
Debug	Remove bugs from a program.
Desktop	An icon-based user interface that enables the user to load software easily. When you load Microsoft Windows, you see the desktop.
Digital	Something that is represented in numerical form typically in binary numbers.
Direct-mail	Advertising a product by sending details directly to potential buyers through the post.
Directory	A group of files. A disk may have several directories and subdirectories to make finding files easier and to aid security.
Dongle	A piece of hardware, for example, a lead that has to be plugged in to the computer before software will run. Usually used to protect copyright.
DOS	Disk Operating System
Dot.com	A company usually trading exclusively via the Internet.
DPI	Dots per inch – describes the performance of a printer.
DVD	Digital Versatile Disk. An optical disk which has greater capacity than a CD-ROM.
e-banking	The use of the Internet to communicate with your bank.
e-commerce	The use of computers and electronic communications in business transactions, including websites, EDI, online databases and EFTPOS systems.
EDI	Electronic Data Interchange. Transferring information such as orders and invoices electronically between two organisations.
e-tailors	Retailers who do business on the Internet.

e-shopping	Using the Internet to purchase goods and services.
EFTPOS	Electronic Funds Transfer at Point of Sale. The system where customers can pay by debit (Switch) card and the money is taken electronically from their bank account.
Embedding	Including one file (such as an image or a document) in another file. See OLE (Object Linking and Embedding).
Emoticon	Little text-based faces you may see in e-mail and online chat. For example, :-)
Encryption	To scramble data into a secure code to prevent it being read by unauthorised users.
Extranet	The linking of two intranets usually to assist business transaction, for example, linking a customer and a supplier.
FAQ	Frequently Asked Questions. A file containing answers to common questions, for example, about using a program.
Fax modem	A modem that enables a computer to send and receive faxes.
Fibre optic	A cable made out of glass fibre and used in communications.
Filters	An option in a program enabling the user to import files from, or export files to, another program.
Firewall	Either hardware or software used to protect a networked computer system from damage by unauthorised users.
Flatbed scanner	A scanner in which the item to be scanned is placed on a flat piece of glass.
Floppy disk	A small removable disk in a hard plastic case, used to store data.
GIF	Graphics Interchange Format. A format used for storing compressed images on World Wide Web pages. These images are usually called a 'gif'.
Gigabyte (GB)	A measure of memory capacity equal to roughly 1,000,000,000 bytes (it is exactly 2 to the power 30 or 1,073,741,824).
GUI	Graphical User Interface, for example, Windows. It is sometimes pronounced 'gooey'.
Hacking	Unauthorised access to a computer system, possibly for criminal purposes.
Hand scanner	A small device, held in the hand and dragged over the item to be scanned.
Hard disk	A magnetic disk inside a computer that can store much more data than a floppy disk. Usually it cannot be removed but removable hard disks are becoming more common.
Hardware	The physical parts of the computer, such as the processor, keyboard and printer.
Hotdesking	The practice of office workers sharing desks. Workers come in, sit at the next available desk and log into the computer network.
HTML	Hypertext Markup Language. The language that web pages are written in.
HTTP	Hypertext Transfer Protocol. The standard protocol for sending and receiving data on the Internet.
Integrated package	A package which combines several different applications such as a wordprocessor, a graphics package, database, communications software and spreadsheet.
Interactive	A system where there is communication between the user and the computer.

Internet	International WAN providing information pages and e-mail facilities for millions of users.
Intranet	A private internal network using Internet software, that can be used for internal e-mail and information.
IRC	Internet Relay Chat. A function of the Internet allowing users to send and receive real-time text messages.
ISDN	Integrated Services Digital Network. A telecommunications digital network which is faster than an analogue network using a modem.
ISP	Internet Service Provider. A company that offers a connection to the Internet.
JavaScript	A programming language used to add interactive features to web pages.
JPG or JPEG	Joint Photographic Expert Group. An ISO standard for storing images in compressed form. Pronounced jay-peg.
Kilobyte (Kb)	A measure of memory capacity equal to 1,024 bytes.
LCD	Liquid Crystal Display
Licence agreement	The document which defines how software can be used, particularly how many people can use it.
Macro	A small program routine usually defined by the user.
Magnetic disk	A small disk coated with magnetic material on which data is stored. It can be a floppy disk or a hard disk.
Magnetic tape	A long plastic tape coated with magnetic material on which data is stored.
Mail-merge	A feature of a word processing program that combines details from a file of names and addresses into personal letters.
Master file	The file where the master data is stored. Data from this file is updated with data from the transaction file.
Megabyte (Mb)	A measure of memory capacity equal to 1,000,000 bytes (it is exactly 2 to the power 20 or 1,048,576).
Megahertz	See Clock speed
Memory stick	Small portable storage device that plugs into the USB port.
MICR	Magnetic Ink Character recognition. The input method used to read cheques.
Modem	Modulator/demodulator. The device that converts digital computer data into a form that can be sent over the telephone network.
MS-DOS	Microsoft Disk Operating System. The operating system developed for the PC.
Multi-access	A computer system allowing more than one user to access the system at the same time.
Multimedia	A computer system combining text, graphics, sound and video, typically using data stored on CD-ROM.
Multitasking	A computer system that can run more than one program simultaneously.
Network	A number of computers connected together.
OCR	Optical Character Recognition
OLE	Object Linking and Embedding. A method of taking data from one file (the source file) and placing it in another file (the destination file). Linked data is stored in the source file and updated if you modify the source file. On the other hand, embedded files are part of the destination file.

Open Source Software	Software for which the underlying programming code is available to the users so that they may read it, make changes to it, and build new versions of the software incorporating their changes.
Operating system	The software that controls the hardware of a computer.
Package	A program or programs for a specific purpose.
Palmtop	A small hand held computer around the size of a pocket calculator.
PDA	Personal Digital Assistant. A hand held portable computer. See also palmtop.
Peer-to-peer	A type of network where there is no server, with each station sharing the tasks.
Pentium™	A processor developed by the Intel Corporation™ for the PC.
Peripheral	Any hardware item that is connected to a computer such as printers, mice or keyboards.
PIN	Personal Identification Number, used to check that the user is the person they claim to be, for example, at an ATM.
Platform	Used to describe a hardware or software environment.
Port	A socket usually at the back of the computer.
Portability	The ability to use software, hardware or data files on different systems.
Primary Key	A unique identifier in a record in a database.
Protocol	A set of rules for communication between different devices.
QBE	Query By Example. Graphical method of specifying a search. Usually used to search a database.
RAID	Redundant Array of Inexpensive Disks. A fault tolerant system using two disks to store the same data.
RAM	Random Access Memory. The computer's internal memory used to store the program and data in use. The contents are lost when the power is turned off.
Redundant data	Data that is repeated unnecessarily (in a database).
ROM	Read Only Memory. Part of the computer's memory that is retained even when the power is turned off. Used to store start up program and settings.
Serial access	Accessing data items one after the other until the required one is found. Associated with magnetic tape.
Server	A dedicated computer that controls a network.
Shareware	Software that can legally be distributed freely but users are expected to register with and pay a fee to the copyright holder.
Smart card	A plastic card, like a credit card, with an embedded microchip. The information in the chip can be updated, for example, when cash has been withdrawn from an ATM.
Software copyright	Laws restricting copying of software.
Software	A computer program or programs.
Spam	The sending of unrequested e-mails (usually advertisements) to many e-mail addresses.
Systems analyst	A person whose job involves analysing whether a task could be carried out more efficiently by computer.
TFT	Thin-film Transistor
Toggle switch	A switch or button which if pressed once turns a feature on. If pressed again it turns the feature off. The Caps Lock button is an example.

Transaction file	A file containing new transaction details or changes to old data, which is merged with the master file.
USB	Universal Serial Bus – a port on a computer used to connect peripherals such as scanners or a palmtop.
USB hub	A device that plugs into the USB port that enables several peripherals to connect to the computer at once.
URL	Uniform Resource Locator – the Internet address, e.g. http://www.hodderheadline.co.uk
Vector graphics	Image system that stores lines by the length and direction rather than the individual pixels (as in a bit map).
Webcam	Any video camera whose output is available for viewing via the Internet.
WIMP	Windows, Icons, Menus, Pointers.
Windows™	A GUI for the PC produced by Microsoft.
Wireless network	A network that uses radio waves to transmit data rather than cables.
WWW	The World Wide Web
WYSIWYG	What You See Is What You Get